The Music Men

The Story of Professional Gospel Quartet Singing

By BOB TERRELL

Printed in the United States of America.

Library of Congress Catalog Card Number: 90-90225

ISBN 1-878894-00-5

OTHER BOOKS BY BOB TERRELL

J. D. Sumner—Gospel Music Is My Life!
Fun Is Where You Find It!
Holy Land: A Journey Into Time
A Touch Of Terrell
Billy Graham In Hungary
Grandpa's Town
Woody (with Barbara Shelton)
Old Gold
The Peace That Passeth Understanding
    (with Connie Hopper)
Disorder In The Court
    (with Marcellus Buchanan)
Billy Graham In the Soviet Union
Keep 'em Laughing
Papa Coke (with Sanders Rowland)
The Ralph Sexton Story
The Chuck Wagon Gang—A Legend Lives On

Contents

Foreword

In a book of this type, one might expect to read about the organizations and agencies that make the industry of gospel music operate as smoothly as it does, but that is not the nature of this book.

This is a *people* book. It is the story of the people who made gospel music what it is today, the story of the pioneers who rode from town to town in automobiles—sometimes in pickup trucks—to sing the gospel in harmony. Thus, I have made no great effort to emphasize organizations, agencies, and events except as they relate to the characters.

I have taken some liberty with subject matter, such as reconstructing conversations of long ago, but none with history. This book is written as historically accurate as checking, double-checking, and cross-checking facts, dates, and events will make it.

Those characters in the book who are no longer with us are constructed as carefully as research and interviewing their relatives and contemporaries can make them.

No effort was made to cover the present day period in gospel music. Because of the length of this work, I must leave that for a future volume.

In these pages you will meet the men—and some women—who pioneered gospel music in every way, who lived for it, and some of whom died for it. Although there are many references to the present in the book, it deals primarily with the people in the business from the time the first professional quartet went on the road in 1910 through, roughly, the 1960s.

Also, I could not do full justice to all of the quartets and people who sang during that period because, as they say in newspaper writing, of a lack of space; but you'll get the idea of what quartet singing was all about in the old days after you read to the end of the book.

I hope you meet some old friends along the way.

*   *   *

Finally, I must thank those who helped me compile the information in these pages. I am tremendously indebted to Robin Clayton of Radio Station WLRC in Walnut, Mississippi, who actually saved my bacon in writing this book. He provided huge boxes full of materials and information on the early Vaughan dynasty, and also made available to me tapes of several interviews he did with old-timers, some of whom were dead before I could personally get around to them.

Thanks to Tommy Wheeler of DeSoto, Texas, son of Palmer Wheeler, the first tenor singer in that great 1927 Stamps Quartet. Tommy provided much of the information about the Stamps empire.

Jack Callaway of Knoxville, Tennessee, a gospel historian, made available to me many of the details on the Rangers Quartet. First-hand information on two gospel greats who were killed in automobile crashes in the early 1950s was supplied by Juanita Slater Guice of Geraldine, Alabama, the daughter of Erman Slater, killed in a wreck with the Rangers Quartet; and J. B. Strickland of Hondo, Texas, brother of Bobby Strickland, who died in the wreck of a Crusaders Quartet car.

I drew heavily on historical data that I compiled while writing stories for *The Singing News*, and I must thank that magazine for the opportunity to gather that material in the first place.

And then, I am grateful to those countless singers who sat for interviews and patiently answered my questions while I probed and dug and exercised their memories for information I needed. Many of these singers performed in the 1930s and 1940s, and their memories of those days are keen. I cannot name them for there are far too many to list.

Some of these interviews were done under fairly extreme conditions, at the National Quartet Convention, on board the *Emerald Seas* sailing the Caribbean, backstage in the hubbub of the Grand Old Gospel Reunion in Greenville, South Carolina, in many auditoriums and quartet buses, and over long-distance telephone lines.

Whatever place this book turns out to occupy in gospel music, it would not have been possible without the help of all of these people who contributed, and for their efforts I have heartfelt thanks.

Bob Terrell
55 Dillingham Road
Asheville, NC 28805

March 15, 1990

CHAPTER ONE

The Waypavers

Two huge motorcoaches thundered through the night, bearing down on Detroit. Setting a rapid pace, the forward coach carried the famed Statesmen Quartet of Atlanta, Georgia. Following closely behind was the coach with the Blackwood Brothers Quartet of Memphis, Tennessee, aboard.

The hour was late; actually, the wee hours of the morning had arrived. The Statesmen driver wore a look of weariness from the all-night run. He would be happy to reach the hotel in Detroit. So would Bundy Brewster, wheeling the other bus.

Suddenly, the Statesmen driver snapped his eyes open, realizing he had dozed for just a second. He also realized something was in the road immediately in front of his bus.

He slammed on the brakes, but the coach crashed through a detour barrier and careened to a stop.

Bundy saw the lumber fly from the front of the Statesmen bus when it hit the barrier and jammed on the brakes of the second bus. It stopped just on the other side of the barrier.

The Blackwood Brothers were thrown out of their beds into a jumbled heap on the floor, jolted awake, frightened out of their wits, and shaken to the bone.

J. D. Sumner, the Blackwood bass singer who was in charge of the bus, thought about the incident during the two days the quartets sang in Detroit, then fired his driver, Bundy Brewster.

"You've got the lives of the Blackwood Brothers in your hands,

Bundy," J. D. said, "and lately you've become too careless. We can't afford to take chances."

J. D. had no real intention of turning Bundy loose; he only wanted to impress upon him the importance of his job.

"You make the rest of this trip with us," J. D. told Bundy, "and I'm going to teach you something about driving. After that, we'll talk about letting you re-apply for your job."

The Statesmen and Blackwood Brothers left Detroit en route to an engagement in El Paso, Texas, 1,700 long miles away, and after that they were going on to the West Coast.

Leaving the hotel in Detroit, J. D. purposely let everyone get on the bus ahead of him, then he stepped aboard, opened his brief case, and extracted a water glass.

As he filled the glass with water, he had everyone's attention. He placed the glass on the flat dashboard and took his seat at the steering wheel.

"Now," he said, "I'm going to show all of you how to drive this bus three hundred miles without spilling that water. Not even a drop."

All eyes were riveted on the water glass for three hundred miles, and even to J. D.'s surprise, not a drop sloshed out.

Then Bundy drove two hundred miles without spilling the water, and Cecil Blackwood, the baritone, replaced him and drove another two hundred miles with one eye on the road and the other on the glass of water.

All the Blackwood Brothers who could drive the bus took turns, and when Cecil Blackwood wheeled into El Paso at three o'clock in the morning, the glass still contained the water.

The others were asleep in the back of the bus and Cecil drove down the main street, looking for a place to get a cup of coffee.

Ahead, the driver of a pickup truck full of inebriated farm workers suddenly cranked up his engine and pulled the truck directly into the path of the bus.

Fortunately, Cecil wasn't driving fast, but he was driving fast enough to knock the truck out of the road and scatter Mexicans all over the street and the adjoining landscape.

The jolt woke the others in the rear of the bus, and J. D. was struggling upward, trying to shake the fog of sleep from his brain, when Cecil rushed back, grabbed him by the shoulders and shook him violently.

"J. D.!" Cecil shouted. "Wake up, J. D.! I spilled that glass of water!"

* * *

Bundy Brewster drove the Blackwood Brothers another dozen years without having even a close call. His only major foulup in those twelve years came when he drove out of Las Vegas, Nevada, one night, heading for Phoenix, turned the wrong way, and wound up in Salt Lake City the next morning. The Blackwood Brothers had to fly back to Phoenix to make their date that evening.

Those incidents, certainly the latter one, were typical of the things that happen to gospel quartets on the road.

These people are—and always were—among the nomads of America. They practically live on the road, so demanding and so different are their schedules from those of others in the entertainment business.

Gospel singers are the only entertainers in America who have their own "circuit," which they work every week. While country and rock and pop singers schedule one or two tours a year, singing in a string of cities for several weeks, gospel quartets go on tour every week, singing in every town, hamlet, and big city in which they think they can draw a crowd.

While country singers like to believe they sing "the people's music," gospel singers sing of the roots of Americana.

Professional quartets began singing in 1910, and they sang both popular and gospel tunes in public appearances. The gospel songs were written in a peculiar style of shaped notes. Where others sang notes according to which line of the scale they were on, gospel singers sang notes by their shapes—round, triangular, square, flag-shaped, bowl-shaped—and called them *Do, Re, Mi, Fa, Sol, La, Ti, Do.*

Perhaps the trend of the times shaped the style of music for gospel singers more than any other. Professional gospel quartet singing hit full stride in the late 1920s, just as the Great Depression spread across the nation, and in an apocalyptic measure, quartets began singing of joy and the abounding love of God and of better times to come. They sang not only songs of faith, but songs of hope as well—exactly what the people wanted to hear.

The music outlived the depression, and just as hard times came to an end, the world exploded with the second worldwide war in a quarter of a century, and gospel songs remained especially meaningful.

Coming out of the war, quartets and their songs were established, and the singing groups became outstanding entertainment units across the Southern United States.

Gospel singers were especially talented people, attuned to the hardships of the times; committed to what they were doing; and musical men and women through and through.

You have only to talk for a moment to men like Connor B. Hall, James Blackwood, Glen Payne, Roy Carter, and Jake Hess to realize how musical their voices are. Strangers might even guess they were singers.

Most of these singers possess extraordinary qualities. James Blackwood can reach back in his memory and bring forth any one of four hundred songs—and sing it without missing a word or a note.

J. D. Sumner, who didn't know a formal note of music, other than how to chord a guitar, once wrote eight Hawaiian gospel songs while the Blackwood Brothers rode the sixty miles from Terre Haute to Indianapolis, Indiana. He roughed out each song with words and chords, sang them for James Blackwood in Indianapolis—and all were recorded on a Hawaiian gospel album which became the second best selling album the Blackwood Brothers ever did. J. D. wrote more than five hundred songs that were recorded by quartets.

In gospel, as in any other type of music, many voices sound the same. There are numerous quartets and singing groups today that most people cannot tell apart by sound because they sound very much alike. The same was true in the "old days" which will be covered within the pages of this book: Some of the quartets sounded just like others. But not all.

No one who knows this business could mistake the sound of the Chuck Wagon Gang for that of any other group, or vice versa. The sound of the Swanee River Boys was easily distinguished, as were those of the Statesmen, the Blackwood Brothers, the Homeland Harmony, and a dozen others.

It's the same with the singers. James Blackwood has a voice no one has duplicated. One could easily recognize the first tenor voices of Jerry Redd or Calvin Newton, the basses of J. D. Sumner, "Big Chief" Wetherington, Big Jim Waits, and countless others.

The most unfortunate part of gospel singing, hindsight tells us, is that the singers were so close to the people—many on a first-name basis—that the people adopted favorites, and showed them fierce loyalty. Often, when another quartet came on stage, the fans of the Statesmen, for example, paid little or no attention, and sometimes even left the arena to go and talk with the Statesmen at the table where they sold their records. Such devoted fans managed to miss a tremendous amount of great singing.

Musicians were distinctive. One could pick Eva Mae LeFevre's piano-playing out of a crowd. Or Hovie Lister's. Certainly Wally Varner's, whom most singers consider to have been the finest quartet pianist who ever plunked the ivory.

When male quartet singing became popular, some adjustments had to be made to make the male voice fit the parts of song written with both male and female voices in mind.

Male quartets were made up of a high tenor, or first tenor; a lead singer, or second tenor; a baritone, or, in the early days, a tenor; and a bass.

Songs were written for alto, soprano, tenor, and bass. A group like the Chuck Wagon Gang, which always contained two women and two men, could sing any song just as it was written. But when a male quartet got hold of it, when the lead singer tackled the soprano line, he usually found himself out of reach, unable to clearly hit the high notes.

Thus, adjustments had to be made. Sometimes the quartet could simply change the song's key, but sometimes it couldn't. Then the first tenor sang the alto line where it was written; the lead singer dropped the soprano line an octave and sang it there; the baritone sang the tenor line where it was written; and the bass sang the bass line anywhere he could reach.

After a pianist named Jackie Marshall came into the business as accompanist for the Blackwood Brothers in 1950, the practice of singing parts changed somewhat, because Jackie introduced the idea of swapping parts, and in some gospel harmony singing today, people would be surprised to know what part each of the singers is singing. The high tenor, lead, and baritone frequently change parts to make for better harmony.

Gospel singing today is a much more sophisticated business than it was seventy years ago when it was developed. It is that way only because of its pioneers, those who came before, those who led the way, those who showed each other what could be done with the human voice (make that plural!).

As in every great endeavor, someone had to pave the way.

This book is the story of the waypavers.

CHAPTER TWO

In the
Beginning...

America had been torn asunder by the Civil War. Atlanta lay in smoldering ruin and General William Tecumseh Sherman and sixty thousand Union troops were approaching Savannah, cutting a fifty-mile-wide swath through the Georgia countryside from Atlanta to the sea. The entire South was devastated by the war. On the evening of December 14, 1864, with Sherman only a week out of Savannah, a baby boy was born to George Washington and Eliza Shores Vaughan in Giles County, Tennessee. The boy's parents named him James David Vaughan. His life spanned seventy-seven years, ending February 9, 1941, ten months before Pearl Harbor.

What happened to James D. Vaughan between the burning of Atlanta and the bombing of Pearl Harbor was significant in the annals of American music.

He helped develop and popularize a new folk form of American music. It is known today as Gospel Music.

While James D. Vaughan was yet a baby in homemade diapers, something happened up North that would affect his life tremendously in later years. Ephraim Ruebush, a Union soldier, rescued a bright young Southern musician, Aldine S. Kieffer, from a Union camp for prisoners-of-war, and in the next few years the two became brothers-in-law and business partners. They founded a publishing company in New Market, Virginia, called Ruebush/Kieffer Publishing Company, and printed books of sacred and gospel songs.

Until that time, Southern sacred songbooks had been written in a four-note system known today as "Sacred Harp." The Ruebush/Kieffer book contained songs written on a seven-note scale that provided a completely different style of harmony and certainly a different sound.

Ruebush/Kieffer started two more things that influenced later publishers: a monthly publication known as *Musical Million*, which began in January 1870 and grew to 1,200 circulation in its first year; and in 1874 a singing school known as the *Ruebush Kieffer Normal School*. From 1874 to 1882 the principal of the Ruebush Kieffer normals was Benjamin Carl Unseld, a highly trained music man who adhered to the standard round-note system of music.

Ruebush and Kieffer wanted shaped-note music taught in the school, but Unseld held out for round notes, and finally, as a compromise, they agreed to teach both forms. Eventually, the shaped notes won the battle and round-note training was dropped from the school's curriculum in 1875.

A. J. Showalter, destined to become a giant among Southern music publishers, got much of his training in the Ruebush Kieffer Normal in 1876.

About 1883 James D. Vaughan became a pupil of B. C. Unseld in the Ruebush Kieffer Normal. Vaughan and his three brothers, Charles, Will, and John, had first attended a singing school under a teacher named James Berry in 1881 when James D. was seventeen years old. It was said that Berry had a songbook that contained songs with 16th notes that no one in the school, not even Berry himself, could sing—with the exception of James D. Vaughan, who sang them perfectly.

After this school, Vaughan taught his first singing school, and organized his brothers and himself into a quartet; Charles singing the high part, the alto line; James D. singing soprano; Will singing tenor; and John singing bass.

Aldine Kieffer, the shaped-note champion, and R. A. Glenn, a song compiler for Ruebush/Kieffer, made such a lasting impression on James D. Vaughan that ten years later Vaughan named his son after them, Glenn Kieffer Vaughan.

Vaughan was married to Jennie E. Freeman on May 15, 1890, and to their union a daughter, Grace, was born July 23, 1891. The next year, 1892, the entire Vaughan family moved to Cisco, Texas, where the grass appeared to be a bit greener. There, E. T. Hilderbrand, a Ruebush/Kieffer disciple, taught a singing school which James D. Vaughan attended, and it served to whet his appetite for music even more.

The year 1893 was significant for James D. Three important things happened in his life.

His father died in Cisco. Then his son, Glenn Kieffer, was born on March 20. And six weeks later, a devastating cyclone hit Cisco, killing twenty-nine people and destroying everything the Vaughan family owned.

With the help of friends, James D. Vaughan moved his family to Elkmont Springs, Tennessee, and became a school teacher.

Music continued to nag at him, however, and in 1900 he succumbed to the urge and printed a songbook which he entitled "Gospel Chimes."

With two young mouths to feed, Vaughan took the biggest step of his life in 1902. He moved to Lawrenceburg, Tennessee, about fifteen miles away, giving up his job as principal of Elkmont Springs school, and opened the *James D. Vaughan Publishing Company*. His younger brother, Charles, joined him a year later, in 1903, and went into the music business with him.

The company grew slowly. In 1909 the Vaughan brothers sold about 30,000 songbooks. They planned to publish a great new book entitled *Voices For Jesus* in 1910, and James D. came up with an idea that really put the Vaughan company on the map. Why not put a quartet on the road to promote the book? he reasoned, and the more he and Charles discussed the idea, the better he liked it.

So it was that in May of 1910, the first professional all-male gospel quartet in America hit the road. Charles Vaughan was manager of the quartet. In it he was joined by George W. Sebren, who would later run his own music company in Asheville, North Carolina; Joe M. Allen, who became a preacher of note in Georgia, preaching James D. Vaughan's funeral in 1941; and Ira T. Foust, who found his place as a music teacher and songwriter. The four were on salary to James D. Vaughan Publishing Company. Sebren trained the quartet.

There were no other quartets in the country at that time singing gospel songs as a regular work. The Vaughan Quartet sang in as many places as it could, always pushing the new Vaughan songbook, and sales doubled to 60,000 that year. The next year Vaughan sold 75,000 books, and in 1912 he sold 85,000, and the quartet grew more popular all the time.

The Vaughans concluded that the quartet idea was a success and made plans to expand it when the occasion arose.

In 1911 Vaughan started the famed Vaughan School of Music in

Lawrenceburg, and gave B. C. Unseld, his old teacher and friend, the principal's chair. By this time Unseld had made his peace with shaped-note music. He held the principal's position until his death in 1923.

Unseld and all the others who taught in the Vaughan schools did not consider themselves to be gospel singers; they thought of themselves simply as music men. The school was not limited to gospel but taught all types of music and related subjects.

Ottis J. Knippers, a retired Tennessee state senator and judge, attended the Vaughan School of Music and sang in the Vaughan Trio. "The school featured high voice culture," he said. "Some of our teachers studied under the best teachers in New York and brought this knowledge back to us. They studied operatic singing. They used to tell us how Caruso did this and that.

"We were taught how to breathe, how to shape the lips for singing, how to enunciate correctly. They taught many courses in the school: rudiments of music, sight reading, ear training, harmony, composition, counterpoint, directing, voice culture, piano and other instruments, even piano tuning, radio broadcasting, and radio engineering. This was a thorough music school."

Striving to make his company as complete as possible, Vaughan in 1912 started his own publication, called the *Musical Visitor*. George W. Sebren was the editor for two years until he moved away about 1914. Then Unseld became editor and the publication's name was changed to the *Vaughan Family Visitor*. Published monthly, the magazine caught on immediately and down through the years carried news of all the Vaughan operations. It was an all-important cog in the Vaughan machine.

The magazine was well-rounded, with space devoted to music, poetry, and good home literature. Every issue carried the words and music to new songs. Vaughan advertised it as "the leading music journal of the South," noting that it was "safe, pure, and clean, and should be in every home."

As America rolled out of the first World War and into the Roarin' Twenties, the Vaughan company really began to balloon.

The phonograph that Thomas Edison invented in 1877 brought a new source of revenue to Vaughan, and in 1921 he instituted a new branch of the James D. Vaughan Music Company: Vaughan Phonograph Records.

These early Vaughan recordings were made under the Vaughan custom label and were advertised as the "first and only Southern records to be placed on the market. They are safe for the boys and girls, the kind that Father and Mother will enjoy. If you buy these records you will have a Vaughan Quartet in your home every day in the year."

Homer Rodeheaver and others had made sacred records in the teens, but Vaughan was the first to put a quartet on record.

In 1921, a year before the first country music recording was cut, a Vaughan quartet consisting of Hillman Barnard, first tenor; Kieffer Vaughan, lead; Walter B. Seale, baritone; and Ray Collins, bass, cut the first gospel quartet record ever. The first song recorded was "I Couldn't Hear Nobody Pray," a repetitious number, as many songs were then:

"I couldn't hear nobody pray;
"Way down yonder by myself
"I couldn't hear nobody pray.
"Ohhh, way down yonder by myself
"With Jesus in the valley,
"I couldn't hear nobody pray."

The song had characteristics of a Negro spiritual.

On the other side of that original record was a song entitled "Look For Me," written by V. O. Stamps, a name that was to become famous in gospel quartet music. He was employed by Vaughan at the time and wrote this song for the Vaughan book of 1921: *Temple Bells*.

The first song was recorded with Ted Shaw accompanying on the piano, but the Stamps song was recorded with a full orchestra backing the quartet.

Business became so good that Vaughan opened branch offices in Mansfield, Arkansas; Laurel, Mississippi; Greenville, South Carolina; and Jacksonville, Texas. V. O. Stamps became Vaughan's Texas manager, maintaining the office in Jacksonville.

V. O. and his younger brother, Frank, both studied in the Vaughan Conservatory, as the school of music was known, and both joined the Vaughan company as employees. Frank managed one of the Vaughan quartets for at least a couple of years, perhaps longer.

By the middle twenties, Vaughan had sixteen quartets on the road, all on salary, most traveling in Dodge automobiles furnished by the company, and all selling Vaughan songbooks and records and carrying the Vaughan name far and wide.

CHAPTER THREE

The Catapult: Radio

Fred Green, a Lawrence County man who had been a communications officer in World War I and who would later rise to the rank of colonel in World War II, met James D. Vaughan in Lawrenceburg one day in 1922, and the two struck up a friendly conversation.

Their talk turned to the late war, and Vaughan asked, "What was your work in the army?"

"I was in communications, " Green replied. "A new form of communications, actually, called radio. It works like a telephone but there are no wires involved."

"Can it carry a voice wireless?" Vaughan asked.

"It can."

"That's interesting," Vaughan mused.

"Radio," Green said thoughtfully, "is going to be the bigget thing that's happened to this country. Everybody will have a radio set."

Vaughan, who had been wondering what other fields he could incorporate into his company to improve his products, suddenly showed a deep interest.

"Tell me more about radio, Fred," he said. "That's maybe something we ought to think about here."

The two sat on a park bench, and Fred Green told Vaughan everything he could think of the new medium.

Vaughan suddenly fixed Green with a close stare through his *pince-nez* eyeglasses.

"Fred, could you build me a radio station?"

"Why, yes," Fred said. "But I would have to round up the parts. They're not available here."

"You do that," Vaughan said. "Let's go to my office and settle the deal. We will build a radio station and broadcast this gospel music all over the country."

In his office, Vaughan gave Green a checkbook. "Get on the train, Fred, and go wherever you need to go to buy the parts."

They shook hands and Fred Green set forth on a monumental and history-making journey.

By the late fall of 1922, Green had the radio station ready to go on the air. The control room was in the back of the Vaughan Music Company building. Vaughan chose and registered the call letters *WOAN*, which stood for "Watch Our Annual Normal."

The station was licensed to operate by the United States Department of Commerce. This was even before the creation of the Federal Radio Commission, forerunner of the Federal Communications Commission.

Vaughan received his license on November 21, 1922, and WOAN went on the air immediately—the first radio station in the state of Tennessee. The largest drawback to radio was that it was so new that few people owned radio receivers, and those that existed were mostly battery operated and inclined to static. But the airwaves were uncluttered and a signal traveled far—and receiving sets were improved tremendously during the years that WOAN was on the air. Too, the Vaughan Music Company began selling radio sets when WOAN went on the air.

WOAN had the 600-kilocycle wave length and operated on only 250 watts of power, but the channel was clear and the signal boomed across Tennessee and into many other states. Its antenna of eight copper wires was suspended horizontally between two tall windmill towers about two hundred feet apart.

After two years, WOAN was allowed to increase its power to five hundred watts, and before long the station and the *Vaughan Family Visitor* received mail from people who had listened to the station in such distant locales as Pekin, Illinois; Wichita Falls, Texas; Erie, Pennsylvania; St. Paul, Minnesota; Owego, New York; Creston, Iowa; Rapid City, South Dakota; Ardmore, Oklahoma; and, of course, from all over the state of Tennessee and the states adjoining.

Vaughan called his station the *James D. Vaughan Radiophone Broadcasting Station.*

WOAN was certainly a novelty. Fred Green was the engineer and when he pushed the switch to turn on the power, electric lights glowed in several nearby houses and in a garage across the street.

Others were quick to follow Vaughan's leadership in radio. Hoyt Wooten of Coldwater, Tennessee, opened a radio station called WREC and in a few months moved the station to Memphis. Since the low numbers on the radio dial were choice, Wooten asked Vaughan if he would divide time with him at 600 kilocycles.

"Why, sure," Vaughan said. "You can operate there any time we don't. We'll tell you the time we're not going to be on and let the FRC authorize you to be on anytime we're not."

WOAN went off about 8:30 each evening and WREC came on at that time. In the mornings, WREC was on until WOAN came on at noon for about an hour, and then WREC took over again until 6:30 when WOAN came back on for two hours.

Many stations divided time on the same wave length in those early days. WFAA and WBAP of Fort Worth, Texas, split air time. So did WOWO of Fort Wayne, Indiana, and WWVA of Wheeling, West Virginia.

Vaughan used WOAN more when the School of Music was in session. He broadcast a lot of programs coming from the School of Music. The December 14, 1924, *Nashville Tennessean* carried a story about the fine musicians who played on the air over WOAN, including a twelve-piece orchestra under the direction of Professor Herschel L. Raines, who had previously directed the Barnum & Bailey circus band; and the newspaper story paid attention to the Vaughan Quartet which had been giving concerts all over the South and in a number of northern cities, and which, according to the paper, had only a few weeks previously been in New York making records for the Edison Company. In that quartet were Kieffer Vaughan, Barnard, Seale, and Collins.

Radio stations such as WOAN catapulted quartets into widespread notoriety, and gospel quartet music was accepted and enjoyed in our largest cities. It was not considered to be a cult music, but simply good music.

In 1925 Edwin Craig, owner of the National Life and Accident Insurance Company in Nashville, paid Vaughan a visit. He told Vaughan that he planned to put a radio station on the air in Nashville with the call letters of WSM. He wanted the 650-kilocycle wave length but wanted to clear it with Vaughan because it was so near WOAN at 600.

"I don't want to interfere with your operation," Craig said.

Vaughan had Green check it out and when Green told him that WSM would not interfere, Vaughan said to Craig, "Go right ahead and take the 650 spot. It won't hurt us in the least."

WSM went on the air in 1925.

That bit of generosity helped Vaughan in later years. The Vaughan quartets went off the air when WOAN folded in 1929 and had been off of radio for a few years in the mid 1930s. The quartets of Frank and V. O. Stamps, who had pulled away from Vaughan in 1924, were broadcasting over several stations, including the high-watt behemoths just south of the Mexican border, and they were killing Vaughan in sales.

"We've simply got to get back on radio," Vaughan told his brother Charles. "Let's get our best quartet on WSM."

That quartet consisted of Kieffer Vaughan, John Cook, Palmer Wheeler, and Big Jim Waits, with Dwight Brock accompanying.

But when the Vaughans asked for time on WSM, the station refused to sell it to them. Charles Vaughan, the family's politician, drove to Nashville and collared Craig in his insurance offices.

"Do you remember my brother allowing you to take that place on the dial so near to his?" Charles asked.

"Yes, of course, I remember," Craig said.

"Okay, look," Charles said, "you owe this to us."

Craig relented. He sold Vaughan Wednesday afternoon and Thursday morning time periods and the Vaughan Radio Quartet went on WSM in Nashville.

The night broadcast over WOAN from 1921 to 1929 was the farthest-reaching, most popular program. In addition to his quartets, Vaughan paraded student quartets, soloists, duets, trios, choruses, and the Vaughan orchestra to the microphones. So many telegrams were received each night that Western Union had to stay open until the station went off the air.

The studio was equipped with a Baldwin grand piano given by the Baldwin company in exchange for mentions on the air; so when the Vaughan Quartet came on, Vaughan would announce, "Luther Heatwole at the Baldwin Grand."

Alas, the depression was fatal to WOAN. Vaughan had to cut back his operation when Wall Street collapsed in 1929, and in order to save the school and the *Visitor* and the quartet and songbook operation, he took WOAN off the air and dismantled the station, selling the equipment and the remainder of the air time to WREC in Memphis.

* * *

The year 1923 was typical of the successful years Vaughan enjoyed during the decade of the twenties. On New Year's Day, a Vaughan Quartet composed of R. C. Deaton, Jeff Duncan, M. D. McWhorter, and Frank Stamps sang at the annual New Year Celebration at County Line, Raine County, Texas. During that month, V. O. Stamps sang with Zeke and Bill Kitts, M. L. Yandell, and Jeff Duncan at a Texas convention. V. O. limited his singing to special engagements in order to devote full time to office business in Jacksonville, Texas.

The April issue of *Vaughan Family Visitor* reported that the Vaughan Quartet of Barnard, Kieffer Vaughan, Seale, and Collins was at Richmond, Indiana, making records at the Star Piano Company.

Between April 21 and May 1, that quartet cut numerous recordings to be sold on the Vaughan custom label. Among the songs recorded were "Echoes From The Glory Shore," "I Need The Prayers of Those I Love," "Beautiful Harbor Lights," a solo by Seale on "When They Ring Those Golden Bells," "Music In My Soul," a solo by Kieffer on "Jesus Is All I Need," "Only A Step," "Mother And Home," "The Old Fashioned Cabin," "They Left Him Alone," "Go To Jesus With It All," and "Singing A Wonderful Song," all from the 1923 Vaughan songbook, *Awakening Praises*.

They also recorded some other favorites, including "When You And I Were Young, Maggie," especially arranged for male voices by Adger M. Pace.

There was a Vaughan Quartet that summer composed of J. L. Jimerson, F. X. Trigg, J. E. Hamilton, and Robert Vaughan; and later in the year Jimerson teamed with W. T. Richardson, M. D. McWhorter, and a man named Kimbell in yet another Vaughan Quartet.

Still another quartet had P. B. Burress, J. E. Wheeler, E. C. Brooks, and H. O. Walter, who was replaced in midseason by Cullie Wilson.

Two quartets were based in Texas, one managed by Frank Stamps, who sang bass in it, with Jeff Duncan, F. H. Prine, and Thomas Ware; and another, called the Vaughan Texas Quartet, containing V. M. Nipper, Will Fincannon, Raymond Elliott, and Lee Myers.

Reports in the *Vaughan Family Visitor* of April 1923 showed the extent of the Texas operation and provided a glimpse of quartet life. Frank Stamps gave a report on his quartet:

We got together in Jacksonville, Texas, about the first of March, and after a couple of weeks there we left for parts unknown. The first stop was at Post City, Texas, where we attended the Garza County convention. We must say that we enjoyed the day very much, although we had Texas weather; and it rained a little, snowed a little, then the sun came out for a spell and so on the rest of the day. . . . Next we went to Floyd County, Texas, and spent a pleasant week there.

Then we attended the Castro County convention at Dimmitt, Texas, where we met many old friends and made many new ones. I believe that this is one of the best conventions that we have ever attended. . . .

Last Sunday, April 1st, we stepped on the starter of the old Buick and headed for New Mexico to be with the people at the Roosevelt County convention at Portales. We enjoyed the day very much. . . .

We are at home now and consider this one of the best fields in the west.

V. M. Nipper, who managed the Vaughan Texas Quartet, reported on his quartet's activities like this:

We left Jacksonville for a convention at Hartshorne, Okla., on the 24th and 25th of March. This was a dandy good convention. J. S. Brown is the president of this convention, and he certainly knows how to treat a music man. . . . We spent the following week in that area concerting. We gave our first concert in that section at Cambria, a mining town. . . .

The first Sunday in April found us in the Sanboise District Convention in Le Flore County. This was a splendid convention. The second Sunday found us in the Canadian Valley convention in Muskogee County. . . . The third Sunday we attended the Haskell County convention. I believe this is the best convention we attended since we have been in Oklahoma. Charles W. Rainwater is president of this convention and, believe me, he sure knows how to treat a quartet for he once made his dollars as a music man.

We will be in Eastern Oklahoma until the last of May. This is a fine country and is fast developing into one of the leading countries musically.

During the months when the weather was good, the Vaughan quartets stayed on the road. Between conventions they usually made enough money concerting to pay expenses.

A quartet called the Dixon Bros. Quartet represented Vaughan in East Tennessee's hill country, one of the few Vaughan quartets that did not carry the Vaughan name. Three Dixon brothers, Sam, West, and Frank, teamed with Claude Sharpe in this quartet. Sharpe later came to Lawrenceburg and sang with the Vaughan quartets before moving on to Nashville where he organized the Old Hickory Singers and sang on the Grand Ole Opry for years.

The arrangement Vaughan had with his quartets, keeping the men on salary and on the road, probably was the first example in rural America of a company serving as agent for a stable of performers.

Back in Lawrenceburg, Tennessee, was the most unusual Vaughan Quartet of all—the Vaughan Office Quartet, or, as it was better known, the Vaughan Saxophone Quartet. These were four men who played the saxophone and sang: H. E. Barnett, first tenor and alto sax; Ted R. Shaw, second tenor and C Melody sax; W. B. Walbert, baritone and alto sax; and Adger M. Pace, bass and baritone sax. Sometimes they were joined by an office employee named Ed Teske who played the violin and the sax. Later, Otis L. McCoy was a member of this quartet.

The quartet, or quintet, whichever it might be at the moment, started by playing a verse of a song on saxophones, then singing the chorus and perhaps another verse and chorus *a cappella*, and winding up playing the song again on the instruments.

The Vaughan Saxophone Quartet was a favorite over WOAN and sometime during 1923 the quartet made a lengthy road trip. The *Visitor* reported that the quartet "received favorable attention from many cities, including New York, Chicago, Cleveland, Toronto, Erysipalas, and others."

This quartet was quite a sensation wherever it went.

In the early 1920s, Vaughan was the biggest thing in music from Florida to New Mexico and north to the Mason-Dixon Line. Vaughan schools were held all over the country. Typical was a Vaughan Normal held in Clovis, New Mexico, August 13 through September 7, 1923.

Students came from miles around, many boarding in Clovis homes. The three-week school required only a ten dollar tuition, and private lessons cost one dollar for voice and seventy-five cents for piano.

V. O. Stamps taught theory, harmony, and methods. M. L. Yandell taught harmony and piano; F. X. Trigg instructed in voice culture and piano; Zeke Kitts taught sight-reading and theory; and Jeff Duncan served the school as secretary. All members of the faculty had sung in Vaughan's Texas quartets that summer.

V. O. Stamps had risen high in the Vaughan company. He and his brother Frank had been with Vaughan since the mid-teens when they came to Lawrenceburg to attend the music school. By 1923 V. O.'s name, along with Charles W. Vaughan and W. W. McGlamry, was carried as a contributing editor on the masthead of the *Visitor*. James D. Vaughan was listed as managing editor; B. C. Unseld, who died later that year, as literary editor; and James Rowe, a poet, was a special contributor.

An editorial by Charles W. Vaughan in the June 1923 *Visitor* told of the current state of quartets and conventions, and gave an insight to the quartet business:

> Many people do not appreciate the good that the right kind of a quartet does by being in a convention or community. If a quartet is up to the Vaughan standard—it will be an incentive to local singers to sing better. I say 'Vaughan standard' because no other music publisher does what James D. Vaughan and his associates do to produce the best quartets, and only a very few music publishers, and that in a limited way, send out any singers. Some of them do get four men together for a short time to make a few conventions, without much cost to the publisher, but they soon disband.
>
> Vaughan quartets are made up of trained singers, men whose voices are suited to the parts they sing; then they are trained for weeks before they are ready to go out and sing to the people. This is done at considerable expense, but that part is not the chief consideration; the main idea is to have them so they can 'deliver the goods' when they do go before the people. The majority of them have been trained in the Vaughan schools and know the value of being able to interpret a song, be it simple or difficult. But back to the sense of appreciation, many leaders and presidents of conventions expect a quartet of this caliber to attend their conventions without any remuneration (which cannot be done) or any preparation for the quartet's entertainment. At times local singers, who hardly know enough to stand up and sing a song, let alone direct one, are given as much or more time than one of these quartets. This is the pathetic side of the question, but I am glad to say that places of this kind are woefully in the minority. At almost all conventions the quartets visit now,

concerts are arranged for them before they go, usually on Saturday night of the convention, which usually takes care of all expenses. Lots of times a full week's dates are arranged for them between conventions.

The progressive people, musically, realize that a quartet like a Vaughan quartet, is a big asset and inspiration to any convention. They are mighty nice indeed to the boys, wherever they go and it is highly appreciated by the man who sends them out as well as by the quartet members. For if it were not for the cooperation and help of the people, the quartets could not attend the singings and the quartet boys would not have a job.

When I started with the first Vaughan quartet, there were no quartets at conventions except ours in the section of the country we traveled; now there are many good local quartets at different places over the territory. And while I do not feel exalted over it, I do feel that the Vaughan quartets have been instrumental in building the singing interest over our great Southland and a part of the North. Not only have the quartets helped, but good singers and directors have done their bit also. Conventions are better conducted; there are more good singers and more conventions. The singers are waking up and better preparing themselves by attending schools that teach something. A better day is in sight for gospel song, and the Vaughan quartets are getting better because there are more good singers to select from. . . .

CHAPTER FOUR

A Man of Principle

Had all gospel singers and musicians—those of today and those of yesteryear—been given the opportunity to vote for the man to father the business of professional gospel singing, they could not have made a better choice than James D. Vaughan.

Vaughan, of course, was self-appointed in this role, having been a man in the right place at the right time with fortitude enough to put his sound ideas to work. He was, fortunately, a man of good business acumen and a man of adventure. He accepted major challenges without the blink of an eye.

But above all else, he was a man of principle.

Saved by the Grace of God at the age of ten, Vaughan never indulged in the earthly pleasures that attract boys and young men. He never used tobacco in any form, never swore an oath, and never drank intoxicating beverages.

"The worse word I ever heard him say was 'Pshaw!'" said his grandson and namesake, James D. Walbert.

James D. Vaughan lived an exemplary Christian life. He was ever a student, and he knew the Bible as few men did.

Vaughan had his distractions and hobbies. He took sports seriously and loved athletic games. He had a baseball team in Lawrenceburg at one time and attended all of its games.

"I wish he had lived to see television," said James D. Walbert. "He would have enjoyed all the games. I've seen him with his ear glued to the radio, listening to the World Series. He loved all sports."

Vaughan's favorite hymn was "Amazing Grace," and he would request it at conventions. Usually he requested that his grandson, the same James D. Walbert, play it; Vaughan loved the piano arrangement Walbert worked out.

It has been said of James D. Vaughan that he was a "well-intentioned man," that he had compassion for the human race.

"The beggar was never turned away from his door," said Adger M. Pace, who worked with Vaughan twenty-seven years. "It was almost a daily occurrence that the down-and-out came to his office for help. They never got too ragged but that he would take time to shake hands and say a few words of encouragement and give them help."

The Rev. J. M. Allen, who preached Vaughan's funeral, said, "Thousands of students left his school prepared for Christian work and living through his love for humanity. He never turned them away, whether they had money to pay him or not. Many of his students went on to preach and sing the gospel. Truly his influence for good was far-reaching. He lived his religion every day."

Many boys and girls came to his school without financial means to pay tuition, and he accepted them without question. He also paid the board of many students who had no money for that. If a student had talent but not money, James D. Vaughan paid the student's way, even furnishing private lessons; and so that his associates would not think he was giving the lessons away, he usually said, "They'll pay me sometime."

In the latter months of B. C. Unseld's life in 1923, Vaughan paid him a pension of $50 a month, even though Unseld was too ill to work.

Two of Vaughan's teachers said to him once that they needed to go to New York City for further study, and Vaughan not only paid their way but paid their salaries while they were gone.

Vaughan was a prolific writer, despite his busy schedule. He wrote more than five hundred songs, most of them printed in the songbooks he sold. At his death, his company had printed and sold almost seven million songbooks. For a long while he kept Southern America singing.

James D. Vaughan died February 9, 1941, of a coronary thrombosis. His funeral was held in the Nazarene Tabernacle, which he attended, in Lawrenceburg. The church seated five hundred; and when seven thousand people came for the funeral, a public address system was rigged in the churchyard so those standing outside could hear.

When undertakers prepared Vaughan's body for burial, they were disturbed to find callouses the size of a quarter on each of his knees.

They checked with the family and found that the callouses were caused by Vaughan's spending so much time on his knees in prayer.

Otis L. McCoy was typical of the young people Vaughan helped start in musical careers.

Born February 7, 1897, at Old Ninety-Six, South Carolina, Otis was taken to Alabama with his family in 1900, settling in the redlands country.

His grandfather, S. M. Denson, a teacher of Sacred Harp music, taught Otis the four-note system when he was eight years old.

In his ninetieth year, Otis McCoy looked back and explained the four-note musical system:

"The four-note system does not have an absolute pitch," Otis said. "It only has the bass, tenor, and treble. Only four notes represent the eight tones of the scale. You have to hear the other pitches. The scale was *Fa Sol La Fa Sol La Mi Fa.*

"There are so many repetitions of the same note in there that you can't have an absolute pitch. You couldn't match this to the notes of the scale, *C D E F G A B C.*

"Sacred Harp is 'Semi Demi Quaver Flaver' music. That's what they called it. An eighth note is 'Semi Quaver.' A sixteenth note is 'Semi Demi Quaver.' A thirty-second note is 'Semi Demi Quaver Demi Quaver.' And a sixty-fourth note is 'Semi Demi Quaver Semi Demi Quaver Quaver.'

"I learned all that when I was eight years old."

At the age of seventeen, Otis studied music with W. P. Ganus of Birmingham, one of the great music teachers. Ganus was the father of four sons, who sang as the Ganus Brothers Quartet. The four—Clarence Powell, Claude Patton, Clyde Patterson, and Cecil Palmer Ganus—each had the initials C. P., and Otis remembers that when one of them received a letter from his girlfriend addressed to C. P. Ganus, they all had to read it to determine which brother it was intended for.

By 1923 when he was twenty-six years old, Otis McCoy had decided he didn't want to be a farmer; so, quite naturally, he turned to music. But he knew he needed more study. The Vaughan School of Music intrigued him, and he decided to make his way to Lawrenceburg and give it a shot. He was a married man with two children at the time.

"I put all of my household utensils and one thing and another in one big box," he said, "and rolled it out on the platform of the depot at

Carbon Hill, Alabama. The depot agent heard those tin pans rattling and smelled the old kerosene stove in the box and asked me, 'Are you gonna take this stuff out when you get to Lawrenceburg?' I said, 'Yes, sir,' but I didn't have a dollar to put on it at the time I was talking.

"What I did have," Otis said, "was the faith to believe that something would happen when I got there."

As soon as he arrived in Lawrenceburg, Otis made his way to James D. Vaughan's office.

After introductions, Otis charged ahead. "Now, Mr. Vaughan," he said, "I am here to go to school, and I couldn't promise you any money under three months, but if you'll let me go to school I'll pay you every penny; I'll work around at anything I can get to do to make the money to pay you."

"That's fine," Vaughan said. "You go ahead and I'll take care of you on your tuition."

Next, Otis went to a neighborly grocer. He explained his plight and made the grocer the same offer that Vaughan had accepted.

"All right," the grocer said, apparently recognizing Otis McCoy's sincerity. "I'll feed your wife and babies, and you get your schooling and pay me when you can get the money."

So Otis McCoy went to school, and before a year was over he had taught 160 days of singing schools and worked in five weeks of revivals, all out of town. When he returned to Lawrenceburg after the last revival, he cleared all of his accounts, paying Vaughan and the grocer every cent he owed them.

Then it was Vaughan's turn to make an offer. "I would like to have you with my institution," Vaughan said. "You can sing with one of my quartets." In that way, Otis joined the Vaughan family of quartets and sang with them for seven years. He also finished the Vaughan Conservatory during that time, and his music education was extensive.

In 1927 McCoy joined the Vaughan quartet of Hillman Barnard, W. B. Walbert, and Adger M. Pace—the Saxophone Quartet—and made a road trip with them that covered twenty states and two Canadian provinces. They sang in New York, Chicago, Philadelphia, St. Louis, Lincoln (Neb.), Cedar Rapids (Iowa), Champaign (Ill.), and dozens of other cities and received rave notices wherever they performed.

Because of James D. Vaughan's philanthropy, Otis McCoy went on to accomplish many things in music. He started the Tennessee Music and Printing Company in Cleveland, Tennessee, in 1930, which became the music department of Lee College, the higher education unit of the Church of God. In 1932 Otis organized the Bible Training School Quartet, which became the Homeland Harmony Quartet. He gave Aycel Soward his first musical training and later thought Soward became one of the best bass singers ever. "He could knock the bottom out of those Gs below low C," Otis said.

Otis sang the lead with first tenor Eugene Whitt, baritone Fred C. Maples, and Soward in the first Tennessee Music Company Quartet in 1931, recording for Okeh Records with Frances Johnson at the piano. At the same time, he sang first tenor in the Bible Training School Quartet with lead singer J. H. Walker, baritone Lloyd McLain, and bass B. C. Robinson.

Alf and Urias LeFevre, Fred C. Maples, and songwriter Vep Ellis studied under Otis at the Bible Training School in Cleveland. Alf drew the cover page for the songbook entitled *Homeland Harmony* from which the quartet later took its name.

It was unfortunate that the depression struck the quartet business at its height; otherwise James D. Vaughan and his sprawling empire might have accomplished even greater things.

But the depression cut songbook sales in half, and according to Charles W. Vaughan, no quartet could make a living singing, except by working in evangelistic meetings. The Vaughan Radio Quartet worked revivals almost exclusively for four years during the depression.

Too, by that time, V. O. and Frank Stamps, who formed their own music company in 1924, were going full steam and were rapidly approaching a role of domination in quartet singing.

There was disappointment in the Vaughan company when the Stamps brothers pulled out, because it was quickly recognized that Vaughan suddenly had a strong competitor. But the quartets and representatives of the two companies usually got along well—at least superficially—when their trails crossed at conventions. They finally decided in general that there was room for all.

But competition between the company quartets on stage was ferocious. Friendly, but ferocious!

In 1939 when the nation was snapping out of the depression, the Vaughan Quartet of Leroy Carver, first tenor; Charles Helton, lead; W. B. Walbert, baritone; and Chalmers Walker, bass, with James D. Walbert at the keyboard, went up against the Blackwood Brothers, then a Stamps-Baxter quartet, at the Tri-State Singing Convention in Shreveport, Louisiana.

Both quartets had jobs singing on radio stations in Shreveport, and both were very popular. The convention auditorium seated ten thousand persons, and it was packed out for this event.

Joe Roper, the Blackwood Brothers' pianist, had left the quartet, and Walbert had played piano for the Blackwoods for about a month, doing double duty with both quartets on the radio, until Stamps-Baxter sent Marion Snyder to replace Roper.

Snyder was a showy pianist. He constantly grinned at the audience and threw his hands up and down above the keyboard as he played.

The success of quartets at singing conventions then was measured largely by the number of encores the group received. At this convention, two encores insured a quartet of the status of "greatness."

The convention people scheduled the Blackwood Brothers and the Vaughan Quartet back to back on the program, with the Blackwoods singing first.

Snyder was his usual great self that day, and the Blackwoods were typically tuneful—a great quartet, really—and the group received two encores.

W. B. Walbert, who managed the Vaughan Quartet, was a spiritual man who did not believe that a quartet should do anything showy to detract from the gospel messages in the songs.

But in W. B.'s absence from home during working hours, his son, James D. Walbert, had worked up a routine in which he played the piano backward. He had to play with opposite hands, the octave with his left and the chord with his right—but he mastered the trick and felt fairly comfortable when he went out with the Vaughan Quartet at the convention and began playing the big concert grand.

The Vaughans finished and drew their first encore, and gave it enough flourish to earn the second, equalling the Blackwood Brothers' performance. But in that second encore, Walbert suddenly leaped off the piano bench, shoved the bench out of the way, turned around, and began whomping the piano backward, and the crowd went wild, demanding a third encore, which won the day for the Vaughan Quartet—with the Blackwood Brothers standing in the wings watching and enjoying the show as much as anyone in the house.

"I know Dad didn't care for that stunt," James said later, "but he didn't dislike it enough to mention it, because it got us our third encore. Still, I never tried the trick again."

One trick that he did try later, however, was playing the piano with his elbows.

Walbert was trained in the classics, and was one of the great pianists, but he could ham it up when he thought it necessary.

He had a solo of "Stars and Stripes Forever," which was all right to use at conventions because it was a patriotic song, and with World War II approaching, any patriotic song was acceptable.

He had worked up a routine in which he played the song with his elbows and kept the melody going with his hands in the middle, but one day at a big convention, adversity struck. Walbert hit his funny bone while playing with his elbows and the resulting dance he did on stage brought the house down.

Quartets in the late 1930s had become so versatile, and were so musically educated, that they could solve almost any problem in mid-song.

In 1936 the Vaughan Trio—Ottis and Cecil Knippers and Cullie Wilson—was singing on WOWO, Fort Wayne, Indiana, "the Voice of Indiana," 10,000 watts, clear channel, and they knew their songs were booming across the continent to millions of homes.

The guys were strictly a trio, singing without accompaniment. They got their pitch from a pitch pipe which Ottis manipulated. For one song, he made the pitch without checking the pipe, and pitched it in G instead of C—five notes off. They were already into the song before they realized what Ottis had done.

"We looked at each other and our eyes got bigger and bigger," Ottis said, "and we knew that when we started to go up we were going to be in trouble."

He thought about stopping and starting the song all over but was too embarrassed to do that before such a vast listening audience.

The three, he thought, had sung together enough to handle the problem. They had ways of communicating with their eyes, and in that way they began to swap parts.

"The high tenor would grab the soprano's part," Ottis said, "and the soprano would take the high tenor and drop it an octave. We just switched around when we came to a difficult part, and we finished the song in pretty good shape."

Many years later, part-switching became an everyday thing in quartet singing.

By 1939, James D. Vaughan knew that his business had survived the depression very well.

The summer school of music in the Vaughan Conservatory in June of 1939 was the largest school Vaughan had ever had.

Charles W. Vaughan wrote in the *Visitor* that students "came from Dan to Beersheba." So many were taking private lessons that the private teachers worked day and night. Every piano in every studio and five pianos at the M. E. Church, South, were busy from early morning until 10 p.m. Nine regular organized quartets were in attendance and great local crowds attended the daily chorus practice every afternoon at three.

The school was so large that the regular faculty of G. Kieffer Vaughan, W. B. Walbert, Adger M. Pace, G. T. Speer, Luther Drummond, Dewey Yeager, Brock Speer, Dwight Brock, and Leroy Carter had to be supplemented by three additional teachers, Austin Williams, Pearl Claborn, and E. M. Bartlett.

Such were the fortunes of hard work and righteous living for James D. Vaughan.

CHAPTER FIVE

The Stamps Act

The first hint James D. Vaughan had of a split in his ranks came from Otis McCoy. V. O. Stamps, running Vaughan's Jacksonville, Texas, branch office, far, far away from the home office in Lawrenceburg, Tennessee, had wanted to go into business for himself for some time. Frugally, he saved his money until he thought he had enough to weather through the first year, and he made definite plans to resign from Vaughan and open up the V. O. Stamps Music Company. His brother, Frank, was ready to join him, not on a full partnership basis but as a quartet manager.

The Showalter Music Company of Dalton, Georgia, had printed a rudiments book, and V. O. apparently was selling it on the side to make some extra money.

He mailed one of the books in a Vaughan package C.O.D. to a man on Vaughan's mailing list, and the man refused to accept the package. The book was mailed from the Jacksonville office but under a label listing the return address as Lawrenceburg, as all Vaughan merchandise was mailed.

So instead of the package being returned to Stamps, it was returned to the Lawrenceburg office where Otis McCoy was working as Vaughan's C.O.D. manager.

McCoy took the book to Vaughan and asked what should be done with it, and Vaughan recognized what V. O. Stamps was doing—selling other merchandise under the name of Vaughan.

When word circulated around the Vaughan Lawrenceburg office, most of the employees were convinced that V. O. Stamps had been filling cash orders with his own books.

Also, to this day, there are those in the music business who believe that V. O. Stamps had been squirreling away the best songs that Vaughan's Southwestern songwriters sent to the Jacksonville office, saving them for publication in his first book, which was an excellent book that came out in 1924.

At any rate, V. O. Stamps finalized the split in 1924 and opened the V. O. Stamps Music Company in Jacksonville, Texas.

Frank Stamps organized the first Stamps Quartet in 1924. While V. O. (Virgil Oliver) ran the office and edited that first Stamps songbook, Frank formed a quartet composed of J. E. Wheeler, Lee Myers, and J. E. Hamilton, all former Vaughan singers. Frank sang bass and played piano for accompaniment.

They sang at local singing schools, forming their style, but the quartet made no great splash of interest among the good church-going folk of Texas, and within two years, by 1926, after several personnel changes, it disbanded.

V. O. Stamps found himself in financial difficulties in 1926, in dire danger of losing his company, and almost floundered before bringing J. R. Baxter, Jr., of Chattanooga, Tennessee, into the company as a partner. Baxter, who had studied and worked with Showalter, bought forty-nine percent of the company. They changed the name to the Stamps-Baxter Music Company and moved the offices to Dallas, Texas.

Stamps and Baxter proved to be a perfect combo. J. R. was a harmonist, deep in music theory, and V. O. was a promoter extraordinaire. They published songs that were singable. J. R. made sure the words fit the music, and that there was no funny meter in any of the Stamps-Baxter songs. The songs had good voice lead ins, no abrupt jumps and skips in the voice lines, and were easily sung.

In no time at all, the company was back on sound financial footing.

And then 1927 rolled around. That was a big, big year all over.

Babe Ruth hit a record sixty home runs for the New York Yankees that summer; Charles Lindberg flew nonstop across the Atlantic in a perilous, one-man, daredevil attempt to accomplish what had previously been impossible; Gene Tunney decisioned Jack Dempsey in the famous "long count" fight; and Warner Bros. premiered "The Jazz Singer" with Al Jolson, heralding the age of talking pictures.

The twenties were really roaring. Americans thrilled to glitz and glamor.

Down South, this new style of pure American Christian folk music was still somewhat in it's infancy, but it was about to come of age.

The Stamps Quartet, a failure three years previously, was about to gain a tremendous amount of popularity because of a young man who played strange but appealing accompaniment on the piano. His name was Dwight Brock, and he played for a Stamps Quartet composed of two brothers, Palmer Wheeler on first tenor and Roy Wheeler on second tenor, Odis Echols on the baritone, and Frank Stamps singing a rolling, unamplified, yet sometimes booming bass.

Brock played a rhythm piano style; some thought it sounded a little like Dixieland or razzamatazz. He was developing a style in which he would eventually play the first line or two of a song and then, without stopping, wheel directly into the melody and the quartet would come in on the fly. At the end of the verse, he would do the same thing, playing an interlude, and again without stopping, as pianists of the day were wont to do, the quartet would catch on again on the fly. Dwight's interludes would become known as turnarounds, exciting changes that established a precedent and heralded the growth of professional gospel quartet singing in America to heights that were hard to measure. Thousands of pianists would copy his style in the years to come.

Whether Brock was the very first to play turnarounds is debatable. Lee Roy Abernathy, the sage of Canton, Georgia, who has taught a multitude of people how to play and sing, may have been the first. He believes he was. Lee Roy began singing with a quartet when he was three years old in 1916, and by 1926 said he was playing piano turnarounds for his dad's Atco Quartet before Brock played them for the Stamps.

Brock, however, was the man who carried this style of playing to America, for he traveled far and wide with the Stamps Quartet.

Whoever began it, the way Dwight Brock and Lee Roy Abernathy played the piano was an exciting change that established a precedent. Gospel quartet singing grew into big business.

Brock was the first man hired to play the piano for a quartet without doubling as a singer. The Vaughan quartets included only four men, one of whom played piano while he also sang.

Brock's unique style was a boyhood dream come true. It was revolutionary because it jazzed up gospel music just enough for the secular public to catch on.

Dwight's nephew, Brock Speer, who sings bass for the Speer Family today, said that when his uncle was a boy in the early teens—he was born in 1905—he heard a circus drummer playing syncopated rhythms on snare drums, and said to himself, "I wonder if I could do that on the piano." He developed some piano licks like nobody had ever heard in those days. Brock Speer's brother, Ben, remembers his uncle talking about the experience but remembers the instrument that activated Dwight Brock's piano licks as being a calliope.

When he finally developed the style and put it to work for Frank Stamps and his All-Star Quartet, Dwight Brock's piano playing thrilled crowds so that people climbed up on benches just to get a glimpse of him playing.

He was thrilling to hear.

With Brock at the piano, the style of music presented by the All-Star Quartet was far more pleasing to the ear than that of the 1924 Stamps Quartet had been.

Chattanooga, Tennessee, site of a Stamps-Baxter office run by J. R. Baxter, Jr., was more centrally located in the territory in which the Stamps-Baxter company wished to build its business, and from Chattanooga Frank Stamps took his quartet out to sing. Chattanooga was also nearer Lawrenceburg and the chief competition for the Stamps Quartet, the Vaughan quartets. Stamps brought his quartet on stage sharp in appearance, dressed alike in matching suits. One set of suits was handsome black tuxedoes with wide, shiny-silk lapels.

The Stamps Quartet was an entertaining fivesome. It not only sang the most popular gospel songs of the day, but gave an all-around entertainment program, singing popular and standard songs. Each member of the quartet sang his own specialty number, songs such as "Me and My Shadow," "Ah, Sweet Mystery of Life," and others of a similar theme. All the gospel quartets sang secular music in those days. G. T. (Dad) Speer, coming along as a gospel singer in Alabama, frequently sang such songs as "My Blue Heaven," and "My Blue Skies," and the old Gene Austin songs.

Frank Stamps' All-Star Quartet adopted a song written in 1925 by piano-playing M. L. Yandell and singer Otis Deaton called "Give The World A Smile" as its theme song, and it caught the public's fancy in a big way. It was a happy rhythm number with a bass lead in the chorus. While the bass sang the strong melody, the upper trio voices sang an afterbeat. Then, on the repeat chorus, they sang a boom, boom, pang, pang effect like a rhythm guitar.

Wherever the Stamps Quartet appeared in concert, it sang "Give

The World A Smile," and audiences went crazy with applause over the number.

The Stamps All-Star Quartet's popularity grew to such proportions that a talent scout from the Victor Talking Machine Company approached Frank Stamps with the offer of a recording contract for his quartet. This was the opportunity that really opened the door of fame for them. Frank signed the contract and the Stamps Quartet became the first gospel quartet to record for a major record company.

Its first recording session was in the Victor Studio in Atlanta, Georgia, October 20, 1927. The A&R man for Victor wanted the quartet to record two of his favorite hymns, "Bringing In The Sheaves," and Fanny Crosby's famous song, "Rescue The Perishing." These went on both sides of one record, a 78 rpm disk; and the quartet recorded "Give The World A Smile" and "Love Leads The Way" for another record.

That latter record, because of the popularity of "Give The World A Smile," sold more than a million copies, and both the Victor Talking Machine Company and the Stamps All-Star Quartet knew they had formed an alliance that would be of major import.

The record was handy financially, too. Dwight Brock often talked about that 1927 quartet and how its traveling expenses almost ran it into the red at first. It was on the verge of disbanding, flat broke, Brock said, when a big check, like $1,500—a fortune in those days—came through from the Victor company for record royalties and got the quartet back on its feet.

Other quartets began to use "Give The World A Smile" for their theme song, and before long many of the professional quartets had adopted it for an introductory theme. All the Stamps quartets used it. Even the Blackwood Brothers used it for a theme song in the 1930s when they sold Stamps-Baxter songbooks to supplement their income.

Still popular today, "Give The World A Smile" is sometimes recorded by male quartets now.

V. O. and Frank Stamps were strong bass singers, V. O. a bit stronger than Frank; both were tremendous singers, capable of filling huge rooms with their voices. Forcing the bass voice as they had to do, without amplification, resulted in slurred words and a totally different sound than quartets achieved years later when amplification came into use.

The Stamps brothers were great personalities. Many quartet old-timers today say, "I wonder where gospel music would be if V. O. Stamps had lived." He was an innovative man, filled with ideas that he wasn't afraid to put into action.

Quartets attended singing conventions on weekends and went head-to-head in competition with quartets of other publishing companies. Through the week they gave concerts wherever they could. They carried songbooks with them but sold only the books of the companies they represented. Later, when more quartets began making records, they also carried their own records and sold them, too.

J. D. Sumner recalls that once during the 1940s when he was singing with the Stamps Sunny South Quartet in Florida, his quartet went against the Melody Masters, a Vaughan quartet featuring Jake Hess and Jim Wetherington, at a Sunday afternoon singing convention at which all singers sat on stage. Frank Stamps was there to hear and support the Sunny South. The Melody Masters crowded around the one microphone and began singing, and when they hit their stride and really opened up, Frank Stamps got up and walked across the stage, ostensibly to get a drink of water. When he crossed over the electric cord to the public address system, he kicked the cord out of the wall, the mike went dead, and the Melody Masters, going great at that point, were suddenly cut off.

Frank shrugged and spread his hands, saying, "Sorry, fellows," and the Melody Masters could not get it back together again when electricity was restored.

Quartet men were troubadours in the truest sense. Good singers, good storytellers, good men they were, wandering vagabonds whose senses of humor, accomplishment, and entertainment were sharp.

Frank Stamps once said that his quartet chose places to do concerts by driving through the countryside until they came to a town with smokestacks, and there they did a concert.

"Where there were smokestacks," Frank said, "there was a payroll."

They had no public address equipment, no means of amplification, but that made no difference. The quartets hired only those singers who could fill large buildings with their voices—and especially some of the basses were quite spectacular.

A person with an average voice stood little chance of getting a position with a professional quartet in the 1920s. Quartets demanded two things: good voices and music readers. Even though many of them taught singing schools in the summer, these men still sought out the best music teachers and studied voice regularly. People like W. W. Combs, Harley Lester, Walter B. Seale, Millard Massey, Robert and Vera Vaughan, Kieffer Vaughan, Luther Drummond, and Dewey Yeager were great teachers. They instilled in those early quartet singers the rudiments of proper breathing, enunciation, and such correct singing procedures that few were ever bothered by voice or throat problems.

The advent of the music company quartets made the Sunday afternoon singing convention a thrilling experience. Quartets sat together on stage, rising from their chairs to step forward and sing when their turns came, and they sang with all the other competitive quartets sitting just behind them.

Folks came from miles around to attend the singing conventions, traveling over dirt and gravel roads in all kinds of weather, sometimes over no roads at all, to spend the day in an oven-hot auditorium or church, sweating and fanning, but happily whiling away the hours listening to great singing.

Some of the singers established reputations early and became popular. While the early Vaughan quartets were thrilling America, there was also something especially appealing about G. T. and Lena Speer, later called Dad and Mom Speer, who began singing in Double Springs, Alabama, in 1921, and as the years passed formed a family-singing group with their children.

Two brothers, Alphus and Urias LeFevre, walked out of the Tennessee hills in 1921 and sang their way across America, gaining immense popularity as the LeFevre Trio after Urias married Eva Mae Whittington early in the 1930s.

Two other great singers, Lloyd Gilbert and Harley Lester, began traveling in the middle of 1926 as the "Personality Two," and then in 1928, when the Stamps and Vaughan quartets were putting quartet singing into the upper echelon of Southern music, they joined Walter B. Seale and Eiland Scarborough in the Vaughan Texas Quartet.

In 1925, with Frank Stamps's original 1924-model Stamps Quartet still struggling for a foothold, V. O. Stamps used the three Wheeler brothers, J. E. (called Johnny), Roy, and Palmer, in a quartet for which V. O. himself sang bass and played piano or organ, when a church was equipped with one. That lively group sang on occasion for about a year.

Garland May of Monroe, Louisiana, remembers attending the 1926 Louisiana State Singing Convention at which V. O. Stamps sang with a quartet composed of Millard Massey, Kay Baird, and Bill Fincannon, and one of the quartets singing against them was a Vaughan quartet with M. D. McWhorter, John Pickering, C. B. Ribble, and a fourth man whose identity has long since escaped May's memory.

After Frank Stamps's All-Star Quartet cut those records in 1927, a lot more professional quartets began singing, no doubt hoping for lucrative recording contracts. V. O. Stamps organized a new V. O. Stamps Quartet in 1928 with Bill and Zeke Kitts, Jeff Duncan, V. O. singing bass, and M. L. Yandell playing piano. V. O. and his quartet recorded on the Brunswick label under the name of the Stamps Quartet. Frank Stamps reorganized his own quartet in 1929 with E. T. Burgess, Henry Long, Andy Hughes, and himself, with Dwight Brock still playing the piano. They continued to record for RCA Victor under the name of the Frank Stamps All-Star Quartet.

In the late 1920s a quartet called the "Owens Brothers and Ellis" became popular. Four Owens brothers, Arch, Aubrey, Babe, and Hub, from Gilbert, Texas, hired a bass singer by the name of Oglesby Ellis and came up with a quartet good enough to record for the Columbia Recording Company. They traveled exclusively for the Stamps-Baxter Music Company, selling songbooks and records.

Otis Deaton had a good quartet somewhere in that 1920s time frame with Henry Long, Theo Casey, and Eddie Glossom.

Quartet singing grew in popularity by leaps and bounds. Almost every community had its own quartet, whether it could sing or not.

Those big quartets, especially the radio quartets, made rural kids of the 1930s thirst to be singers. Because of the depression, most rural people in the Southern United States were well grounded in their faith in God; God was the only power most of them could look to during those trying days. Thus, when quartets began singing God's Good News over the radio, which provided the most entertainment that rural people could find—when they could find it—the songs and the music became especially appealing to youngsters trying to decide what to do for a vocation in a world that had cracked apart at the seams.

When James Blackwood was a kid, still on the farm in Mississippi, the Vaughan Quartet had two programs every week on WSM in Nashville. The quartet drove from Lawrenceburg to Nashville on Wednesday afternoon, sang on the air from 4:30 to 5 p.m., spent the night in Nashville, and the following morning sang on the radio again from 6:30 to 7 o'clock. Vaughan paid for the air time so he could not only get his quartet before the listening public, but could advertise his song-books as well.

"Most of the time I listened," James Blackwood said, "the quartet consisted of Palmer Wheeler singing first tenor, Kieffer Vaughan singing lead, Johnny Cook singing baritone, and Adger M. Pace singing bass. Mr. Pace was replaced sometime in there by Jim Waits."

The Blackwoods didn't have a radio on their sharecropping farm in Mississippi, but a neighbor about a mile away had one. James was so interested in hearing the Vaughan Quartet that, with the permission of the neighbor, he walked the mile to the neighbor's house in the afternoon and listened to the thirty-minute program, then walked back home. The following morning, James walked back to the neighbor's to hear that program, then walked home again.

"I couldn't wait," he said, "to get old enough to sing."

Frank Stamps's All-Star Quartet continued to make records for Victor through 1928, using recording studios in Atlanta, Memphis, and Bristol, Tennessee. They recorded newly-written songs published by the Stamps-Baxter Company, and recorded at least one unpublished song, "Let Me Live Close To Thee," which they recorded off the manuscript. A lot of quartets do that today, but it was unusual in the days of company quartets.

V. O.'s quartet in Dallas (Bill and Zeke Kitts, Jeff Duncan, V. O., and M. L. Yandell) had two recording sessions in Dallas with the Brunswick Record Company, one on October 27, 1929, and the other on November 29, 1930, recording several songs at a time. Some of the songs recorded were "Cling To The Cross," "City of Gold," and "Jesus Taught Me How To Smile."

This was the quartet which began to sing on Dallas Radio Station KRLD, an association that continued into the 1950s.

V. O. also joined with Yandell and recorded several sides for Victor as a duet. Yandell played the piano and sang. They recorded "You Must Come In At The Door," "When Jesus Comes," and several others. All were recorded in Dallas in 1928 and 1929.

Late in 1929, Palmer and Roy Wheeler and Odis Echols left Frank's quartet. The Wheelers joined their older brother, J. E., to form the Wheeler Brothers Trio, performing through Tennessee, Kentucky and Alabama. Soon after this, Palmer joined the Sunshine Quartet in Kentucky.

Meanwhile, Frank regrouped with Andy Hughes, Henry Long, and E. T. Burgess, with Dwight Brock at the piano. They continued to record for Victor, cutting such songs as "Working For The Master," "Singing In My Soul," and "Living For Jesus."

During this time, 1929 and 1930, Vaughan had two quartets to record for Victor. In October of 1928 at the Victor Studio in Nashville, the Vaughan Quartet, composed of Hillman Barnard, Otis McCoy, W. B. Walbert, and Adger M. Pace, with Johnnie Jernings playing piano, made a series of recordings, including "In Steps Of Light," "What A Morning That Will Be," and "Sunlight and Shadows." This group also recorded in Memphis in September 1929 and May 1930. Otis McCoy later sang with Frank Stamps and then with the Homeland Harmony Quartet, which he founded.

The second quartet, known as the Vaughan Texas Quartet, recorded six songs for Victor in Dallas October 9, 1929, including "I Walk With Jesus" and "The King Needs Workers." Lloyd Gilbert, Harley Lester, Eiland Scarborough, and Walter Seale made up this group, with Lee Myers at the piano. Lester became one of the great voice teachers. He sang with the Stamps Quartet later, then formed his own group, Lester's Stamps Quartet.

The nation sank into the depths of depression in 1930, slowing some quartets, and taking others off the road. The depression is reflected in the personnel changes Frank Stamps made in his quartet that year. Otis McCoy came over from the Vaughan Quartet, and all other personnel came from the ranks of the Stamps-Baxter Music Company. Dwight Brock, who would spend most of the rest of his life working with the company, eventually retiring in 1974 as president and one-third owner of Stamps-Baxter, switched from the piano bench to a singing part, handling the baritone. J. R. Baxter, Jr., sang the lead, and Naomi Stamps, Frank's wife, played the piano. This group finished the recording contract with Victor, making the last records in February of 1932, cutting "The Great Redeemer," "I Want To Hear Him Call My Name," and others.

In 1934 Dwight Brock left temporarily. He switched to the Vaughan Radio Quartet to play piano again. Palmer Wheeler came with him to Vaughan, and they joined Kieffer Vaughan, John Cook, and Big Jim Waits. The quartet sang twice weekly over WSM in Nashville and traveled extensively throughout the South, giving concerts and public appearances and singing in a lot of revivals.

Unfortunately, the quartet made no commercial records, which old-timers say is a pity because this was one of the best blended quartets in the business.

Depression days continued to disrupt quartet singing, and this group, too, broke apart. Dwight Brock left to sing and play with his own family group and to manage the Stamps-Baxter Music Company office in Chattanooga. He was replaced on the Vaughan piano bench by James D. Walbert.

W. T. (Deacon) Utley, who later organized and conducted the Smile-A-While Stamps Quartet, emerged during the 1930s, singing in a Hartford Music Company quartet with Zelmer Lee, John Cauthron, and Bob Allison, with Burgess Bell accompanying. At the same time, Hartford put another quartet on the road, composed of Clyde Garner, Albert Houpe, J. T. McClung, and Austin Arnold, with an Oklahoma Indian named Doy Ott playing piano.

Sometime in the mid-1930s, V. O. Stamps reorganized the Stamps Quartet with Walter Rippetoe, Bob Bacon, Jim Gaither, V. O. singing bass, of course, and Marion Snyder playing the piano. Marion was V. O.'s brother-in-law. This was the group that became so well recognized as the V. O. Stamps Quartet, broadcasting twice daily over radio station KRLD in Dallas. They made numerous transcriptions that were used on many other radio stations internationally, stations such as WSM in Nashville, WOAI in San Antonio, and XERL and XENT in Mexico.

V. O.'s quartet did a live program every morning at 6:30 and another live one at 12:30 p.m. on KRLD, a powerful, 50,000-watt station that covered Texas and surrounding areas like a blanket.

Then V. O. made a deal with XERL in Mexico. This was the station that broadcast out of Del Rio, Texas, over a 500,000-watt transmitter located across the border in Mexico. The station was established and owned by Dr. John R. (Doc) Brinkley, who gained international fame with goat gland medicine which he developed on a farm on which he grew up in Tuckaseigee, North Carolina, just a hop and skip down the road from where Martin Cook of the Inspirations lives today.

Brinkley had a deal with the Mexican government that allowed him to do almost anything he pleased—and what he pleased to do was cover North America with a radio station advertising his medicines.

The station penetrated Mexico only for about fifty miles. Its transmitter was fan-shaped and pointed directly toward Texas. Its signal came in so powerfully at night all over North America that it zapped any station near it on the dial. With half-a-million watts, XERL drowned out all competition.

V. O.'s deal with XERL was to furnish fifteen-minute transcriptions in bulk, and the station played them several times every night, starting around 9 p.m. and lasting until midnight, and then the next morning XERL began broadcasting the Stamps Quartet again at 4, 5, or 6 a.m.

This coverage really put V. O. Stamps, his quartet, and his company, on the map. James Blackwood remembers going into the Stamps-Baxter office in Dallas in the mid-1930s when V. O. was selling a songbook entitled "V. O. Stamps Quartet Radio Favorites," and the mail came in that morning in several trucks.

"Most of the mail was orders for that songbook," James said. "They had orders that day from twenty-some states, all Canadian provinces, and even from some islands in the Pacific Ocean."

Frank Stamps, too, wanted to reorganize. He had lost both Otis McCoy and Dwight Brock to the Vaughan Quartet and had completed his recording contract with Victor. Frank, however, was not one to remain out of the spotlight very long; he wished to regain the popularity that had made the name of Stamps so famous. He therefore called the original members of the 1927 quartet back, Palmer and Roy Wheeler and Odis Echols, and hired Lawrence Ivey to play piano.

They made their home base in Greenville, South Carolina, where they sang on radio, but after a short while they moved to Hot Springs, Arkansas, and sang over radio station KTHS, traveling from there to fill personal appearances.

Perhaps because of the scarcity of money in the depression, this group made no records, but attained a blend and sound that surpassed the original recordings made for Victor in 1927. Through men like these, quartet singing constantly improved in quality.

They made several transcriptions, and even sang with V. O.'s quartet as guests on some of his transcribed programs.

By 1938 the end of the depression was in sight, but war clouds began to gather over Europe. Significant things started happening again for the Stamps-Baxter Music Company that year. V. O. signed a recording contract with Columbia Records. On May 13 in Dallas the quartet recorded several songs, among them "Just A Little Talk With Jesus," "Farther Along," Albert E. Brumley's "There's A Little Pine Log Cabin," and, naturally, "Give The World A Smile."

The Stamps company patterned a lot of its activities after the things V. O. learned from Vaughan, who, of course, had patterned his after Ruebush/Kieffer and other earlier publishers.

The Stamps School of Music, begun by V. O. Stamps when he opened the Stamps Music Company in 1924, thrived during the depression and continued full blast into the 1950s, teaching all phases of quartet singing and managing and piano-playing to youngsters from all over the country. Each year, at the end of the school in June, an all-night singing was held in the Sportatorium in Dallas, featuring kids from the school, and the program was broadcast over KRLD. CBS took a half-hour of the program and broadcast it coast-to-coast. Out of these schools came hundreds of men and women who went into professional gospel singing. Some of the notable ones were Hovie Lister of the Statesmen Quartet; Glen Payne of the Stamps-Ozark Quartet and later the Weatherfords and Cathedrals; Gordon Stoker of the Jordanaires; and so many others that a list would fill this page.

The schools averaged a thousand youngsters in attendance, and one year the enrollment was 1,176. Glen Payne, a kid from Josephine, Texas, did not have the financial means to attend the school, but his grandmother swallowed her pride and wrote to V. O. Stamps about her grandson's great love of gospel music and strong desire to attend the school. V. O. wrote back, "Please send the boy on over here. It won't cost him a dime." Even though V. O. died in 1940, Glen Payne attended the Stamps School of Music tuition-free in 1939, 1940, 1941, and 1942. He sang a year with Frank Stamps's quartet before going into the army, and when he returned in 1946, Frank Stamps gave him his job back.

Glen taught in the Stamps School of Music in 1950 and 1951. "The most embarrassed I've ever been," he said, "was at one of those all-night broadcasts from the auditorium in Dallas. We always had our best students sing on that program, and one year I had taught a woman from Portales, New Mexico, who had a beautiful voice; I was extremely proud of the way she improved during the school and really wanted her to show off her voice that night. When her turn came, I stood with my chest puffed out, thinking how everybody would see how much I had taught her; but when she got to the microphone, she puckered up and whistled 'Peace In The Valley.' I was never so deflated in my life."

Frank Stamps's quartet in Hot Springs stayed together until the fall of 1938 when Palmer Wheeler finally made up his mind to leave quartet singing. He began full-time work with the Church as a singer and teacher and never again returned to quartet singing. He began in a good position with Freed-Hardeman College in Henderson, Tennessee.

Odis Echols left the quartet to form his own group, the Odis Echols Melody Boys, in Louisville, Kentucky.

Frank replaced Palmer with Alton Floyd and Odis with Wilkin

Bacon. Roy Wheeler remained with the group. They moved their home base to Tulsa, Oklahoma, where they sang over radio station KVOO, moving in 1939 to Iowa. The Stamps Quartet found fertile ground in the Corn Belt and loved it, but the untimely death of V. O. Stamps in 1940 forced Frank Stamps to return to the South. At that time, the Blackwood Brothers were a Stamps-backed group, singing in Shreveport, Louisiana. Frank switched places with the Blackwoods, calling them to Iowa where they settled at KMA in Shenandoah, and the Stamps Quartet came to Shreveport and replaced the Blackwoods on the radio there. Not long after that, Frank Stamps left the quartet and returned to Dallas to take up some of the slack in the company offices created by V. O.'s death.

The Frank Stamps Quartet in Shreveport consisted of Aubrey Low, Roy Wheeler, Wilkin Bacon, and Harley Lester, with Lawrence Ivey at the piano.

In Dallas, Frank Stamps replaced V. O. in V. O.'s Stamps Quartet, and if all this is confusing now, it was pretty much the same then. The new Stamps Quartet in Dallas had Walter Rippetoe, Bob Bacon, John Jordan, and Frank Stamps, with Marion Snyder playing the piano.

The Stamps Company always kept several good pianists on its payroll and moved them around like checkers to help out its far-flung affiliated quartets. The first piano player the Blackwood Brothers had was Smilin' Joe Roper in 1938. He was assigned to them by the Stamps-Baxter Music Company.

Frank found that he could not sing full time, so he called in Big Jim Waits to replace himself and settled in to work in the Dallas office. J. R. Baxter, Jr., succeeded V. O. as president of the company. There were dire personality conflicts and other problems between Frank Stamps and J. R. Baxter; and in 1946, Frank packed up and left Stamps-Baxter, taking his quartet and a few key men with him. He organized his own music company and called it the Stamps Quartet Music Company. The move created a permanent split with the Stamps-Baxter Music Company and with J. R. Baxter himself.

Baxter took full control of Stamps-Baxter and Frank had what he wanted, a company all his own. Bitterness remained between the two companies and the two men for the remainder of their existence. Baxter formed several quartets to represent the Stamps-Baxter Company, and they sang over local radio stations in Dallas, but Frank's quartet remained on powerful KRLD. Some who sang in the Stamps-Baxter groups were Clyde and Wilford Roach, Gene Moss, who later sang with the Rangers, Charles Collier, Bert Carroll, Joe Roper, and Herschel Foshee.

But the Baxter quartets never attained the popularity and favor of the public that Frank's quartet had throughout its existence. The name of Stamps spelled magic in the quartet world. Both Frank and V. O.'s quartets from beginning to end were known as the V. O. Stamps Quartet, or Frank Stamps and his All-Star Quartet, or simply as the Stamps Quartet. The name of Baxter was never used in the title of the Stamps quartets.

The quartets that sang for the Stamps-Baxter Company after the split carried the name of Baxter—the Stamps-Baxter Quartet, the Baxter Quartet, the Stamps-Baxter Men's Quartet, the Stamps-Baxter Song Fellows, the Stamps-Baxter Melody Boys, and so on. They were excellent quartets, but the full magic was not there. One area in which the Stamps-Baxter quartets prided themselves was enunciation; no one ever had trouble understanding the words of the songs they sang.

After 1945, Frank's quartet remained static for a while. On their radio programs, Frank often referred to them as "The Old Men Themselves," signifying first that all the men in the quartet were above fifty years of age, older than most men who made up the vast number of groups singing then; and also that this was the oldest male quartet in the business, having survived from 1927.

Sometime in 1946, the Stamps Quartet began to record again, for Sellers Recording Company in Dallas. The quartet made only two records, containing four songs: "Precious Memories," Albert E. Brumley's new favorite "I'll Meet You In The Morning," "I'll Be Listening," and "When The Saints Go Marching In." The quartet's personnel included Walter Rippetoe, Bob Bacon, Bob Arnold, Frank Stamps, and Harvey Shelton at the piano.

Later, either in late 1946 or early 1947, Frank signed a contract with Mercury Records, and when he recorded for that firm, his only personnel change was at the keyboard where Jack Hendrix replaced Shelton.

During the first Mercury recording session, the Stamps Quartet cut its version of the most recorded gospel song ever written, "Hide Me, Rock of Ages." Frank also recorded the Stamps' theme song again, "Give The World A Smile," but this version by the Stamps Quartet did not compare with the original recording on Victor in 1927 that made

the Stamps Quartet famous. The Mercury version was the fastest anyone ever sang the song, and it did not score well with those who knew
and loved to hear the song.

After the Mercury sessions, Frank switched to Bibletone Records,
and cut twelve songs on six recordings. Among the titles recorded were
"If We Never Meet Again" and "The Little Chapel In The Vale." These
were far better sounding recordings than the Mercury disks, perhaps
due to a better selection of songs.

Early in 1950, Frank Stamps signed a recording contract with Co-
lumbia Records, which billed the quartet as the "original" Stamps
Quartet. This was a misnomer, of course, since Frank Stamps was the
only original member left, and too, in 1940 after the death of V. O.
Stamps, Frank left his "original" quartet in Shreveport and returned to
Dallas where he took over V. O.'s quartet.

Columbia chose to bill the quartet as original, however, to set it
apart from all other quartets using Stamps in their names—the Stamps
True Tone Quartet, the Stamps-Ozark Quartet, the Stamps Sunny
South Quartet, the Stamps Friendly Five, the Smile-A-While Stamps
Quartet.

The first recording date with Columbia, January 31, 1950, produced recordings like "Good News," a great quartet song featuring an
exciting bass lead; "Just A Closer Walk With Thee," "What A Savior,"
and "I'm A Little Bit Closer." The quartet returned to the studio May 2
to record "Whispering Hope," "Lead-a My Children," "A Hallelujah
Day," and "That Lonely Mile."

For those two sessions, the Stamps Quartet included Walter Rippetoe, Loy Hooker, Albert Houpe, and Frank Stamps, with Harvey
Shelton back at the piano.

No one knew it then, perhaps not even Frank Stamps, but these
were the last recordings he made as a member of his own quartet.
Sometime between that recording session in May and the first of November, 1950, Frank left the quartet as an active singing member. He
continued to travel with the groups as its spokesman, and managed the
group through the office of the Stamps Quartet Music Company. And
though the quartet continued to perform together for several more
years, that was the end of the Stamps Quartet as it was known from the
beginning. There was no longer a member of the quartet named
Stamps. Only the Stamps Quartet name lived on.

From its beginning to this point, the Stamps Quartet sang and
promoted only those songs published by either the Stamps-Baxter Mu-

sic Company or the Stamps Quartet Music Company. It did not sing songs by other publishers.

On November 7, 1950, the Stamps Quartet returned to the Columbia studios to record again. The personnel included Clyde Garner, Roger Clark, Glen Payne, and Haskell Mitchell. Jack Taylor played the piano. They recorded songs like "The Lord Is Coming By and By," and "Paradise Island."

Payne, who had been associated with the Stamps-Baxter and Stamps Quartet Music companies and with the Stamps Quartet since 1939, left the group in 1951 and moved to Wichita Falls, Texas, to sing with the Stamps-Ozark Quartet until the group ran into rough times in 1956. Glen left it then, and it disbanded some time thereafter.

The Stamps Quartet struggled through many personnel changes in the 1950s. Until 1957, some who sang with the Stamps Quartet included Don Randall, Bill Randall, Randall Mathis, Harley Lester, Vernon Bright, James Barnett, Benny Dugger, Howard Welborn, and a heavy basso named Joe B. Davis. The group that stayed together longest included Welborn, Don Randall, Bill Randall, Davis, with Easmon Napier at the piano.

Through the life of the Stamps Quartet, as it was in that period from 1927 through 1957, the sound of the quartet was a rather heavy, robust sound. When listening to the records the quartet made, this quality is noticably heavier than the softer blend of other quartets of the day.

The Stamps Quartet grew to such uncertainty in personnel by 1957 that a quartet that had developed within the Stamps Quartet Music Company—the Office Quartet—had to finish the recording contract with Columbia. This group had Loy Hooker, Rommy Grissom, Jimmy Grisham, and Arthur Watson, with Cecil Pollock at the piano. The last recording session for Columbia was on August 15, 1957. A couple of songs recorded were "The Walls of Jericho" and "My Lord Grows More Precious To Me."

Frank Stamps recorded "Maybe It's You, Maybe It's Me" that day with the quartet backing him. That was the last recording Frank made.

Before Frank Stamps died in 1964, he sold the Stamps Quartet Music Company and the Stamps Quartet to J. D. Sumner and James and Cecil Blackwood. He knew that the Blackwoods and Sumner were looking for a music company; so he called and offered his. He sold the printing plant, all copyrights, the entire business, and the name of the Stamps Quartet.

The Stamps Quartet did not disband in 1957. It went to Word Record Company in Waco, Texas, and recorded a series of records, about fifteen of them, and issued them under the Stamps label. In these recordings were "He's A Personal Savior," "Precious Lord, Take My Hand," and "Heavenly Love." Soon after that, this quartet decided to venture out under its own flag. It dropped its affiliation with the Stamps Quartet Music Company and became the Plainsmen Quartet, and under that name sang harmoniously for several more years.

J. D. Sumner and James Blackwood reorganized the Stamps Quartet in 1964 with Jerry Redd singing tenor; Terry Blackwood, lead; Roger McDuff, baritone; and Big John Hall, bass. Smilin' Joe Roper—remember him from the early Blackwood days?—was pianist and manager of the group.

The Stamps Quartet struggled along, recording for Skylite, but actually made little headway until 1965 when Sumner switched over from the Blackwood Brothers to sing bass and manage the Stamps Quartet, and John Hall went to the Blackwood Brothers. This move heralded the rebirth of the Stamps Quartet, and in the years since, which is recent history, it has grown into a mighty quartet again. For six years, it backed Elvis Presley on all his stage appearances and recordings.

Sumner swapped his shares in the Blackwood Brothers Quartet for full ownership of the Stamps Quartet, and it is among the finest quartets in the business today.

Since J. D. took over the quartet, it has been known for its fine harmony singing and its extreme discipline and stage presence, qualities that many groups sadly lack.

CHAPTER SIX

The
Old Perfesser

Lee Roy Abernathy, the "old per-fesser of Canton, Georgia," has seen it all. Born August 13, 1913, he has been around gospel singing forever. He is one of the few who go back beyond World War I to the days when most quartets were mixed quartets that sang in their churches simply for the spiritual edification of the congregation.

Lee Roy and his dad, Dee Abernathy, were probably ahead of their time. Not long after James D. Vaughan organized that first professional all-male quartet in 1910 to peddle songbooks, Dee Abernathy had a quartet of all male voices, albeit all were not men. One of the voices belonged to Dee's three-year-old son, Lee Roy.

That was the year 1916, when George M. Cohan was writing spirited songs for Broadway and the automobile was still making a gallant effort to replace the horse and buggy in many areas of the country.

Dee Abernathy usually stacked two Coca-Cola crates and stood his young son on them, or put him in a chair, and let him sing first tenor. Amazingly, Lee Roy could memorize the songs, and even more surprising, he could sing them in a high, clear voice with which the other men of the Atco Quartet, Will Hartsey, Grady Looney, Bill Cagle, and Dee himself, could harmonize. Dee's daughter, Velma, five years older than Lee Roy, played the piano for the quartet.

Dee Abernathy was a sharecropper who later left the fields to work in a textile mill in Canton, Georgia, where Lee Roy still lives. Dee knew music; he was a music teacher who conducted singing schools all over the countryside, and was a choir director and some-times an evangelistic singer.

Later, after Lee Roy learned music, Dee wrote several songs, like "Don't Be Knocking," which the Blackwood Brothers recorded and the Kingsmen Quartet revived and recorded more than a half-century later. He also wrote "Won't We Have A Good Time Up In Heaven" and "My Labor Will Be O'er." Dee would write the words, hand them to Lee Roy, and say, "Put some music on this."

The Abernathy family was happy when it settled in Canton, Georgia. It had lived in Cartersville and other places during its share-cropping days, and settling down was a welcome change. Lee Roy at-tended many of his father's singing schools. Some were ten-night schools; others ran four weeks with day and night sessions.

"I didn't realize how much I was learning then," Lee Roy said years later. "I learned a lot. Students don't know how hard it is to learn, and teachers should realize that. I think as I've worked through the years that I have gleaned that knowledge, but I didn't know it then. After a while, I realized that music just came to me. I absorbed it."

The Atco Quartet was so good and so novel that it sang by invita-tion in many places, and usually had singing engagements on Friday and Saturday nights and Sunday afternoons.

Lee Roy came out of grammar school at the age of thirteen in 1926 at about the same time his father signed a recording contract with Co-lumbia Records. The Atco Quartet made a recording that summer on which Lee Roy sang first tenor. The recorded songs were "Rich Young Ruler" and "Don't Forget To Pray," but the record apparently did not sell well, for Columbia cancelled the contract.

Unfortunately, Lee Roy's early singing career came to a halt soon after that. Singing so high, he strained his vocal cords and suddenly realized his singing voice was gone. He couldn't sing a note! He over-heard the doctor tell his dad, "Uncle Dee, that boy of yours will never sing again. He's just torn up his vocal cords."

So it was that when Dee Abernathy signed a recording contract with the Victor Talking Machine Company in 1928 and made a record on that label, Lee Roy's voice was not on the recording. One of the recorded songs was "I'm Redeemed By Faith Divine."

And a few weeks after that, an old nemesis of a lot of early quartets—wedding bells—struck a blow to the Atco Quartet. Velma Abernathy, eighteen years of age, announced that she was getting mar-ried and would no longer be able to play for the quartet.

Dee took Lee Roy aside and said, "Well, now, Velma's getting married and I'm gonna need a piano player. You've been fiddling around with it, and now you must get serious. You're going to have to learn to play the piano."

Lee Roy didn't want to learn. His mother was a piano teacher who taught both organ and piano lessons; and Velma taught piano, too. Neither, however, would take on the task of teaching Lee Roy.

Dee started Lee Roy's lessons with Charlie West, who had studied music in Germany. He was a fabulous teacher who had once been a piano tuner for the famed Polish pianist, composer, statesman Paderewski. But Lee Roy had no appreciation for West's skills and credentials. He hated piano; and he resisted it. He decided not to practice, but his daddy told him whether he practiced or not, he must sit at the piano for an hour every day.

For six and a half months, Lee Roy spent his hour each day idling at the piano, never tapping a key, never playing a note.

"I didn't realize I was stubborn," Lee Roy said. "I was mad because I felt the Lord had taken something away from me that I cherished—my high tenor voice. Before I lost my voice, I felt I could sing as high as anybody in the world."

One day Dee Abernathy walked into the room where Lee Roy sat unmoving on the piano bench. "Son, I want to talk to you just a minute," he said.

He sat down beside Lee Roy. "I know you can learn to play this instrument," he said. "Maybe I ought to tell you that I don't care whether you ever play the piano or not, but I think you ought to know this: I don't have any worldly goods to give you, and I think that every father ought to give his son whatever he's got. If you never play, I want you to leave out of this house able to do so."

He left and let his words soak in.

"That was precious," Lee Roy said later. "His words put me to thinking. He went out of that room and in five minutes I began to practice."

Soon Lee Roy had learned enough to play for the quartet, and as time passed he became more accomplished on the keyboards. With proficiency came confidence, and Lee Roy began to add all sorts of curlicues to the quartet's sound.

"Nobody had ever done a turnaround in the middle of a song," Lee Roy said. "They didn't even know that existed. I started that. Even in 1927 when I heard Dwight Brock and the Stamps Quartet, he would stop and they'd start another verse. He began doing the turnarounds later." The 1927 recordings of the Stamps All-Star Quartet, for which Brock played, support Lee Roy on this.

Lee Roy and his father were doing a "Happy Two" act in West Lafayette, Georgia, in 1927, and the Stamps Quartet was there. Dwight Brock listened to the two, then put his arm around Lee Roy's small shoulders. Lee Roy only weighed ninety pounds at age fifteen. "Son," Dwight said, "you just keep up what you're doing there, and some of these days you'll make somebody live hard."

More than fifty years later, Lee Roy had the occasion to tell that story in Dwight Brock's presence. "He'll never know," Lee Roy said, "what the weight of his arm on my shoulders meant when he said that. Those words came from the greatest piano-player who ever lived.

"But I was doing turnarounds before he was," Lee Roy added, "and I promise you it was me who played the piano so that a quartet could come in on the fly."

In 1928 Lee Roy played for a while for the Electrical Workers Quartet in Atlanta, one of the early quartets that featured the big bass voice of Big Jim Waits.

"We were in a contest," Lee Roy said. "My daddy had his Atco Quartet in the contest, and the Electrical Workers were in it. We won the contest. They had Big Jim at the time, but my daddy was the lowest bass singer who had come along. He could sing Fs below low C with no mike, because there wasn't no mikes.

"The Electrical Workers," Lee Roy remembered, "had Bruce Stroud as manager. The lead singer was John Cook. Fred Thomas was the tenor, a precious tenor. And Jim Waits was the bass. They were all the same height—they looked good, standing up there singing—and they all wore blue serge suits. I was used to that, though; we had manipulated around and got matching suits and polka dot ties for everybody in the Atco Quartet. In fact, we set the pace: We were the first ever to use the dress-alike deal."

Lee Roy left the Electrical Workers because of his age. "I wasn't old enough to play for them," he said, "but I didn't know that. They didn't either. I wasn't but fifteen but I looked twenty or twenty-five. When I come up to join the union after I'd been there about two months, they said they couldn't hire me because I wasn't old enough. I had to be eighteen. So they regretfully paid me two weeks severance and let me go."

Lee Roy claims a couple more "firsts."

"I had the first PA set for many years," he said. "I had mikes special-made by RCA in '28. Nobody knew what a PA set was. Sometimes they wouldn't even let me plug the set in because they thought I'd use too much power. In an auditorium for a singing they would let me plug in, but in a building like a church or school they wouldn't let me use that much electricity. I just had inside speakers; I never had over two."

Lee Roy was giving Brock Speer a voice lesson in 1968 and said, "Brock, you know your biggest problem in singing?"

"What's that?" Brock asked.

"You don't know how to work a mike," Lee Roy said.

Brock wasn't upset over that revelation. He only said, "Well, let's see, now, I remember the first microphone I ever worked was in '36—that was thirty-two years ago—in Hogansville, Georgia. . . . Wait a minute! That was your mike, wasn't it?"

"Yep," Lee Roy beamed. "Shore was."

Lee Roy fiddled around with everything. He bought recording equipment in 1933 but didn't learn to use it till 1936. He said he cut the Speer Family's first record in 1936.

"I got that equipment to going," he said, "and carried it with me to singings, and I'd say, 'For three dollars and a half I'll cut you a record.' I cut a good many records. Cut one for J. B. Vick's quartet. J. B. Vick was in Chattanooga. He was not a singer; he was a booster. When he walked in a room, it lit up. He raised a daughter who was the greatest singer I've ever heard in my life. She took Kate Smith's place for two weeks on the CBS network when she was only eighteen. Melba Vick was her name.

"Fred Elrod sang with J. B. Vick. Even Shorty Bradford sang with him some in the thirties. In '37, Vick took me to Corbin, Kentucky. I'd never been farther away than Chattanooga, and that was the greatest deal I ever had in my life, to go to Corbin and play for J. B. Vick's quartet. And that's when I met the Rangers. They were on their way to Louisville. . . ."

Lee Roy is a voice teacher. Singers come from all over the South to study with him. Ask London Parris what kind of teacher he is. Ask Brock Speer, who still takes voice lessons from Lee Roy as Brock closes in on seventy years of age. He must think Lee Roy can still teach him something—and Brock is proving that one never gets too old to learn or to improve himself.

"I've always studied voice, have for years," Brock said. "I studied at Belmont College and with various teachers. The older you get and the longer you sing, the more habits you develop. Sometimes you develop bad habits you are unaware of, and you need a coach. Lee Roy is my coach. Golfers on the pro tour often develop bad habits and have to take lessons from a coach to rid themselves of the things they're doing wrong. It's the same with singing. Big opera singers go on tour and come back and start taking lessons because they develop bad singing habits they don't realize.

"Another thing is this: In a family group you can't always choose the part you sing; you sometimes have to take whatever you must. We never had a bass singer. Daddy used to sing the bass part, but he was a baritone. When my voice started changing at around fourteen years, I couldn't sing anything. I did less harm on the bass part, and he put me on it. That kinda stuck with me. I still didn't have a bass voice. My voice would be natural about like my brother Ben's, I guess.

"I had to almost manufacture a bass sound. Lee Roy Abernathy is the best trainer of bass singers of anybody I know. I think the thing to do if you want to keep singing is to have a coach who can help you."

Another reason Brock Speer needs help is because he lost the hearing in his left ear. "I woke up one morning a few years ago," he said, "and couldn't hear. I still can't. There's a hissing sound there. I began to sing off pitch. Ben noticed it and would tell me I was off pitch. Lee Roy has helped me by giving me some different techniques."

Lee Roy began teaching in 1927 when he was fourteen, as soon as he learned to play the piano a bit. He charged twenty-five cents a lesson and walked to his students' homes to teach.

"I'd get enough to pay for my own lessons that weekend," he said. "I took lessons on Saturday in Atlanta. Cost me five dollars for thirty minutes. I'd get to Atlanta the best way I could; most of the time I walked. I took my lesson at six-thirty and at seven I started back to Canton. Wasn't many cars and I had to walk the forty-four miles. I'd get back home close to noon on Sunday. If I trotted I could get in early enough for Sunday School, but if I just walked I couldn't make it in time."

He has taught constantly since the age of fourteen.

"It's been a ball," he said, "I've enjoyed it. I never even slowed down. If you slow down, it takes more time and effort to get up speed again. I'm into more teaching now, sure enough, than I've ever been before, by far. I teach sixty hours every week, and most of the time seventy. Lots of days I teach fifteen hours."

Not only did Lee Roy show others how to sing in his studios at home, he also showed them on stage. He had some of the finest honed quartets in the business. He and Shorty Bradford teamed for years in a "Happy Two" act that was in great demand. His Miracle Men Quartet with Earl Terry singing first tenor, Shorty Bradford on the lead, Idis Spivey singing baritone, and A. D. Soward on bass was one of the great quartets in the early 1950s.

During World War II, Lee Roy had a quartet that sang full time, despite the hostilities and the shortages of gasoline and everything else. He called his group "The Four Tones" and they sang over WPTF in Raleigh, North Carolina. Sponsors paid each man in the quartet $82.50 a week to sing a fifteen-minute show each day.

Two of the Four Tones, Little Johnny New, the tenor, and Curley Kinsey, the bass, became original members of the Oak Ridge Quartet in 1945 when the Four Tones disbanded. The other two members, Lee Roy and Shorty, returned home and began singing as a duet.

The Four Tones sang popular music, not gospel, and because of that they made few public appearances. "Pop music didn't draw a lot of people to concerts," Lee Roy said, "but folks loved it on the radio." WPTF had Carl Raines's Lone Star Quartet singing gospel, and the Lone Star did a lot of personal appearances. Sometimes the Four Tones went with the Lone Star and sang gospel at the concerts, and people loved them.

Raines had great singers in the Lone Star—Milton Estes, Burt Frye, Clarence Turbyfill—and they knew how to put on a show. "They knew how to get to the people," Lee Roy said. "They had a different sound from other quartets."

Lee Roy was an innovator. He had ideas, and he put them to work for him and his quartets. Harking back to the 1920s, Lee Roy dressed his quartet men alike, usually in white suits, which made them stand out when in the company of other quartets.

He knew how competitive the business was. In those days just after the war, and before, too, for that matter, quartets competed with each other. Each strove to get the upper hand in any decent way. No one really resorted to underhanded work, but not any of the quartets was above pulling shenanigans on the other groups.

Sometimes, when Lee Roy really wanted to compete, he would buy five front-row tickets, and just when a rival quartet hit its stride on stage, Lee Roy and his quartet, dressed in loud white suits, made their way slowly down the aisle and took their seats on the front row. By the time they reached the front of the house, everybody in the audience would be staring at them.

Lee Roy and Shorty were a perfect pair. They sang well together, and Shorty's great range enabled them to sing anything they wanted to. Sometimes the two sounded like a quartet.

Their comedy gags were simple, but effective. For example:

Lee Roy had a little act in which he played off the end of the piano, and Shorty would ask, "What's the matter? That piano not long enough?"

"No," Lee Roy said, "it don't have enough notes on it."

"How many notes does it have?" Shorty asked.

"I don't know how many this one has."

"How many does yours have?"

"Mine has eighty-eight notes."

"Reckon you'll ever get 'em all paid off?" Shorty asked, and the audience usually broke up with laughter.

Then Shorty would ask, "Are those ivory keys?"

"No," Lee Roy patiently answered. "They made that against the law. You can't make ivory keys any more."

"Why not?" Shorty asked.

"Well," Lee Roy explained, "it takes three elephants to make one piano."

"It's a sight," Shorty sighed, "what you can teach them animals to do, isn't it?"

Lee Roy said he drove by Shorty's place to pick him up once, but before he got to Shorty's house, he saw Shorty coming. Shorty took a short cut through a pasture and Lee Roy stopped to wait for him.

In the pasture was a mean bull, and when the bull saw Shorty he began to snort and paw the earth, and Shorty began to run. The bull took off after him.

Lee Roy jumped out of the car, raced to the fence, raised one strand of wire with his hand, and lowered the other with his foot, and Shorty dove through the opening a step and a half ahead of the bull.

"Boy!" Lee Roy exclaimed, "it almost got you that time."

"It nearly gets me every time," Shorty answered.

* * *

Lee Roy's teaching methods are not always the most orthodox, but they are effective.

Once when he tried to teach Brock Speer to hit a B-flat, the following conversation ensued:

Lee Roy: "Brock, you can't hit that B-flat."

Lee Roy lowered his chin and knocked the bottom out of a B-flat.

Brock: "Why can't I do that?"

Lee Roy: "You don't sing in the spirit. That's your problem. You learned (to sing) because you thought your dad had to have you, and you were doing what your dad said."

Brock: "Well, that's right."

Lee Roy: "You got to do what the Lord says."

Brock: "I thought I was doing that."

Lee Roy: "You're not. Be still and know that it is I. Be not afraid. Put your hand out there (in front, down low) and hit that low note."

When Brock went down to hit the note, his voice quivered. He tried again. And again.

Brock: "You know why I can't hit that, Lee Roy?"

Lee Roy: "Why?"

Brock: "I don't believe it's in there."

Lee Roy: "You're on your way."

He figured Brock was then in the proper frame of mind.

Lee Roy: "When you admit that you don't believe that much, that you don't have that much faith, then you're on your way to success. You see, we are physical human beings and our consciousness is our brain. You sing unconsciously, and if you're reading the music, you don't have time to think of yourself, you're reading."

Brock: "How am I going to get where I can sing that note?"

Lee Roy: "That's your problem."

He didn't leave Brock dangling. He simply programmed Brock in the only way he thought Brock could hit the B-flat. He put the monkey on Brock's shoulders; he challenged him. Then Lee Roy hit the note again, and again.

"There's not a bass singer on earth can sing lower than I can if I'm teaching him," Lee Roy said. "I don't care who it is. I could sing below J. D. Sumner if I were teaching him. But I can't do it to show out. My voice just closes up. I think that's what brought me off the road, for one thing. I was out there trying to show people up, and I didn't want to do that. I wanted to help 'em, and I'll do anything in the world for 'em."

Lee Roy came off the road in 1968. Five years earlier, he and

Shorty quit singing when Shorty's arthritis prevented his traveling comfortably. Lee Roy traveled on for five more years, working with other groups. Sometimes a group hired him to travel with them for a while to try to improve their singing, and Lee Roy loved the challenge.

Lee Roy liked not having to travel all the time. He liked staying at home and teaching others to sing. And by doing this, he contributed far more to the business than if he had stayed on the road these last twenty years.

He has taught hundreds to sing properly. His contribution can never be evaluated.

CHAPTER SEVEN

Altos and Sopranos

Some significant advances occurred in quartet singing in 1920 and 1921. Joyously, the World War had ended in November, 1918, but the human slaughter in Europe was still very real in the minds of Americans. With peace at hand and prosperity ahead, however, Americans moved into the twenties with songs in their hearts—and those songs were bound to come out.

Down South, the songs were gospel, hymns of praise, hymns of thanks for God's goodness, songs of joy, and, perhaps best of all, songs of a better life to come.

In Double Springs, Alabama, G. T. and Lena Speer began singing together anywhere they found an opportunity. A farmer, G. T. perhaps saw in singing a way out of the fields.

Up in Tennessee, a couple of brothers, Urias and Alphus LeFevre, walked out of the Cumberland Mountains in 1921 and began singing toe-tapping tunes in the churches of East Tennessee.

These four people helped bring the new music to the American culture.

G. T. Speer had been singing for some time. He always attended the all-day singing conventions in various Alabama churches. At those gatherings, a church filled with people sang with various music directors, usually from different churches, who led the congregation in singing both their favorite songs and new songs, too. The "known" singers sat up front, or on the stage if the singing were held in a school auditorium, as many were, for some churches would not permit these "jazzy"

singers to perform in church houses. Those who came to hear the singing, and to lend their voices to the congregational singing, took seats
behind the better singers.

The directors chose songs out of songbooks, some of them old favorites, but some new songs out of the Vaughan or other songbooks.
The director took his pitch from a pitch pipe or tuning fork, or from
piano or organ when the churches were equipped with them, and then
marked time and led the congregation through the songs.

At noon, after a couple of hours of preliminary singing, the convention broke for dinner-on-the-ground, during which the ladies of the
community showed off their culinary skills, weighting long tables in
the churchyard with bowls and platters of country ham, fried chicken,
roast beef, peas, beans, corn, banana pudding, fried apple and peach
pies, baked pies and cakes of every flavor, and jugs of iced tea, lemon-
ade, and coffee.

When the convention reconvened, usually around one o'clock,
they got down to business, full stomachs or no. Congregational singing
started the afternoon, and when the congregation tired of singing,
some of the directors picked out three others and sang a "quartet number." Each sang one of the four parts—soprano, alto, tenor, and bass—
thus giving the congregation a rest and a treat at the same time. Good
singers took these occasions to show off their voices, and out of these
conventions came a lot of professional quartet singers.

People decided they liked the four-part harmony with just four
voices singing, and the quartets were born all around. Some of the
quartets learned to sing together very well.

In the late teens, around the end of the World War, G. T. Speer sang
frequently with different quartets. Later in his life, he showed his sons,
Brock and Ben Speer, a little church in Shiloh Park on the Tennessee
River in West Tennessee where he had sung in concert with his male
quartet. One of the other singers was named Amos Box, the only name
Brock Speer remembers today.

Some of these quartets became so good they were considered to be
"drawing cards," and churches that sponsored all-day singings, usually
in connection with homecoming or decoration day for the church ceme-
tery, often hired a good quartet to be featured at the church's singing.
These quartets usually brought in the latest printed songbooks and put
them on sale at the church that day.

For these singing conventions, the buildings were usually packed
to overflowing. Most of the time, people stood in all available floor

space, jammed the doorways, sat in the windows, blocking off ventilation, so that the only circulation of air in the stifling hot auditorium came from the waving of big cardboard fans.

G. T. Speer studied music from the age of seventeen, at first under a teacher named Tom Lane who came from Oklahoma to the little community of Houston, Alabama, where G. T. grew up. When he got a taste of gospel music, G. T. Speer fell in love with it. He continued to study with George W. Bacon and C. A. Brock, who eventually became his father-in-law.

Lena Brock played the pump organ at her father's singing schools, and she and G. T. Speer met at a singing convention. They were married February 27, 1920, and their first child, a boy they named Brock, after Lena's family, came along on December 28, 1920.

In February of 1921 G. T. and Lena organized the Speer Quartet with her sister, Pearl, and Pearl's husband, Logan Claborn. For four or five years they sang together at singing conventions, in churches, and sometimes in school auditoriums—and now and then they made a little money singing.

Mom Speer had a fine soprano voice, and Pearl Claborn was a powerful alto. Logan sang tenor and G. T., bass. They had a really good mixed quartet.

Rosa Nell was the second child born to G. T. and Lena Speer.

In 1925, Logan Claborn, a carpenter by trade, decided to devote all his time to carpentry, and he and Pearl quit singing in the quartet. Brock and Rosa Nell, though young, began going to conventions with their mother and dad. They sang two or three songs on a program, then Lena bedded them down backstage on quilts she brought with her. Usually she had a bag of homemade cookies and a fruit jar of water for the kids to snack on while she and G. T. finished the program.

The first song Brock remembers singing was "Jesus Has Full Control." The family sang it in a little country church in Walker County, Alabama, near Jasper.

Folks began to call G. T. Speer "Dad," and it followed naturally that Lena would be tagged "Mom."

The family sang somewhere almost every weekend, mostly in the spring, summer, and fall. Winter was tough on travelers in those days.

Dad Speer, born in 1892 and reared on a farm, began farming on his own when he married, but figured out that his singing schools and the revival meetings at which he sang were supporting the farm and feeding his mules, and he said, "Why put up with this!" and sold his farm. He moved his family to Double Springs where he bought a small home.

Then he was free to do his music.

He taught Brock and Rosa Nell to read music, and as they grew older he gave them bigger parts in the family's singing appearances.

Mary Tom was the third of the Speer children, and Ben was the fourth, and when they grew old enough to sing, Mom and Dad took them into the group. They became known as the "Singing Speer Family"—mother and daddy, two daughters, and two sons—and they could sing!

The male quartet became the predominant unit of singing in this new field of entertainment, often singing *a cappella*—but Mom Speer decided she would play for the Speers. She played the organ and later the piano. The Speers became a very musical, six-member singing group, and they were in demand.

Through part of the 1920s, the Speers traveled to singing conventions and church and schoolhouse appearances in a two-horse wagon. Transportation limited their range drastically, but there were enough places within reach to keep them reasonably busy.

Roads were almost nonexistent. What roads there were were farm roads or community roads of dirt that usually turned to quagmires in hard rains. A big novelty was getting to Haleyville, twenty miles from Double Springs, where the nearest railroad passed through. Haleyville had a paved street down the middle of town, but to get to that paved strip in the winter was sometimes a day's work.

Automobiles often got stuck in mudholes in or beside the road, and drivers sometimes had to hire farmers to pull their automobiles out of the muck with a team of horses. Some cars carried pry poles which were used to pry the car wheels out of ruts in bad weather.

The Speers got their first automobile in 1925, a new Model-T Ford, for which they paid $475, and then they could range farther afield, provided the primitive roads went where they wanted to go.

The Speer Family's income came from singing. They were as professional as a group could get.

When Brock was ten years old in 1930, the Speers moved to Lawrenceburg, Tennessee, home of the James D. Vaughan Music Company. Oddly enough, Dad Speer didn't make the move to work for the music company, but for an insurance company that promised him a job. The job didn't pay off; so the Speers continued to sing, and Dad taught all four of his children to sing parts, improving the family's music. He was a stickler for correct singing—every pitch right, every harmony spot right, no clashes or discords. He made his children learn to sing correctly.

By that time, the Speers had a 1927 Chevrolet touring car, complete with side curtains and a cloth top. Often, they piled in the car and headed out through the countryside, looking for a schoolhouse in which they could sing. When they found one, they struck a deal with the principal, filled out the date and time on pre-printed posters and put them up in town and around the countryside. Admission price was usually fifteen cents for children and a quarter for adults.

Times began to improve when Franklin D. Roosevelt took over the White House, and Dad Speer accepted a job with the Vaughan company, writing and editing songs, and working in the mail room and the printing plant next door. At home he taught his family to play instruments: Brock the guitar, Mom the accordion, Rosa Nell the piano, and Ben was so small that he could manage only the ukelele.

At about the age of fourteen or fifteen, Brock's voice changed. Dad Speer wanted him to continue to sing; so he let Brock sing bass, and Dad moved up to baritone, which was his natural part.

By 1940 the Speers wanted to get on the radio, like most professional quartets, and the best avenue seemed to be with the Stamps Music Company; so after communicating with V. O. Stamps, Dad Speer took his family to sing at a revival meeting in Atlanta, Texas. Following that, they were to drive to Dallas and finalize their deal with Stamps.

However, while on the road from Atlanta to Dallas, they heard that V. O. Stamps was dead. Dad Speer just kept going, returning home to Lawrenceburg, and when the Stamps company began to recover from V. O.'s death, he worked out the deal with J. R. Baxter, Jr., who moved the Speers to Montgomery, Alabama, where he had them a job singing on WSFA Radio.

The Speers sang two shows daily, one at 6:30 a.m. and the other in the afternoon following a thirty-minute country show by a good-natured fellow named Hank Williams. Calling himself "Hank the Drifter," Williams went out at night and played honky-tonks.

Came World War II and Brock Speer went into service. Although he was gone more than three years, the family continued to sing. With tires and gasoline strictly rationed, the family could not range far, but usually when they were asked to come to a singing convention, some of the people in the community involved not only provided enough money to pay the Speers to sing, but managed to send along a few gasoline stamps, and on occasion stamps for tires.

After the war, taking advantage of the G. I. Bill, Brock went to college at Trevecca Nazarene College in Nashville and the Speer Family moved there and got a radio job on WSIX. Ralph Emery ran the board for the Speers' early-morning show, and introduced them on the air each day.

After graduation from Trevecca, Brock continued through Vanderbilt University, earning a master's degree in religion, a Masters of Divinity, which qualified him to preach the gospel.

The war had shifted enough population out of the South that certain areas in the northern states began to open up for gospel singers just after hostilities ceased. The quartets referred to that as going "up north" to sing, and the Speers were among those who pioneered those trails, going into Detroit, Akron, Chicago, and other places where enough of the South's population had remained following wartime jobs in the defense plants to support gospel music shows.

When television became an entertainment medium in the United States, the Speers sang over WLAC-TV in Nashville and did concerts at night. Their popularity spread widely and quickly and their date book was always filled.

While male quartets enjoyed a dominance in gospel singing, the Speers and a handful of others kept mixed-quartet singing alive and popular.

Dad and Mom Speer spent the rest of their lives singing, but in the late 1940s the personnel in their group began to change. Rosa Nell married in 1948 and left the group. Brock married in 1948 and his wife, Faye, began singing with the family. In 1952 Mary Tom was married and left, and at that point the Speers had to start hiring people outside the family. Joyce Black was the first.

Dad Speer died in 1966 and Harold Lane joined the Speers, remaining twenty-two years. Mom died a year later, in 1967, and Faye took her place for a while, then Jeannie Johnson came along to sing the alto.

The Speer Family is active today singing the gospel, having done so actually for more than seventy years. They pioneered singing in the mixed quartet field.

The LeFevre brothers, Urias and Alphus, like the Speers, were musical. They came from a musical family. Their great grandfather played music in the Mexican War. Their grandfather played a flute, and their father, Silas Abraham LeFevre, played a guitar. Their mother, Martha, played the organ.

Both boys were taught to play instruments as youngsters, and when they started singing publicly in 1921 they were proficient musicians. Around Smithfield, Tennessee, where they grew up, they learned that people especially loved instrumental music, and when they added their voices in song, the people seemed to like it even more.

In 1927 they got their first paying job on radio at WSM in Nashville. That was the year Alphus entered high school. When he finished high school and enrolled at Lee College in Cleveland, Tennessee— actually the Bible Training School of the Church of God then—Urias was already there. They joined with Johnny Yates and James McCoy as a quartet and sang as the Bible Training School Quartet Number Two. The Number One quartet had J. H. Walker, Lloyd McLain, Otis McCoy, and B. C. Robinson.

"Our BTS quartet was very smooth," Uncle Alf said many years later. "We had teamwork down to perfection, and we could sing *a cappella* or do counterpoint, or anything that we wanted to. Later, with the LeFevres, we always tried to sing so the people could understand the words and get the message of the song."

Urias married Eva Mae Whittington, a preacher's daughter who could sing alto and play the daylights out of a piano; and she and Urias and Alf became the LeFevre Trio. The men sang variously as a trio or quartet for several years, depending on Eva Mae's maternal condition. But anytime the LeFevres came on stage the audience knew some music was about to be made, for between Urias, Uncle Alf, and Eva Mae they could play any instrument that could be carried, rolled, or dragged on stage.

The depression years were tough on the LeFevre Trio. Once Eva Mae and Urias had to sell their furniture to keep the trio on the road, but they were one of the few groups that did not have a breakup during the depression.

On the road, they stayed in people's homes because most of the time they couldn't afford the four dollars a good hotel room cost. "We ate with people," Uncle Alf said, "not in restaurants. When we sang for a campmeeting they usually let us eat in the mess hall and sleep in the dormitories, and that way we got by with a bare minimum of expenses. We operated our car, bought our clothes—what weren't given to us— and managed."

In the deepest part of the depression, the LeFevres signed on with the James D. Vaughan Music Company. Money was scarce, and even the Vaughan name sometimes failed to help their financial condition.

Once the LeFevres traveled 1,200 miles and worked a whole week for $25.

Then Vaughan offered to put the group on salary if it moved to Lawrenceburg, which it did. The LeFevres worked in the printing office during the week and went out singing on weekends. Competition was keen with the Stamps quartets and audiences usually were polarized: some for Vaughan, some for Stamps. Competition became more fierce as time passed, and once when a big singing was held in a schoolhouse with both Stamps and Vaughan represented, each quartet distributed songbooks to the crowd before the singing, hoping to be able to sell some for 35 cents each after the singing. In the midst of the singing, some of the singers from one quartet saw some from the other quartet poking rival songbooks through a big crack in the floor.

Uncle Alf had a short career singing with the Stamps Quartet. One of Eva Mae's pregnancies brought their job with Vaughan to an end, and Alf joined the Stamps Quartet as first tenor. They sang at the Texas Centennial in 1936 over three networks, NBC, CBS, and the Texas Quality Network. Alf didn't make enough to live on and when he asked for a raise and V. O. Stamps refused it, Alf quit.

"I went back to sing with Urias and Eva Mae," he said, "and she was pregnant again."

Times were still bad in 1937 and the LeFevres moved to Charleston, South Carolina. "There looked to be no end to the depression," Alf said. "I worked in a music store and Urias sold cars, and we got on a radio program and sometimes sang for a church. We needed a sponsor for the radio program in order to make any money off of it, and the only firm in Charleston that offered to sponsor us was Pabst Blue Ribbon Beer. Of course, we turned that down, as bad as we needed the money."

After wandering through the remainder of the depression, the LeFevres moved to Atlanta in 1939 and almost immediately struck gold.

"That's where we really got our start," Alf said. "When we went on WGST, a ten thousand watt station that reached into several states, we began to make some headway. You could walk down the street and from house to house you could hear the LeFevres singing on the radios in those homes. We put out some recordings in 1940, made at WGST, and one, 'Beautiful Flowers,' sold fifty thousand copies in ten days in the Atlanta market alone."

Mail response was tremendous. In one week the LeFevres received 10,000 cards and letters in response to their WGST program.

And then came December 7, 1941. The LeFevres were singing live on WGST and an announcer broke into their program and announced that the Japanese had bombed Pearl Harbor.

Alf remembered thinking that going from the depression into another world war was like jumping out of the frying pan into the fire. He spent thirty-four months in the Signal Corps, most of it in New Guinea and the Philippines, and when he returned home the LeFevres were waiting for him.

Their post-war singing was mostly success. With some ups and downs thrown in, the LeFevres built an empire. They had their own television show, owned their own building in Atlanta, and had one of the first twenty-four-track recording studios, and in one year their income reached $750,000. A lot of the glitter was taken off of that year when the government hit them for a ten-percent excise tax, and instead of drawing a big bonus that Christmas, Alf and Urias had to use their savings to pay the tax.

Such were the fortunes of many in this business.

Uncle Alf probably summed it up best. "Gospel music," he said, "is not like rock 'n roll or country music. In rock you can become a millionaire in a month, but this music was a slow struggle for me all my life."

The LeFevres remained in the upper echelon of gospel music until age took its toll and one by one the trio retired from the road. Rex Nelon came to the LeFevres as bass singer in 1957, and it was to Rex that the LeFevres turned when they wanted to sell the group. In the 1970s Rex changed the group name to "The Rex Nelon Singers," and a bit later, at the suggestion of his recording company, to "The Nelons"—and today they are going strong, one of the most popular of the mixed groups.

The third of America's early mixed gospel groups began in 1935 when D. P. (Dad) Carter sought a way to remove his family from the back-breaking itinerant labor in the Texas cotton fields.

All nine of his children could sing. They had learned to sing to entertain themselves, as had many other families of that dreary depressed era. Dad called on three of his children, Rose, Anna, and Jim, to join him in forming a quartet. The kids' real names were Rosa Lola, Effie, and Ernest, but their names were changed to make them ring better on the air.

At first, the Carters called themselves the Carter Quartet. They learned several songs, mostly Western, with what they considered to be good messages for that day and time, and, armed with these, found a place to sing on Radio Station KFYO in Lubbock, Texas. The station paid the Carter Quartet fifteen dollars a week.

Within a year, the Carter Quartet was the most popular show on the Lubbock station, and before that first year was up, they moved to WBAP in Fort Worth, one of the largest stations in the nation.

Their weekly Saturday afternoon program, called "The Round-Up," was sponsored by Morton Salt. The huge Bewley Flour Mills also sponsored a group on WBAP, a male group known as the "Chuck Wagon Gang," which sang Western songs.

Three months after the Carters arrived in Fort Worth, Bewley Mills pulled the Chuck Wagon Gang off the air and sent it into the hinterlands of Texas to make personal singing appearances advertising Bewley Flour. At the same time, Bewley asked the Carter Quartet to fill the Chuck Wagon Gang slot on the radio, and the offer was too lucrative for Dad Carter to turn down. Thus, the Carter Quartet became the "Chuck Wagon Gang of the Air," and when the original Chuck Wagon Gang disbanded not long afterward, the Carters continued to sing as the Chuck Wagon Gang.

Western music was popular in that day, with groups like Roy Rogers and the Sons of the Pioneers rendering beautiful harmony, so the Chuck Wagon Gang adopted a repertoire of all Western songs except for one gospel song on each program.

More than ninety percent of their mail over the next few months requested more gospel songs, and the Chuck Wagon Gang eventually switched to an all-gospel format. They sang on WBAP for fifteen years, and their popularity increased each year. Once, Bewley Mills offered free pictures of the Chuck Wagon Gang to anyone sending in a coupon found inside a sack of Bewley's flour, and more than 100,000 requests came in.

This, remember, was during the heyday of the Stamps-Baxter dynasty in nearby Dallas, when gospel programming grew by leaps and bounds on radio, and the popularity of gospel groups grew every day.

The Chuck Wagon Gang's first recording session was on November 25, 1936, for Columbia Records. They recorded in a small studio set up in a San Antonio hotel. Their first recording was of the song "The Son Hath Made Me Free." For more than forty years they recorded on the same label.

Through the years their records have sold more than thirty million copies in the United States and foreign countries.

While other gospel groups used the airways to advertise their personal appearances, the Chuck Wagon Gang advertised its records. The Gang made few personal appearances, not any outside the Fort Worth area, until promoters, recognizing the popularity of their recordings, asked for personal appearances.

In 1951, the Chuck Wagon Gang made its first tour, a ten-day personal appearance tour. Needing additional personnel as these tours became more popular and lucrative, the Gang added two more Carter brothers, Roy and Eddie, and Anna's husband, Howard Gordon, to the group, replacing Jim and Dad.

"Our first tour was for Wally Fowler," Roy Carter recalled, "and our first concert was an all-night singing in Georgia. We did not know what to expect so we went there to sing out of our songbooks just as we did on our radio show. We didn't think anyone east of the Mississippi River had heard of us, but we were wrong: We had a large crowd of fans that first night."

They also made one more miscalculation. They thought they were supposed to sing Western songs and had no program of gospel songs prepared. Undaunted, the Chuck Wagon Gang simply took their gospel songbooks on stage and sang from them for the entire program.

Gospel fans accustomed to seeing the polished programs of the big professional quartets, thought the Chuck Wagon Gang's style was basic and refreshing, and the Gang was received enthusiastically.

For many years then, the Chuck Wagon Gang made the rounds of Americana, singing gospel songs—which they memorized and sang without books. They sang in Carnegie Hall, before 22,000 people in the Hollywood Bowl, on the Grand Ole Opry, on the silver screen, and to hundreds of thousands at personal appearances. They co-hosted a gospel television show called "Gospel Round-Up."

Never losing their Western flavor, the Chuck Wagon Gang remained different from other gospel groups, and therefore appealing.

Because of having to travel and live in close proximity, in automobiles and later in buses, mixed quartet or group singing in America has almost been limited to family groups. It was extremely tough for a group to include a woman member when it traveled cramped up in a limousine, or even in a bus, which provided relative privacy, but not enough. Still, the family mixed groups have made their marks—the Speer Family, the LeFevres, and their successors, the Nelons, the Chuck Wagon Gang, the Rambos, the Goodman Family, the Hopper Brothers and Connie, the Segos and Naomi, the Johnson Sisters—and today, hundreds of mixed groups who are still mostly family groups make the gospel rounds.

They have made a deep mark on America.

CHAPTER EIGHT

The Rangers: A Different Quartet

Quartets were named for various things. Sometimes a quartet's name came naturally, like the Blackwood Brothers, who were mostly brothers named Blackwood. Hovie Lister named the Statesmen because he wanted a regal-sounding name and because he had a deep, inbred love for politics.

Now and then a name came to a quartet accidentally. Like the Texas Rangers Quartet.

Unless you're a Texan with a memory stretching back to the late 1930s, you probably remember that quartet simply as the Rangers, but at the beginning it had the prefix "Texas," for it was named in honor of those great lawmen who brought order to the state of Texas in the 19th century.

Two Hyles brothers, Arnold and Vernon, born on a farm outside the small town of Italy, in East Texas, were the backbone of this quartet. Arnold was born in 1906 and Vernon in 1910. In 1929, still in their youth, the Hyles brothers attended a Stamps-Baxter singing school in Dallas and sharpened their singing voices, which were developed quite well by that time, both in the lowest range. Arnold sounded lower than any bass singer they had ever heard, and Vernon had the ideal quartet lead voice, low enough to sing bass in most quartets and marvelously controlled.

They sang locally and became quite good at it. By 1935 they were thinking of organizing a quartet of their own, and they wanted a distinctive, superior sound.

They chose their personnel well. George Hughes was a good first tenor, and a friend named Walter Leverette could sing baritone as well as anyone. Vernon sang lead and Arnold sang bass. For accompaniment, Vernon played the guitar.

In October, 1935, they formed what they considered to be the superior-sounding quartet they had dreamed of, and they were in a country where several Stamps quartets held forth.

The quartet, then unnamed, practiced religiously, working their sound to a fine, low harmony. For a couple of months they sang in churches around Luling, Texas, Walter Leverette's home town. Then with the thought in mind of making their way to Dallas to sing at the 1936 Texas Centennial, they began singing farther and farther from Luling.

They sang in churches and school auditoriums and now and then in a lodge hall; like other quartets of the day they sang wherever they could get a date that paid eating money.

In June of 1936, they considered themselves ready for big doings, so they went to Dallas and sang at the Centennial along with the Chuck Wagon Gang and the Stamps quartets. Texas Governor James V. Allred heard them, liked them, and commissioned all four quartet members Honorary Texas Rangers. He made them Good Will Ambassadors for the State of Texas.

Thus was born the Texas Rangers Quartet.

The Rangers stayed in Dallas, singing at the Centennial until the festivities closed in September. With a reputation that extended to the boundaries of the state of Texas, the Rangers sought wider horizons.

In New York, *Major Bowes' Amateur Hour* was one of the nation's favorite radio shows. Everybody listened to the Amateur Hour. Major Bowes had a crew that rounded up talent of all kinds to perform on the show. He awarded prizes. Many an entertainer stepped from the Amateur Hour into national prominence. By the same token, if Major Bowes didn't like what he heard, he hit a gong and cut the act off the air—and those who were gonged made their way back to the farm and whatever obscurity awaited them.

If they could get on that program, the Rangers had no doubt they could win it, and their reputation would spread nationwide.

Then or later, the Rangers were never known for doing anything without flair, and they figured one sure way of gaining a place on Major Bowes' amateur contest would be to make a splash on the way to New York.

They decided that riding bicycles would bring them notoriety wherever they went. They took their idea to Montgomery Ward and talked that huge firm into donating four bicycles. Justin Boot Company threw in high-heeled cowboy boots for each man, and the Ralston Hat Company fitted them with ten-gallon cowboy hats.

Billing themselves as "The Cycling Cowboys" or "The Cycling Rangers, featuring America's Lowest Basso—Arnold Hyles," they gave concerts wherever they found a willing place, picking up expense money along the way.

A fellow named Austin Williams, who later became a songwriter and a good music teacher, was the Rangers' advance man. He went ahead like a scout and arranged bookings for the quartet.

The original idea was for the Rangers to ride bicycles all the way to New York, but pedalling became old stuff 'ere too many miles passed, and they soon fell into a routine of riding between towns in an automobile. At the edge of a town, they unloaded from the car, broke out the bicycles, and pedalled through town to attract attention.

Soon they had worked out a routine. With newspaper ads preceding them, and by trading talent for time on local radio stations and advertising their concerts over the air, they had no trouble drawing crowds to theaters and school auditoriums all along their barnstorming way.

They worked towns in Texas, Arkansas, Tennessee, Ohio, and Kentucky, including appearances on the Grand Ole Opry on WSM in Nashville, and were scheduled on the WLW Barn Dance in Cincinnati.

By the time they reached Ohio, times were so good that they had sold their bicycles. They could do without that leg-aching notoriety; they found that their singing was enough to draw the necessary crowds. They traveled exclusively by automobile and had money in their pockets. They were high up on the side of the hog.

Three months into the tour—the middle of December—they stopped at powerful 50,000-watt WHAS in Louisville and sang on the air. The station manager and his staff liked the singing so well they offered the Rangers a job singing two hours a day, from 5 to 7 a.m., on the station's morning farm program.

The manager said he would put the four men on salary at $32.50 each per week, and more importantly, he would allow them to announce their personal appearances on the air.

The job was too good to turn down. They cancelled their booking on WLW, arranged to go to work at WHAS the first of the year, and headed home for Texas to spend Christmas with their families.

It was typical of the Rangers Quartet that they were so satisfied with present circumstances that they never gave Major Bowes' Amateur Hour another thought!

Up to this time, no quartet had ever made a living singing. Other quartets' members had to have side jobs, or had to be subsidized by selling songbooks for one of the big music publishing companies like Vaughan or Stamps-Baxter.

Later, following the lead of the Texas Rangers Quartet, other singing groups broke away from the publishing giants.

The Rangers at this time moved to the head of the class, quite possibly the most popular quartet in America.

The first and only personnel change the Rangers made for many years, excepting on the piano bench, was at first tenor. In 1938, three years after the organization of the quartet, George Hughes decided to leave, and the Rangers replaced him with a high Irish tenor from Arkansas named Denver Crumpler.

Denver was twenty-five years old, just three years younger than Vernon Hyles, and he had a beautiful voice, perhaps the finest tenor voice in America at that time. He had gone to Dallas to sing, and V. O. Stamps recognized the potential greatness in Denver's voice, and for a while Denver studied voice with V. O.

Denver also played the guitar, providing good accompaniment for those with whom he sang.

When Denver returned to his home in Magnolia, Arkansas, he sang with two cousins, Ernest and Pat Lindsay, and E. T. Burgess as the Stamps Melody Boys, one of the fine Stamps-backed quartets of the day. That was Denver's first professional quartet-singing job.

Through the 1930s he sang with Stamps quartets, and periodically wrote some songs which V. O. Stamps helped put to music.

When the Rangers needed a tenor, they thought immediately of Denver, and hired him. He joined the quartet in June of 1938 and stayed with the Rangers fifteen years until the fall of 1953 when he took a job with Hovie Lister, singing tenor for the Statesmen Quartet.

Through the thirties and forties, the Rangers had a succession of accompanists: Vernon on guitar; Denver on guitar; Marion Snyder, who later had the Imperial Quartet, became their first pianist in 1941. He was succeeded by Charles Friar, then by Larry Walker, Lee Roy Abernathy, Hovie Lister, Doy Ott, David Reece, and in the 1950s, Cecil Pollock and Elmer Childress.

After Denver came to the Rangers, there were no more personnel changes in the singing slots for eleven years. Walter Leverette died in

June of 1949 and was succeeded by Erman Slater, the Sand Mountain baritone.

Just after World War II, in 1946, when singers were returning from military service and restrictions on gasoline were lifted, allowing groups enough fuel to travel again, quartet singing began to flourish, especially across the South—and the Rangers Quartet was at the top of the list, certainly the most popular quartet in America, and the best known.

The Rangers were characters! They had a good time on the road.

Vernon had a cocked eye that went over toward left field when he looked at you. You were never quite sure whether he was looking you in the face, or staring at someone to your left.

Arnold never won a handsome contest, either. David Reece later described him thusly: "Old Arnold, the Lord didn't bless him with good looks. Pore fellow, he was *ugly!*"

Arnold was superstitious. When Lee Roy Abernathy played piano for the Rangers in 1946, he loved to do magic tricks, simple sleight-of-hand stuff. Arnold thought Lee Roy was a witch.

When the Rangers stowed their equipment in their 1942 station wagon and started on tour, they matched to see who sat where. When it came down to Arnold and Lee Roy matching, Arnold would refuse. He'd look at Lee Roy and say, "Well, you get wherever you want," and he took the seat Lee Roy didn't want.

That station wagon was a wreck, but it had to do the quartet until American production of automobiles geared back up from the war effort. Sometimes the wagon wouldn't go in high gear, and Lee Roy remembers the quartet driving from Anderson, South Carolina, to Atlanta in second gear.

The Rangers had a tremendous repertoire of songs. They sang "I've Found A Hiding Place," "He Bore It all," "Wait Till You See Me In My New Home," "Roll On, Jordan," and Arnold gave the quartet great bottom with his rolling bass.

Rex Nelon, who came into the big-time in 1955 as a bass singer with the Homeland Harmony Quartet, remembers the Rangers as having "a different sound from any quartet I ever heard."

"They had the deepest-sounding quartet in the business," Rex said. "Just big, full voices and a bass singer who seemed to have no bottom. He sounded two times lower than J. D. Sumner because Arnold's voice was so much bigger, when in reality he couldn't sing as low as J. D."

For many years, the Rangers said Arnold had a ten thousand dollar check awaiting anyone who could sing lower than he. J. D. could have collected, but he admired Arnold so much he never tried.

Arnold's singing was rough, rough, rough. That's the way both Rex Nelon and James Blackwood described it—but it fit the Rangers' and the public's taste. He could stand at the microphone and belt out low numbers all night. He seemed to have no limit to his capacity. And he sang with such ease that he was easily the envy of all other bass singers. He plowed through the numbers with no effort at all.

Being the superstitious one, Arnold quite naturally became the butt of many of the Rangers' jokes. Vernon was a great trickster. In restaurants, the Rangers would slip silverware into Arnold's pockets, then tell the waiter he'd better search that man.

When the Rangers wore cowboy outfits, they would enter a town and get out to walk around and stretch their legs. The others would let Arnold walk off by himself, someone would yell, "Ride 'em, Cowboy!" and all the other Rangers would duck into a store, leaving Arnold standing there with everyone staring at him, thinking it was he who yelled.

Once in Dothan, Alabama, the Rangers spent the night in a hotel. One by one, they straggled into the hotel dining room for breakfast the next morning. David Reece, Vernon, and Denver arrived early and took a table at the far side of the room. Arnold came in a few minutes later, and failing to see his companions across the room, took a seat at a table near the door.

The waitress came to the table where the three sat, and Reece whispered to her, "Honey, when you wait on that man over there, you better watch yourself. He had a fit out on the street a while ago."

The waitress stared at Arnold, who, still sleepy, quietly resembled a man who had just had a fit. When she went to his table, she stood a distance away and pitched the menu to him. She brought his food and bent over, stretching as far as she could, to place it before him. Then she quickly leaped back.

Arnold stared at her in wonder. Reece, Vernon, and Denver knocked themselves out laughing across the room.

Later when the quartet checked out of the hotel, Arnold muttered, "Last blankety-blank time I'll ever come here."

"Why, Arnold?" Vernon asked.

"They was rude to me," Arnold said. "Acted like I was crazy. Acted like they was scared to death of me."

The other Rangers laughed all the way to the next town.

Vernon was driving the car one night and the other Rangers were trying to sleep. Arnold slept against the door on the passenger's side of the front seat.

Vernon pulled off the road and stopped the car beside a deep ditch. He shook Arnold and said, "How about driving, Arnold; I'm sleepy."

"Okay," Arnold yawned. He opened the door, stepped out—and disappeared into the ditch. Vernon laughed like a hyena, and from the back seat someone said, "Vernon, your ox is in the ditch again."

Sometime later, Arnold, remembering the ditch incident, accompanied Vernon, who did much of the quartet's business, to a theater to try to line up some dates.

The brothers seated themselves in the theater manager's office and Vernon explained what the Rangers could do to help business.

"We can do two shows a night," Vernon said, "one at seven and the other at nine, between motion pictures. You show the movie, then we'll sing, then you show the movie again, and we'll sing again. We can fill up this theater for you both times we sing—that's what we can do for you!"

The theater manager was impressed until Arnold muttered, "Aw, Vernon, you know we can't do that!"

"Well, then," Vernon said, nonplussed, "if we can't do that, let's get the blankety-blank out of here then." He clamped his hat on his head and stalked out with Arnold coming behind him, chuckling softly.

Vernon never let Arnold accompany him on a selling trip again.

Quite possibly the funniest thing that ever happened to this happy-go-lucky quartet occurred in Paris, Tennessee, in the days when motels were a new convenience for Americans, and some motel owners periodically painted the toilet seats in the motel's bathrooms.

Arnold checked the quartet in, and the motel clerk told him the only rooms remaining vacant were those with their toilet seats freshly painted.

"That's all right," Arnold said. "All we want to do is take a shower and dress and get down to the singing."

When he came out, he conveniently forgot to tell the others about the commode seat. Vernon was first into the room. He hurried to the bathroom, dropped his pants, and sat down on the black-painted seat of the toilet.

A few minutes later, he came out, his pants down around his

knees. "Arnold," he asked, "did they say anything about painting the toilet seat?"

"Believe they did," Arnold cracked, trying to stifle a laugh.

Vernon stretched out on his stomach on the bed, with a huge, black semi-circle on his rear end, and David Reece walked in, saw Vernon, and did a double-take.

"Good Lord!" He exclaimed. "What a horse!"

The Rangers got along with each other possibly better than most quartets. Each learned how to handle the other's idiosyncrasies.

Once they stopped at a gasoline station and Vernon went to the rest room. Arnold followed him in with a shaving kit under his arm.

"Get out of here, Vernon," Arnold said. "I've got to shave."

"Now, Arnold," Vernon said, "you just sing bass."

The Rangers adopted that phrase and its modifications. They never had a serious quarrel after that. If Denver Crumpler snapped at one of the others, the other simply said, "Now, Denver, you just sing tenor."

That little ploy worked for the Rangers. That's the way they handled small personal problems as long as they existed as a quartet.

The Rangers broke all the rules of the day for quartets. When others tried to dress alike, the Rangers never did. They were always presentable, but they didn't dress alike. Still, there was magic about them. On stage they were dynamite!

When the Rangers cut a record, they didn't wait around for the engineer to play it back and try to fill in the cracks. They sang the song one time, all singing into one microphone, and then Vernon said, "That's it," and they left.

The Rangers recorded on the White Church label after the war, and a quartet in Florida called the Sunny South Quartet cut two songs for White Church which were pressed into a 78 rpm recording. The Sunny South had a young bass singer, unknown outside the state of Florida, named J. D. Sumner. J. D. idolized Arnold Hyles.

The Sunny South came to Jacksonville for a singing convention on a Sunday afternoon in 1948, and found themselves on the same program with the Rangers Quartet.

"I thought just to be around Arnold Hyles was the greatest thing that ever happened to me," J. D. said.

During the noon hour, when no one was singing on stage, someone played records over the loudspeaker system. Most of what they played were recordings of the Rangers and Homeland Harmony quartets.

After a while, however, they put on the Sunny South's recording of "Marching Up To Heaven," and in the song J. D. had a strong bass run, which he sang masterfully.

As usual, J. D. was following Arnold Hyles around, dogging his footsteps. When J. D. hit that bass run on the record, Arnold stopped in his tracks and J. D. almost ran over him.

Very slowly, Arnold turned around, and in a voice that came from the depths of his belly, asked J. D., "Boy, is that you?"

Dumbfounded that Arnold Hyles would know his voice, J. D. couldn't muster a sound. He swallowed and nodded, and Arnold turned around and continued on his way. But J. D. walked on air the rest of the day, thrilled that Arnold Hyles had noticed his singing.

What goes around comes around. Eight or nine years later, when J. D. was a singing star with the Blackwood Brothers, they sang in Hendersonville, North Carolina. On the program that evening was a local group, the Talley Brothers Quartet, with Rex Nelon singing bass. Rex idolized J. D. the same way J. D. had looked up to Arnold Hyles.

At intermission, J. D. went out on the back porch of the building to have a smoke. He sat there alone as Rex walked out. Neither said a word for a couple of minutes. Then, summoning up his deepest voice, J. D. said, "Boy, when you going to Atlanta?" acknowledging that he knew Rex was joining the Homeland Harmony soon.

Rex was so scared for a minute, being in the presence of such greatness, that he thought he couldn't speak; then he managed to say in a high-pitched, cracking voice, "Next week."

"That was a nerve-wracking thing for a kid like me," Rex said, "just to be spoken to by J. D. Sumner."

Through the nineteen years of its existence, the Rangers Quartet sang on a long list of radio and television stations—WHAS in Louisville: WBT in Charlotte, North Carolina; WWVA in Wheeling, West Virginia; WRVA in Richmond, Virginia; WAGA in Atlanta; WIBW in Topeka, Kansas; WPTF in Raleigh, North Carolina; KWKH in Shreveport, Louisiana; KGKO and WFAA in Dallas; KNBC Radio and KTTV Television in Los Angeles; KANS Radio and KARD Television in Wichita, Kansas; and for two years they sang over the Liberty Broadcasting System, a network that reached coast to coast.

Walter Leverette had a heart attack late in May of 1949, leaving a gap in the Rangers' lineup. They quickly made a desperation call to

Sand Mountain, Alabama, and flew Erman Slater to Kinnett, Missouri, to sing baritone on the evening of June 1, 1949. During that program, word came that Leverette had passed away.

Erman stayed on. He was an excellent singer and fit the quartet well. He sang for a year and a half, until the evening of January 12, 1951, when he was killed in a head-on automobile crash outside Atlanta, Texas. Arnold Hyles, driving the car in which Erman died, was injured so severely with a crushed chest and pelvic bones that he was unconscious for more than a month and hospitalized three months. For the next two years, while Jimmy Jones sang bass with the Rangers, Arnold was in and out of hospitals for various surgical procedures.

David Reece replaced Slater singing baritone while playing piano, too.

When Arnold returned to the Rangers in the fall of 1953, he was as good as new as far as his singing went, but he was in rather constant pain. Jones switched to baritone and Cecil Pollock replaced Reece at the piano.

Denver Crumpler left the Rangers to join the Statesmen in the fall of 1953, and Gene Moss took his place with the Rangers. Gene sang first tenor until the quartet disbanded in April of 1956.

Glenn Sessions sang the lead and baritone with the Rangers in those later years, and Ralph Dailey sang baritone for a while in 1955.

Growing tired of the road and still feeling the effects of the automobile wreck, Arnold Hyles retired from the Rangers in February of 1956, ending his singing career.

Vernon, Gene Moss, and Elmer Childress sang as the Rangers Trio for two more months, but the magic was no longer there. They disbanded the group in April.

Later, David Reece, Roy McNeil, and Clark Thompson revived the Rangers Trio and made some tremendously tuneful recordings. Their harmony was unsurpassed.

Through their long and illustrious career, if the Rangers Quartet taught the gospel singing world anything, it was simply that it was all right to be different.

They certainly were.

Denver Crumpler died while singing for the Statesmen in 1957. Vernon Hyles died in 1973, and Arnold passed on March 15, 1979, his great bass voice finally stilled.

CHAPTER NINE

Death Shakes the Quartet World

The first great problem encountered by professional quartets was not what the average person would guess: It was not bookings, nor was it projection of voice since no adequate sound systems existed then, at least none that were priced within reach of those early vagabond singing groups.

The first great problem to conquer was transportation. In order to make a living singing, quartets had to travel far afield. Since most of the work of these men (and a few women) was in schoolhouses, many of their concerts were staged in the backwoods, and many were scheduled on the spur of the moment. That eliminated travel by rail, which was the best means of long-distance transportation at that time.

The automobile provided the only feasible transportation; so quartets squeezed five men and all their baggage, all the songbooks they thought they could sell, and anything else they wanted to carry, into an automobile and took off. They motored merrily along, probably not very conscious of the fact that they were pioneering a whole new field of entertainment, but merely content to be doing what they were doing.

A fellow named Edward Singletary, whom everyone called "Blocksome," summed up the majority feeling best. Blocksome was the baritone singer for the Gospel Melody Quartet, which later became the Florida Boys. A quiet and reserved man, he burst into enthusiasm one evening while the quartet drove home from an engagement. "You know, boys," he cried, "this is about the greatest thing I've ever known in my life—to sing and enjoy it as much as I do, and get paid for it!"

At first, travel was difficult. Roads were bad, mostly unpaved, some of them just a pair of ruts with holes large enough to burst tires. So distance was a great factor in singing; quartets still had to sing fairly close to home. That was one of the reasons there were so many Vaughan and Stamps quartets in the early days—to cover as much of the country as possible. One quartet couldn't do it.

As time passed and roads improved, travel by quartets became more extensive—and, proportionately, more dangerous. The law of averages was bound to catch up eventually; no one can drive as much as quartets did without incident—or accident.

In 1951, the Sunshine Boys—Ace Richman, Freddie Daniel, Eddie Wallace, and J. D. Sumner—took Freddie's brand-new 1951 Cadillac on one of their forays from Atlanta to Florida.

Going through South Georgia with Ace at the wheel, they came to a treacherously narrow road; and Freddie, knowing Ace to be a most bull-headed man, suddenly found his heart in his throat. They descended a long hill toward a narrow bridge, and across the way, coming down the other hill toward them, was another car. Freddie gauged that the vehicles were destined to meet somewhere on the bridge, and thought a word of caution appropriate.

"Ace," he said, "the bridge is too narrow."

"Naw," Ace said. "We'll make it."

Closer and closer the cars came.

"Ace!" Freddie said sharply, anxiety in his voice, "we're not going to make it."

"No sweat," Ace replied. "We'll make it."

The cars hit the bridge, both going sixty, and Ace passed the other car without touching it. But he touched the side rail of the bridge, wiping out the whole right side of the new Cadillac.

When it came to peculiar driving, however, the Rangers Quartet's bass singer, Arnold Hyles, took first prize. Lee Roy Abernathy learned first hand of Arnold's peculiarities in 1946 when he played piano for the Rangers.

Vernon Hyles told Lee Roy, "Arnold will do anything you tell him to when he's at the wheel."

"What do you mean?" Lee Roy asked.

"Tell him to do something and see," Vernon said.

Lee Roy didn't fully believe Vernon, but one day when they were motoring through Florida, Vernon proved his point.

"Arnold's driving now," Vernon whispered to Lee Roy. "If you told him to make a right turn right now, he'd turn off the road."

"Pshaw!" Lee Roy said. "He wouldn't do that."

A few minutes later they came to a long level stretch where pastureland bordered the road as far as they could see. Vernon punched Lee Roy: "Tell him what you want him to do."

"What?"

"Just holler at him and tell him where you want him to go," Vernon urged.

Thinking all of this was surely a joke, Lee Roy yelled, "Arnold, turn right!"

VARROOOOOMMM!!! Arnold whipped the steering wheel to the right and the quartet took off across the pasture. There was no road, just grass.

A motorist following the Rangers' car turned off too, and the two cars almost collided in the pasture.

Now we come to two great ironies.

One was that the same Arnold Hyles was driving the automobile in which Erman Slater met his death in 1951.

The other was that the first two traffic deaths that shocked the world of quartet singing involved two close friends who came from that famed singing region of northeast Alabama—Sand Mountain. The friends were Erman Slater and Bobby Strickland.

Erman Slater was older than Bobby by seventeen years, but the two sang together both in the Sand Mountain Quartet and with the Harmoneers over Radio Station WNOX in Knoxville, Tennessee.

Born February 2, 1903, in DeKalb County, Alabama, Erman Slater wanted to be a baseball player so badly that he named one of his sons after Cornelius McGillicuddy, known to the sports world as Connie Mack, the great owner-manager of the Philadelphia Athletics. But after an unsuccessful tryout with a minor league team, Erman came back to the farm and married Nora Lee Jolley of Hopewell, Alabama, when he was twenty-one. They reared three children, Myron Elmo, Juanita (Guice), and Connie Mack.

Nora came from a singing family and it was only natural that Erman took an interest in music after their marriage. He learned to sing at singing schools and discovered he could sing very well. By the late 1920s he was singing first tenor with three of Nora's brothers, J. M., Ashton, and Alton, in the Jolley Family Quartet.

The early music that Erman Slater sang was Sacred Harp, but then came the "new book" singing by Stamps-Baxter and Vaughan.

Pap Baxter, one of the pioneers of the new book singing, was a native of Sand Mountain.

Erman sang baritone for the first Sand Mountain Quartet in 1937, singing with first tenor Troy Chafin, lead Alton Jolley, and bass Corby Gardner. Hixon Belle played the guitar and Syble Owens the piano.

Two years later Erman sang with the Friendly Five Quartet, and a year after that—in 1940—he took a job singing baritone with the Stamps Dixie Four over Radio Station WMC in Memphis. In that group, he sang with first tenor Eiland Davis, lead Roosevelt Abney, and a great bass singer, Carl Raines. Reese Crockett played piano.

World War II, which began December 7, 1941, with the bombing of Pearl Harbor, broke up the Stamps Dixie Four, and Erman sang with the Sand Mountain Quartet until 1944 when he and Raines moved to Raleigh, North Carolina, and sang with the Lone Star Quartet over WPTF. Bert Carroll sang first tenor; Milton Estes, lead; and Herschel Collins played piano.

Somewhere in that period of time, Erman sang with Earl Terry in the All-American Quartet.

The year the war ended, 1945, Erman sang with some other names that were destined to make history in quartet singing—with Bobby Strickland in the Sand Mountain Quartet while a youngster named Hovie Lister played piano. Hovie was replaced after a few months by Lee Roy Abernathy. Then in 1946 Erman and Strickland moved to Knoxville to sing with Fred C. Maples and Aycel Soward in the Harmoneers with Charles Key at the piano. They recorded for RCA Victor.

By this time, Erman Slater and Bobby Strickland were at the top of their chosen field. But Erman didn't like to be away from his family as much as the Harmoneers demanded; so he left the Harmoneers and sang for a couple of years with groups called the Radioaires and the Lacey Family Quartet, and finally, in 1949, he replaced Walter Leverette as baritone with the Rangers when Leverette had a heart attack. Leverette died the night that Slater sang his first stand with the Rangers, and Erman took the job permanently.

They were based in Raleigh, singing over WPTF, and included in the Rangers' lineup then were Arnold and Vernon Hyles, Denver Crumpler, Slater, and David Reece. Nora and the Slater kids moved to Raleigh to be with Erman.

For a year and a half the Rangers were based in Raleigh, and in June of 1950 they moved to Shreveport, Louisiana, to perform on the Louisiana Hayride.

It may have been Providence that prompted Erman Slater to insist that a Slater Family Reunion be held at Christmas of 1950 on his farm in Alabama. All the family gathered and had a glorious time.

On December 27, Nora drove Erman to Birmingham to join the Rangers for a two-weeks tour of Georgia, the Carolinas, Tennessee, Arkansas, and Texas.

The Rangers had a great time on the tour. They sang to full houses almost everywhere, for their popularity was at its peak.

The tour was almost over when tragedy struck. After singing in the Concord Baptist Church near Mount Pleasant, Texas, on Friday night, January 12, they headed toward Naples, Texas, on the Douglasville-to-Naples highway. Carrying so much equipment, records, and luggage for an extended, two-weeks trip, the Rangers traveled in two automobiles. Arnold Hyles drove the front car with Slater as his passenger. Vernon Hyles, Crumpler, and Reece rode in the rear car, swapping off the driving.

Newspaper reports claimed that Arnold Hyles "drove at a considerable rate of speed" toward Naples when suddenly, just outside of Atlanta, Texas, he met a pickup truck coming toward him on his side of the road. Arnold swerved desperately to miss the truck, but the truck smashed into the side of the Rangers' car with tremendous impact.

Erman Slater died instantly. Arnold lay crumpled with both legs broken, his lower jaw fractured, his right ankle and hip fractured, his chest ripped and bleeding, and his spine injured. He also had other internal injuries.

Beat and battered though he was, Arnold lived to sing again with the Rangers.

The pickup truck that killed Erman Slater and broke up Arnold Hyles was driven by a Texan who had been drinking considerably. His two brothers, who rode in the pickup with him, had also been drinking—and they were on the wrong side of the road. The driver was convicted of murder with a motor vehicle, and his brothers were convicted of public drunkenness.

Tributes poured in from all over, attesting to Erman Slater's popularity and respect in the gospel singing world. Two who summed it up best were Denver Crumpler and Lee Roy Abernathy.

"The first time I saw Erman and heard him sing," Denver said, "there was no doubt in my mind that he was the greatest baritone I had ever heard."

Abernathy recalled that Erman once said, "Some day I'll sing in the finest quartet there is."

"I felt he succeeded while singing with the Rangers," Lee Roy said. "He was so happy and full of life; it just seems like my neighbor is missing."

Erman Slater's funeral was held in Hopewell Baptist Church near Geraldine, Alabama, on Tuesday, January 16, 1950, and many singers turned out. The Statesmen Quartet and the All-American Quartet sang, and joining in the congregational singing were Bobby Strickland, Lee Higgins, Ward Hurt, Harley Lester, W. O. Pruitt, and many others of musical prominence.

One can hardly help but wonder if Bobby Strickland had any sort of premonition that day, for he would be the next great singer to go.

He had only two and a half years to live.

Tragedy stalked the Hyles family again in 1979, the year of Arnold's death. That he lived twenty-eight years beyond that grinding automobile wreck in Texas was a tribute to his constitution, but Arnold made it. He was a proud man, and one of the things he was proudest of was his family.

At the time of his death, Arnold's son, Gene, was forty. Gene had been a twelve-year-old lad when Arnold was crushed in the wreck, but now Gene had a wife, Faye, thirty-seven; and two children, Steve, fourteen, and Stacey, twelve.

Arnold Hyles was buried on Big Sandy in Upshure County, Texas. Gene and his family rode home from the funeral with a forty-two-year-old Baptist minister, Ralph D. Grice, and the minister's wife, Joyce, of Louisville, Kentucky. The Grices were longtime friends of the younger Hyleses.

Coming up Stemmons Freeway in Dallas, the Grice automobile entered the 3100 block when tragedy struck. A Dallas schoolteacher entered the freeway on the wrong side by coming down an exit ramp. He crossed four lanes of traffic unscathed and crashed head-on into the Grice car. The impact knocked the Grices and Hyleses thirty feet backward where they were struck in the rear by a truck pulling a trailer loaded with five-gallon cans of light blue paint.

The vehicles were crushed beyond repair—and the wreck scene was inundated in a sea of blue paint which lent an eerie atmosphere to the area.

But worst of all, Arnold Hyles' son, Gene; Gene's wife, Faye; and the preacher's wife, Joyce Grice, all lay dead in the wreckage, the life snuffed out of them in the bat of an eye.

* * *

The death of Erman Slater struck Bobby Strickland a severe blow. He liked Erman and loved to sing with him.

They were alike in many ways, though there were seventeen years difference in their ages. Both were from Sand Mountain, both were professional singers and good at their trades. And both had been outstanding athletes in their youth.

Bobby Strickland, the ninth of ten children born to Mr. and Mrs. Sam Strickland of Albertville, Alabama, grew up on a farm where he practiced singing while milking cows by hand. He was a three-letter man at Albertville High School in football, basketball, and baseball. Born January 7, 1920, he came into high school in the early 1930s when football had blossomed into a big sport in Alabama.

His older brother, J. B. Strickland, who lives in Hondo, Texas, today, remembers that Bobby "was kinda fat, but he was one of the best football players around." He was so good, in fact, that he played for Albertville High School the fall following his high school graduation in the spring. Rules were less stringent than now, and he simply studied for and earned another high school diploma while playing a fifth season for Albertville. He studied agriculture and English that extra year in school.

He was captain of the football team two years running, elected by his teammates, attesting to a popularity that remained with him through his singing career to the end of his days.

The Strickland boys were all good singers; at least they had good singing voices, but Bobby was the only one who sang for a living. They were good boys; they did not drink, nor did they have any real bad habits. The Strickland house was like a three-ring circus while the children grew up, with much foolishness going on. Their mother never knew who she was cooking Sunday dinner for; she only knew that it would be eaten by many before supper.

One football game that J. B. Strickland remembers vividly matched Bobby Strickland and Albertville High against their biggest rival, Oneonta High, which was coached by Bobby's older brother, Clair, whom everyone called "Big-'Un."

Big-'Un was a good football strategist, so good that Auburn University offered him its freshman coaching job, but he turned it down and continued to coach high school boys. He confided in J. B. that if he could stop Bobby, he could beat Albertville.

He concentrated two huge tackles on Bobby, and turned loose a fleet running back around the ends. The running back was so fast he had made the Alabama state finals in the 100-yard-dash.

Once those tackles crushed Bobby to the ground, and the fast back sailed around end and set off on a clear course to the end zone, eighty yards away. Bobby recovered, bounded to his feet and ran the back down at the twenty-yard line, hauling him to earth so hard that his teammates had to shake the fleet back to bring him to.

Albertville and Oneonta played to a 6–6 tie that day, and when J. B. asked Bobby where he got the extra speed to run the back down, Bobby said, "I wasn't about to let him outdo me."

That summed up Bobby's life. He did what he could—to the utter limits of his ability. That's the way he sang.

He even helped name himself. When he was just beginning to talk, his father gave him a Holstein calf, and Bobby named the calf Jim. Soon Bobby was calling himself Bobby Jim, and his parents added Jim to his name.

Bobby learned to sing in the cow barn and at local churches and singing schools. He had a fine tenor voice and while still a teen-ager he began singing with Erman Slater and others in the Sand Mountain Quartet.

At the time of the Sand Mountain Quartet's first big break, Strickland and Slater were singing with Alton Jolley and Irby Gardner, with Otis Moore at the piano, and they were invited to come to Chattanooga and sing at a big gathering.

To make themselves as presentable as possible, the quartet bought new matching suits. They rode to Chattanooga, dressed in their new suits, in the back of a cleaned-out cattle truck and those who were married took their wives.

The quartet was a hit. Several times while they sang, the crowd surged to its feet, clapping and yelling, so pleased was it with the Sand Mountain boys' singing.

In 1946, just after World War II ended, Bobby Strickland accepted a singing job with the Harmoneers and moved his family to Knoxville, Tennessee. That quartet generated tremendous harmony, with Strickland singing first tenor; Erman Slater, lead; Fred C. Maples, baritone; and the great Aycel Soward, bass. Charles Key played the piano.

When Erman left the Harmoneers he was replaced by Bob Crews, a tall, handsome man who also came from Sand Mountain. Then Soward departed, and Maples, the quartet's manager, brought in Seals (Low Note) Hilton, another Sand Mountain man, to sing bass. They became one of the finest quartets of the day, singing all over the South.

They were in such demand that they could not fill all the dates requested of them.

The Harmoneers sang over WROL in Knoxville, sponsored by Scalf's Indian River Medicine, and recorded for RCA Victor.

With that quartet, Bobby Strickland established himself in the business as one of the finest first tenors. He was a bit on the heavy side, jolly and friendly, a man who never met a stranger—the ideal quartet man.

In 1948 Hovie Lister organized the Statesmen Quartet and hired Bobby Strickland as the quartet's original first tenor. Bobby moved his family to Atlanta. The Statesmen immediately gained such popularity that they stepped directly onto the top rung of the ladder, and Bobby Strickland enjoyed even more popularity than he had before.

Bobby sang with the Statesmen almost two years, but then opportunity beckoned. Although there were several professional quartets traveling the South, there weren't enough to fill the demand, particularly when quartet-singing became popular in the Midwest and up the East Coast.

Bobby left the Statesmen and organized a quartet of his own. He called his group the Crusaders, and they were an immediate hit. Bobby headquartered the Crusaders in Birmingham where they sang daily on a fifteen-minute show over Radio Station WVOK and recorded on the Bibletone label.

Bobby corralled the best talent he could find to sing with the Crusaders. He had Buddy Parker singing lead, Bervin Kendrick on baritone, and Herschel Wooten singing bass. Dickie Matthews played piano.

Bobby found that his days grew longer when he began to manage his own quartet. He had to keep the quartet busy, and he talked a lot on the telephone, lining up dates with promoters all over the South. He also did the arranging of numbers and choreography (Yes, they practiced stage movements). As a member of the Statesmen Quartet, Bobby had made regular trips to Canton, Georgia, to study piano with Lee Roy Abernathy and voice with Shorty Bradford.

He always said he was a singer, not a pianist, but he studied piano to broaden his musical knowledge and to be able to arrange for his own quartet.

He owned a Hudson automobile without air-conditioning, in which the Crusaders traveled. They packed five men and all their luggage, equipment, and recordings in that car and made the long-distance swings with all the men taking turns driving while the others rested as best they could.

Through his days with the Crusaders, Bobby often sang in Memphis and other towns nearby, and several times he was visited by a young Elvis Presley, who brought his guitar to the concerts and begged Bobby to listen to him play and sing backstage. Patiently, Bobby listened, and gave Elvis advice on singing and performing. Unfortunately, Bobby died before Elvis reached the peak of his popularity. The crux of Bobby's advice to Elvis was to keep practicing and playing. Bervin Kendrick often heard Bobby tell Elvis, "Don't give up; keep practicing. One day you'll make it."

Bobby's family was close-knit. He had married Beatrice Johnston, and they had three children: Rita Jo, who married George Gilbreath and teaches fourth grade at Crossville, Alabama, grammar school; Linda Lou, who married Joe Hawkins and teaches first grade at Crossville; and Bobby Jim, who sells automobiles in Crossville.

As the children came along, Bobby had to supplement his quartet income. Running his own quartet was a costly venture, and he needed more money to support his family; so he taught voice to various students in Birmingham. Among his students were the Thrasher brothers who later became famous on the gospel quartet trail.

Early in 1953, Bobby announced that he planned to enter the ministry, and those who knew him applauded that decision, knowing he would make a fine preacher.

Bobby and his family lived in Midfield, Alabama, near Birmingham, in September 1953. The last concert Bobby Strickland sang was in Kingsport, Tennessee, with Lee Roy and Shorty, and the following week the Crusaders sang in a week-long revival meeting in Chattanooga.

The two single members of the Crusaders, Buddy Parker and Dickie Matthews, spent the nights in Chattanooga that week. The married men—Bobby Strickland, Bervin Kendrick, and Doug Jones, a bass singer who had replaced Wooten—commuted to Chattanooga.

Jones had a new car and on Thursday night of that revival week he drove it to Chattanooga, and after the services Jones drove back to Birmingham with Bobby Strickland sitting in the right front seat and Kendrick asleep in the back seat.

On a hill outside Trussville, Alabama, Jones met two cars coming side by side over the hill at a high rate of speed, one passing the other. A drunk, driving the passing car, gave Jones no place to go and both of the racing cars smashed into Jones's car head-on.

Jones escaped with minor injuries. Bobby Strickland died instantly, and Bervin Kendrick's back was broken.

The date was September 24, 1953.

Bobby Strickland's children were aged ten, eight, and six, and Bobby had just bought a new home and had made one payment on it.

The response to his death was such that his funeral was considered to have been the largest ever in that part of Alabama. People filed by Bobby's casket in two lines for several hours to view the body. So many flowers were sent to the funeral home that hundreds of arrangements were passed on to local hospitals and nursing homes and finally an announcement was made on radio that additional flowers should not be sent.

The radio station, WVOK, offered Bobby's picture for sale at one dollar a copy, and enough pictures were ordered by Bobby's fans that, coupled with the money made at a benefit singing in which several groups took part, the mortgage on the Strickland house was paid off.

One of the groups that participated in the benefit sing was the Blackwood Brothers, who flew into Birmingham in their own airplane to attend the event—an appearance that had portent written all over it, for less than a year later two members of the Blackwood Brothers who sang that night would die in the fiery crash of their airplane.

News of Bobby Stickland's death had a chilling effect on the world of quartet singing. Lee Roy Abernathy told about it this way:

"Shorty and I were with the Crusaders at their last concert in Kingsport, Tennessee, and the next week when they were in that revival in Chattanooga, Shorty and I passed through Birmingham on Thursday, en route to a concert in St. James, Missouri. I telephoned Bobby and he wanted to come downtown and meet me for lunch, but I was in a hurry and told him not to.

"We drove on to St. James and went into concert the next night with the Sunshine Boys. That was the first time I had ever seen the Sunshine Boys flop. Usually they went over great guns, but that night they fell flat on their faces, and I couldn't understand it.

"Then Shorty and I went on, and I did my best to entertain the crowd, but Shorty was distracted. He didn't seem to know where he was or what was taking place. Finally, I got so disgusted, I told Shorty if he didn't intend to sing or crack jokes or something, to just go sit down. He turned and left the stage, and I ended the program quickly

FIRST VAUGHAN QUARTET
1910

The Vaughan Quartet of 1910 was America's first professional gospel quartet. It included, from bottom clockwise, Charles W. Vaughan, Joe M. Allen, George W. Sebren, and Ira T. Foust.

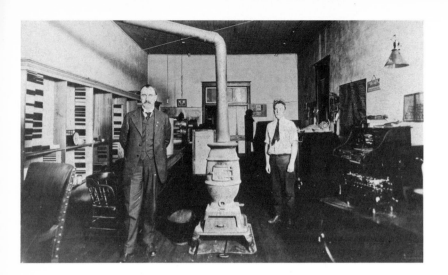

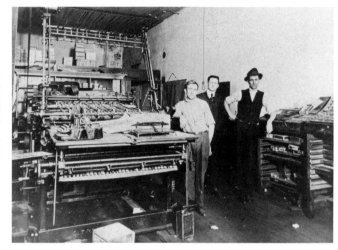

Above, James D. Vaughan stands by pot-bellied stove in the office of the James D. Vaughan Music Company in Lawrenceburg, Tenn. Center, the Vaughan company's press room where millions of songbooks were set into type. These two pictures may date to the teens. Below is the Vaughan Radio Band that played over Radio Station WOAN from 1922 on.

The Vaughan Saxophone Quartet in the 1920s included, L-R, W. B. Walbert, Claude Sharp, Ted Shaw, and A. M. Pace.

James D. Vaughan

The Owen
Brothers and Ellis
were a Vaughan
Quartet in 1928.
L-R: Oglesby Ellis,
Hub Owen,
Aubrey Owen,
Arch Owen, and
Babe Owen seated.

A tremendous quartet was the Vaughan Radio Quartet of the early 1930s which sang over WSM in Nashville. Standing, L-R, Palmer Wheeler, first tenor; G. Kieffer Vaughan, second tenor; John Cook, baritone; Big Jim Waits, bass; and accompanist James D. Walbert is seated.

One of the greatest of the early quartets was the 1928 Stamps Quartet—actually the Frank Stamps All-Star Quartet. L-R: Palmer Wheeler, first tenor; Roy Wheeler, second tenor; Odis Echols, baritone; Frank Stamps, bass; and Dwight Brock is the pianist.

This is the first picture of the Blackwood Brothers Quartet, made in 1934. L-R: R. W. Blackwood, James Blackwood, Roy Blackwood, and Doyle Blackwood.

The Stamps-Baxter Melody Boys of the mid- to late-1930s included Doy Ott at the piano, first tenor Pat Garner, baritone Clarence Heidelberg, second tenor and announcer Art Bowman, and bass and manager Ernest Lindsey.

The Daniel Quartet of about 1937, L-R, Carl Raines, bass; Troy Daniel, baritone; Wallace Fowler, lead; Albert Williams, pianist; and John Daniel, first tenor.

The 1929 Frank Stamps All-Star Quartet, right, had three Wheeler brothers. L-R: Dwight Brock, Frank Stamps, and the Wheeler brothers, Roy, Palmer, and J. E. Center photo is the first studio picture of the Blackwood Brothers, made in Ackerman, Miss., showing, L-R, Doyle, James, R. W., and Roy. Below, the Sunshine Boys of 1943, L-R, Tennessee Smith, Ace Richman, Smitty Smith, and Eddie Wallace.

Top photo: Wally Fowler and the Georgia Clodhoppers of 1945. Wally is seated. Standing are John Gallahar, bass; Chet Atkins, lead guitar; Tony Cinciola, accordion; and Tommy Trent, rhythm guitar. Below, Wally's original Oak Ridge Quartet of 1945 had, L-R, Curly Kinsey, baritone; Johnny New, first tenor; Wally Fowler, lead; and Lon (Deacon) Freeman, bass.

Vep Ellis was one of the great songwriters.

Top, the Blackwood Brothers just after World War II had, L-R, standing, Bill Lyles, R. W., James, Roy, and Doyle. Hilton Griswold was the pianist. At left are the Harmoneers of Knoxville, Tenn. Seated, L-R, Fred C. Maples, baritone, and Aycel Soward, bass; and standing, Charles Key, pianist; Bobby Strickland, first tenor; and Erman Slater, baritone. Below, the Stamps Quartet of 1948 included, L-R, Walter Rippetoe, Bob Jones, Robert E. Arnold, and Frank Stamps.

Stamps Quartet 1948 *Sponsored by the Millers of American Beauty Flour*

Walter Rippetoe

Bob Jones

Robert E. Arnold

Frank H. Stamps

The Rangers Quartet was one of history's greatest. Seated were bass Arnold Hyles, first tenor Denver Crumpler, lead Vernon Hyles, and standing were pianist David Reece and baritone Erman Slater.

Here are two versions of Tampa, Florida's Sunny South Quartet: At left is the 1946 quartet of, L-R, Horace Floyd, first tenor; Lee Kitchens, second tenor; Mosie Lister, baritone; James S. Wetherington, bass; and Quentin Hicks, pianist. Right photo, the 1947 quartet, has Hicks at the piano, and, L-R, Horace Floyd, first tenor; Stacy Selph, second tenor; Roger Clark, baritone; and J. D. Sumner, bass.

The Homeland Harmony Quartet, at left, just after World War II had, L-R, first tenor Connor B. Hall, second tenor Otis McCoy, baritone James McCoy, bass Big Jim Waits, and a kid piano player named Hovie Lister.

The best remembered version of the Harmoneers, top photo, had Charles Key seated at the piano, and, standing, L-R, first tenor Happy Edwards, lead Bob Crews, baritone Fred C. Maples, and bass Seals (Low-Note) Hilton. At center are the smooth-singing Swanee River Boys: George Hughes, Bill Carrier, and brothers Buford and Merle Abner. Sportscaster Bill Stern called them the best quartet he had ever heard. Below are the personnel for the two Blackwood Brothers quartets that sang in 1948: kneeling, L-R, Bill Lyles, Calvin Newton, Cat Freeman, and Johnny Dickson; standing, Warren Holmes, Hilton Griswold, Doyle Blackwood, James Blackwood, R. W. Blackwood, Billy Gewin, and Roy Blackwood.

At top are the Sunshine Boys of 1949, who put swing into gospel music: L-R, Ace Richman, baritone; Eddie Wallace, lead and pianist; J. D. Sumner, bass; and Fred Daniel, first tenor. Center photo is of the Jordanaires, who sang on the circuit for a while before retiring to Nashville to work as backup singers. Below, the Crusaders Quartet, destined to be one of the great ones until the untimely death of Bobby Strickland. Seated are Buddy Parker, lead, and Dickie Matthews, pianist; and standing are Strickland, the first tenor; Herschel Wooten, bass; and Bervin Kendrick, baritone.

At top are two versions of the Carl Raines Lone Star Quartet of Raleigh, N.C., just after the war. Left photo shows, L-R, Bert Carroll, Carl Raines, Milton Estes, Wayne Roseberry, and pianist Hershel Collins. The photo at right shows, kneeling, Jack Pittman, first tenor; Doyce Thompson, pianist; and Clarence Turbyfill, baritone; and standing, Jimmy Frye, second tenor; and Carl Raines, bass. At left is the original Blue Ridge Quartet with, L-R, Clarence Turbyfill, Elmo Fagg, Everett Payne, and Burl Strevel, with Kenny Gates at the piano. Just below is a shot of songwriter and sometimes singer Mosie Lister. At bottom are two famous quartets of bygone days: Left is Deacon Utley and the Smile-A-While Quartet of Macon, Ga., which included, L-R, Clifford Brewton, Earl Peek, Irwin Bridger, Clyde McLain, Deacon Utley, and Dean Winshie at the piano. At lower right is the Dixie Rebel Quartet, L-R, Horace Parrish, first tenor; Lee Kitchens, second tenor; John Matthews, baritone; Norman Almand, bass; and Jimmy Hand at the piano.

The Statesmen Quartet of 1954, above, which the author called "the Perfect Quartet," had, L-R, Denver Crumpler at first tenor; Jakes Hess on the lead; Doy Ott singing baritone; James (Big Chief) Wetherington singing bass; and Hovie Lister at the piano. At left was that great 1952 version of the Blackwood Brothers Quartet. From top: Jackie Marshall, pianist; Bill Shaw, first tenor, and Bill Lyles, bass; and James Blackwood, lead, and R. W. Blackwood, baritone. Below is the Chuck Wagon Gang of 1954, L-R, Dad Carter, Anna, Rose, and Roy Carter.

In the mid-1950s, quartets, like the Statesmen in top photo, sang into one microphone. L-R: Jake Hess, Denver Crumpler, Doy Ott, and Big Chief Wetherington. Center photo shows the early version of the Happy Goodman Family, including, L-R, top row, Bill Huie, bass; Gussie Goodman, tenor; Charles (Rusty) Goodman, baritone; and bottom, Howard Goodman, pianist; Vestal Goodman, soprano; Stella Goodman, alto; and Eloise Goodman, bass. Lower photo shows the Statesmen teaming with the McGuire Sisters on Arthur Godfrey's show in New York.

Top, the Speer Family examines one of its new 78s on the *Bullet* label. Dad and Mom are in front, and standing are Ben, Rosa Nell, Mary Tom, and Brock Speer. At center is the Blue Ridge Quartet with, L-R, Elmo Fagg, Kenny Gates, Jim Hamill, George Younce, and Ed Sprouse. Below are the LeFevres soon after the war with Earl Terry, Uncle Alf LeFevre, and Doug Pratter standing, and Urias and Eva Mae sitting.

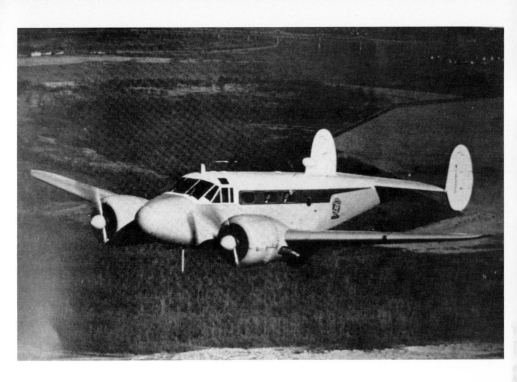

Other quartets were considering taking to the air in 1954 when the Blackwood Brothers' twin-engine Cessna, above, crashed in Clanton, Ala., killing R. W. Blackwood and Bill Lyles, below looking back from cockpit.

Not a year after the air crash, the Blackwood Brothers became the first entertainment unit of any kind to travel in a customized motorcoach, above. The Blackwood Brothers are shown below in the comfortable easy chairs on the bus, L-R, Cecil Blackwood, James Blackwood, Driver Buddy Darvis standing, J. D. Sumner, Bill Shaw, and Jackie Marshall. It was Sumner, lower photo, who dreamed up the idea of traveling in a bus and who built that first bus with hammer and saw, revolutionizing transportation not just in the gospel music world but in the entire entertainment world.

and went backstage to see what was wrong with all the guys. They were all sitting around with long faces and Eddie Wallace of the Sunshine Boys came to me and said, 'Lee Roy, I have been chosen to break some bad news to you.'

"I said, 'Spill it.'

"Eddie said, 'We both lost a good friend last night.'

"I said, 'That's nothing unusual. Quartet men lose friends almost every night.'

"Then he told me: 'Bobby Strickland was killed last night in an automobile accident.'

"Never before had I had such a feeling," Lee Roy said. "I couldn't believe it. Bobby couldn't be dead. I then realized why the Sunshine Boys couldn't sing that night, why Shorty failed to entertain. They kept it from me until the program was over so I could hold up under the strain of losing one of my closest friends."

Only ten days before the accident, Shorty and Lee Roy had dropped in on Bobby Strickland and Beatrice at 2:30 in the morning.

"Beatrice didn't mind a bit," Lee Roy said. "She got up and moved the children and made room for us, and the next morning she fixed a big breakfast for us and really made us feel like two of the family. They were exceptionally fine people."

To keep the Crusaders going, Bill Hefner, now a congressman from North Carolina, came off Sand Mountain to sing tenor in Bobby's place, but soon after that the quartet broke up.

Hefner and Buddy Parker moved to Charlotte and joined Herschel Wooten and Pat Patterson in organizing the Harvesters Quartet, which could be called an outgrowth of the Crusaders Quartet. They, like the Crusaders, achieved top-rung fame over the next few years of the 1950s and 1960s.

Lee Roy Abernathy remembered something that Bobby Strickland had told him while they ate together in a cafe in Columbus, Mississippi.

"Quartets," Bobby had said, "all seem to reach a certain level, and then something happens. Do you know what?"

"What?" Lee Roy asked.

"They don't live right," Bobby said. "I'm working on a building, and when the Lord gets it ready He'll call me home. When He does, I'm ready to go."

Lee Roy added a few words: "I believe Bobby Strickland sent up gold bars to make a mansion of that building he was working on. His singing blessed everyone who heard it, and he sings now with Erman Slater, whom he loved so much, in a heavenly quartet that God has chosen one by one."

CHAPTER TEN

The Blackwood Brothers

The cottonfields of Mississippi are tough places to make a living at any time, but they were especially so during the Great Depression that began in 1929 and stretched through the 1930s.

Ten years old in 1929, James Blackwood grew to manhood in the depression. He was born on a cotton farm in the Mississippi Delta August 4, 1919, the son of William Emmett and Carrie Blackwood. There were three older Blackwood children, Roy, a 1900 Christmas present, born on December 24; Lena, who came along on New Year's Eve, 1905; and Doyle, whose birth was on August 22, 1911.

Roy married Susie Hall early in 1921, and their first son, R. W., was born late that year. Thus, the singers for the famed Blackwood Brothers Quartet, three brothers and a nephew, were all alive and kicking by the early 1920s.

There was little entertainment near those vast fields of cotton. Radio had not yet been perfected, silent movies were too far away from the cottonfields to be considered regular entertainment; so what pleasure those sharecropping families like the Blackwoods had, they provided for themselves.

They sang.

In the cool of the evening, a voice lifted in song, and moments later others joined in—and families sat on the porch, or beneath the huge oaks in the yard, and listened to the children sing. Often the adults sang, too.

Some of the kids learned to sing well. James Blackwood, for instance, began singing with the family when he was seven, and by the time his tenth birthday came along in 1929 he was singing with a quartet.

During that year, James and his eighteen-year-old brother Doyle attended a ten-night singing school taught by Vardiman Ray, who knew shaped-note music inside and out and was excellent in passing his knowledge on to others.

By that time, a few good professional quartets were on the road, most of them bearing either the Stamps or Vaughan names; so singing school teachers kept their eyes peeled for good voices that could be trained for quartet singing. Vard Ray recognized two good ones in James and Doyle Blackwood.

At the end of that singing school, Vard Ray asked James and Doyle if they would like to sing with him in a quartet. He said he knew a bass singer he could get, a fellow named Gene Catledge of Ackerman, the seat of Choctaw County, Mississippi.

Most singings then were all-day affairs with dinner-on-the-ground. The quartet scheduled itself to sing at Concord Baptist Church near Ackerman on a certain Sunday in 1929, and Vard Ray brought along some Stamps-Baxter songbooks. The fellows practiced outside under the live oaks, picked out two or three songs, and headed inside to sing. At the steps of the church, Vard Ray stopped and said, "Fellows, we need a name for this quartet." Before they entered the church, they settled on the name of the Choctaw County Jubilee Singers. Then they went inside, stood the tiny James Blackwood in a chair, and sang their hearts out.

James and Doyle sang a lot as a duet, with Doyle playing the mandolin. The first two songs James can remember singing were "Don't Be Knocking" and "Six Feet of Earth." James remembers singing the songs in the Mount Olive Church of God near Ackerman, the church the Blackwood family attended.

Radio came along and began to look for live entertainment, since there was not enough canned entertainment to sustain stations. Quartet singing became big on radio and thus big throughout the countryside.

By 1934 the Blackwood Brothers were singing together, James singing lead; Roy, first tenor; Roy's son R. W. singing baritone; and Doyle singing bass and accompanying the group on guitar. At first Doyle played an old Russian *balalaika*, which James nicknamed "the Tater Bug" because its round, striped back resembled a potato bug.

Sometime in the mid-1930s, James remembers singing at the Mississippi State Singing Convention in Tupelo when the LeFevre Trio—Urias, Eva Mae, and Alphus—also sang.

"The only groups I knew of then," James said, "were the quartets of V. O. and Frank Stamps and Mr. James D. Vaughan, and the John Daniel Quartet."

When the Blackwood Brothers began to sing together seriously, singing contests became popular in schoolhouses. Gospel, Western, and country singers gathered to compete as solos, duets, trios, quartets, pickers, fiddlers, and such. Prizes were sacks of flour, buckets of lard, and staple things that families could use during those hard depression days. The Blackwood Brothers went to such a contest at Union Schoolhouse one evening, won the quartet singing, and James and Doyle won the duet contest. They took home the groceries that night.

Roy was a preacher, thirty-three years old in 1934, and by that time he had been preaching eighteen years. Doyle was twenty-three, James fifteen, and R. W. was the youngest at thirteen. A quartet with close, pleasing harmony, it was destined for greatness. No one questioned that.

A small new radio station, a 250-watter called WHEF, went on the air in Kosciusko, Mississippi, a one-man outfit in which the station owner served as announcer, manager, janitor, program director, and receptionist. He had access to no network, no recordings, no tapes (they hadn't even been invented), and he had to scramble for live entertainment in a place as small as Kosciusko.

When these four small fellows, the Blackwood Brothers, one carrying a "punkin" guitar, walked in one Sunday and asked for some time on the air, the station owner looked them over sharply and said they could have fifteen minutes.

They sang a couple of songs and the telephone began to ring with people calling in requests. The manager fed the requests to the Blackwood Brothers, and they sang the songs the people wanted to hear. At the end of the fifteen minutes the manager waved to the quartet to keep singing.

They sang an hour and a quarter, and the station received sixty long-distance calls and many more local calls.

It appeared, the Blackwood Brothers thought, that folks liked their singing. They decided right then that they would like to sing for a living and agreed to try it.

They entered an arrangement with the James D. Vaughan Music

Company to sell Vaughan's songbooks for a percentage of the profits. How they made the rest of their living was up to them.

Roy had a car, and in it they drove through the countryside. When they came to a schoolhouse, they went inside and met the principal. Roy usually did the talking. Being a preacher, he had the most persuasive voice in the group. He introduced himself and the others and told the principal they sang together as a quartet. He said they sang in concert in schools in the evenings, and that they would like to sing a concert in his school.

"We charge five cents for children and ten cents for adults," Roy would say. "We will keep two-thirds of the money taken in, and give the other third to the school to be used in any way you see fit. We would expect you to run your school buses to bring the people in, and, of course, you would want to send notices home with the children, telling parents when the concert is."

Most principals were interested in making money for their schools, and they recognized legitimate quartets as being good enough to attract people; so most readily agreed.

The Blackwood Brothers were singing thirty minutes on the Kosciusko station each Sunday morning, and they were allowed to announce their concert dates for the coming week.

Normally, the Blackwood Brothers averaged five to ten dollars per concert, and they had to schedule as many as possible each week in order for the four men to make enough money to live.

They didn't really have much expense. They lived at home with their mother and father, and ate most of their meals there. They had no public address system; so their only expense was gasoline for the car.

The Blackwood Brothers' first big crowd was at Noxapater, Mississippi, where the gate receipts were twenty-seven dollars. Their take was eighteen dollars, which, split four ways, came to $4.50 per man. They couldn't make that much in a day picking cotton!

A few weeks later, at a singing in Houlka, Mississippi, the gate was fifty-five dollars. The Blackwood Brothers' individual shares came to $9.16. Roy got so excited he exclaimed, "Let's just move up here with these good folks!"

Roy's second son, Cecil Stamps Blackwood, was born that year, on October 28, 1934.

The Blackwood Brothers knew that if they were to continue to make a living singing, they had to have greener pastures—or a larger radio station.

They moved to Jackson, Mississippi, where a 5,000-watt station,

WJDX, boomed across the countryside. Unfortunately, the station manager didn't think a full gospel show would be accepted by the listening audience, but the Blackwoods met a country-western singer named Tommy Gentry, who had a daily program on WJDX, and Gentry, always looking for variety, agreed to let the Blackwood Brothers sing one song a day on his program.

That was better than nothing, the Blackwoods agreed, and they accepted. Soon, for that one song daily, the Blackwood Brothers were getting more mail than Tommy Gentry, and the station manager gave the Blackwoods their own show.

The Blackwood Brothers soon became known across the state of Mississippi and beyond. And they perfected their singing every day, becoming sharper and sharper with a certain sound that no other quartet had. That's what most quartets sought to achieve in those early days, an individual sound.

But they still weren't making enough money for the whole quartet to live decently. They had grown up poor and were not accustomed to frivolous things, but growing up on a farm—even a sharecropping farm—they had plenty to eat. At times it was only cornbread and buttermilk for supper, and cornbread and eggs for breakfast, but there was plenty, and it was filling. Because the Blackwoods raised cows and chickens and hogs and cornfields and a garden, they had sufficient food.

But when the quartet moved to Jackson in late 1937, the guys rented two small rooms upstairs in the Kings Hotel on Capitol Street. Across the street was a Krystal Hamburger Palace where hamburgers were five cents each, and much of the time that's what the quartet had to eat—a hamburger for each.

Usually, though, when they sang a concert in the area surrounding Jackson, a family in the community where they were singing would invite the quartet to eat before the concert—and that was the Blackwoods' main meal of the day. If they didn't have a concert, they had to content themselves with nickel hamburgers.

"I can remember a time," James said, "when I didn't have a nickel for a hamburger. There was a kitchen in our little hotel, and one night I got so hungry I slipped down to the kitchen and ate some cornbread and buttermilk."

Those were depression days, though, when a lot of men stood in soup lines. The Blackwoods never had to do that, though they might have been tempted at times.

Still, they wouldn't quit singing. They loved it so much, and their harmony had become so high and sweet that they knew this was what they wanted to do for a living.

They traveled in an old 1935 Ford they had worn out. Some time after they came to Jackson, they found they didn't have money to make the payments on the Ford and eat, too. So they let the payments slide, and soon the finance company repossessed the car, leaving the quartet without transportation.

They had to have a car, but they had no credit at the bank. They looked for someone to sign a note with them to get a car, and after several days one of the engineers at the station came in the studio after the Blackwood Brothers' broadcast and said, "I understand you all need somebody to sign for you at the bank to buy a car."

"We sure do," James said.

"Well, I've got credit at the bank," the engineer said. "If you'll meet me at the bank tomorrow, I'll sign for you."

The man was a godsend. The Blackwood Brothers bought a 1938 two-door Ford.

On Sundays the Blackwood Brothers would find a singing convention to attend, knowing that by this time they sang so well that every time they sang free at a convention they booked some paying dates because of it.

Because of still poor road conditions, and their problems with transportation, the Blackwoods were limited to an area of four or five counties.

The Blackwood Brothers joined many other great quartets at the Mississippi State Singing Convention in Jackson in 1939, and one of the featured quartets was the Stamps All-Star Quartet led by Frank Stamps. As the Blackwood Brothers gathered around the one microphone to sing, Frank Stamps suddenly leaned forward, the better to hear them sing. That evening, Frank called his brother, V. O., in Dallas and told him that he had heard an outstanding quartet that day. "You'd better get in touch with them," Frank said, "They've got a little deal with Vaughan, but nothing like we can offer them."

V. O. Stamps telephoned the Blackwood Brothers the next day and asked if they would like to represent the Stamps-Baxter Music Company. On the spot, the singers said yes.

Thus, the Blackwood Brothers Quartet became the Blackwood Brothers Stamps Quartet.

"Our deal with him was this": James said, "He would furnish us an automobile and songbooks to sell, and from the songbook sales and our concert receipts we got to keep the first $18.50 per man per week. If we made more than that, we sent the overage to Dallas. If we didn't make $18.50 per man, whatever had come in we kept and sent nothing to Dallas.

"The cars Mr. Stamps furnished were not always brand new," James said. "He gave us a 1939 Mercury demonstrator that had about five thousand miles on it, but it was as new a car as any of us had ever been in. That's the same kind of deal he gave all his quartets; the only difference was that the money might have been more for some, and maybe less for others, too—I don't know."

While singing at the 1939 Louisiana State Singing Convention in Shreveport, the Blackwood Brothers and the Hartford Quartet, the latter with Doy Ott at the piano, auditioned for a job on the 10,000-watt station, KWKH, and the Blackwood Brothers won the contract to sing two live programs a day. They moved to Shreveport that April.

The John Daniel Quartet represented the Vaughan Company for several years, and in 1939—in the heyday of the Stamps quartets— V. O. hired the Daniel quartet to sing for Stamps. The quartet came through Shreveport on its way to Dallas to sign the contract with Stamps and stopped off to visit the Blackwood Brothers on their 12:30 p.m. broadcast over KWKH.

"They came up to the studio," James said, "and sang a couple of numbers on our program. They had John Daniel singing first tenor; Wally Fowler singing lead; Troy Daniel, John's brother, singing baritone; and Carl Raines singing bass. Albert Williams played the piano.

"I don't know how much money was involved in John Daniel's deal with Mr. Stamps," James said. "Most of them were older than we were; we were just a bunch of kids. I know Mr. Stamps gave them a Packard automobile, not a new one but a demonstrator like ours. They came back through Shreveport happy as larks, riding in that Packard. They stopped again, sang a number on our show and went with us that night to a concert near Alexandria, Louisiana, and then they went on over to North Alabama. Not long after that, they got on the Grand Ole Opry and had a radio program on WSM."

Frank and V. O. Stamps had affiliated quartets singing all over the South, the Southwest, and the Midwest, and Frank had taken his own quartet to Iowa to sing over Radio Station KMA in Shenandoah.

After sixteen months in Shreveport, the Blackwood Brothers made another move—a major one. V. O. Stamps was in poor health and needed Frank Stamps in Dallas. V. O. suggested the Blackwood Brothers take the Stamps Quartet's place in Iowa so Frank could return south. On August 5, 1940, the move was made, and three weeks later V. O. Stamps died.

The Blackwood Brothers did three shows a day on the radio in Iowa. They sang live at 7:30 a.m. and 12:30 p.m., then transcribed a fifteen-minute show on a sixteen-inch disk that the station played at 5:30 the next morning.

They sang concerts all over Iowa, Kansas, Nebraska, Missouri, South Dakota, and southern Minnesota, and their popularity grew by leaps and bounds.

The station in Shenandoah was only a 5,000-watt station, but it was strategically located on the hub of a lot of major markets and beamed into all of them like a local station. Shenandoah was sixty-five miles from Omaha, eighty miles from Lincoln, a hundred from St. Joseph, a hundred-fifty from Kansas City, Topeka, and Des Moines, and a hundred-sixty-five miles from Sioux City.

"To show you the coverage of that station," James said later, "on the 5:30 morning show during the winter months when radio signals go farther, we got mail regularly from twenty-seven states and three Canadian provinces. Our mother and daddy in Mississippi heard us year-around on that 5:30 program and all during the winter on the 7:30 program."

The Blackwood Brothers had been on KMA only about three weeks when Frank Stamps told them he would run their picture on the front of his magazine, *The Stamps-Baxter News*, and the quartet could offer the magazine for sale. Frank said they could send any requests to him and he would mail the magazine from Dallas. The quartet offered the magazine for two weeks and received more than ten thousand cards and letters, which they passed on to Dallas.

On the basis of that, the station's advertising department estimated that the Blackwood Brothers had a million people listening regularly to their radio programs.

World War II erupted on December 7, 1941, and the Blackwood Brothers moved to California to work in the aircraft industry. R. W. was drafted; James was rejected. James and some others sang some on the West Coast during the war, and when hostilities ceased, the Blackwoods regrouped their original quartet and returned to KMA in Iowa.

Quartet singing reached new heights just after the war. It became bigger than it had ever been, and hundreds of excellent quartets cropped up around the country. Most sang locally, however, and there seemed never to be enough of the professional traveling quartets to satisfy the public's demand.

The Blackwoods increased their popularity, not only in Iowa, but in many other states where they were singing concerts. By this time they were recording on 78s, and their records were in great demand. They had a hard time keeping a supply of records.

Although they were all making good money in 1947, bass singer Don Smith decided to leave the quartet and return to California where his wife was from. James hired a bass singer from Chattanooga named Bill Lyles, sight unseen. Bill had sung with the Swanee River Boys for a while on WSB in Atlanta during the war, but at the time James hired him Bill was singing with Claude Delaney and the Hamilton (County) Harmony Quartet. Doyle Blackwood was by then an announcer on a Chattanooga radio station and when James wrote him that he needed a bass singer, Doyle recommended Lyles, and James wrote back, "Send him on out here, then." Bill went to Iowa by train. He remained with the Blackwood Brothers seven years until he was killed in their 1954 airplane crash.

By 1948, the Blackwoods were in such demand for personal appearances that they couldn't fill all the requests. They discussed the problem and agreed that the Blackwood sound might be duplicated by another quartet, if it had a Blackwood foundation.

So they split the quartet and organized another one, and put two Blackwood Brothers quartets on the road, Blackwood Brothers Number One and Blackwood Brothers Number Two.

James, R. W., and Lyles remained with the original quartet, adding Cat Freeman, one of the great Sand Mountain singers, to sing first tenor. Hilton Griswold joined them at the piano.

Doyle left his radio job in Chattanooga and he and Roy formed the backbone of Quartet Number Two, adding Johnny Dickson on the baritone and Warren Holmes on bass. Roy sang tenor and Doyle, lead. Billy Gewin came out of Texas to play piano for that group.

For most of two years, both groups stayed extremely busy. The Blackwood Brothers were at the apex of popularity, and by this time had probably replaced the Rangers Quartet as America's most popular gospel singers.

By 1950 the Blackwoods wanted to return to the South. They left the Iowa radio station and moved to Memphis. Quartet Number Two disbanded, and Roy and Doyle left the road to run the Blackwoods' growing subsidiary businesses. Quartet Number One began to sing on

Station WMPS in Memphis and immediately started doing concerts across the South.

Alden Toney sang tenor in the quartet, with James, R. W., and Bill Lyles handling the other parts. A kid named Jackie Marshall joined the quartet at the piano.

The Blackwood Brothers sang under contract with Dixie Lily Flour and as soon as television was perfected, the Blackwoods entered that field. They signed a recording contract with RCA Victor, and in 1951 recorded the first album any gospel group ever recorded. It was a ten-inch album, in contrast to the later twelve-inch albums, and today the ten-incher is a valuable collector's item, the most rare of any long-play album.

At that point, the Blackwood Brothers could see only continued success ahead. Things were rosy, indeed, and far better for them than if they had chosen to remain in the cottonpatch.

CHAPTER ELEVEN

The Perfect Quartet

Hovie Lister may be the only pianist in the gospel music business who started out playing for the chain gang.

To place Hovie in time, he was born in 1927, and as he grew up in Greenville, South Carolina, the Blackwood Brothers were already singing professionally.

Hovie's childhood was typical for the 1930s, except for the fact that he took piano lessons from the age of six, which most boys didn't.

Hovie's dad and uncles had a quartet they called the Lister Brothers Quartet, and when Hovie was twelve in 1939, he was good enough on the piano to play for them. It gave Hovie a taste of something he liked—accompanying a quartet, or simply accompanying a singer.

Every Sunday morning, a man named Kestner, a God-fearing Christian who took the commands of Jesus seriously when He said to spread the Word, came by Hovie's house and picked him up. The two made their way to the cells of the Greenville County Chain Gang and Hovie played while Kestner sang and read from the Book to these recalcitrants.

In 1941, Mordecai Ham, the great Kentucky revivalist under whose ministry Billy Graham was saved in 1934, came to Greenville to hold a revival. Ham's songleader was a white-maned, bearded fellow named C. Austin Miles, whose greatest claim to fame was (and still is) that he had written the great old hymns, "In The Garden" and "Dwelling In Beulah Land," which remain to this day among Hovie Lister's favorites.

Miles needed a local accompanist, and Kestner, one of the organiz-
ers and supporters of Ham's campmeeting, recommended Hovie. Even
though he was only fourteen, Hovie rehearsed with Miles and got the
position.

After that, Hovie Lister was known around Greenville, especially
in music circles. He first played on radio over Station WFBC with a
country singer named Baby Ray, who had a gospel group he called the
Swanee River Boys.

By then, Hovie knew what he wanted his life's work to be, but he
needed to learn more about accompanying singers, particularly gospel
singers, on the piano. So in 1943 he took the train to Dallas, Texas, and
attended the Stamps-Baxter School of Music, studying piano under
Jack Hendrix, whom Hovie calls "one of the greatest piano teachers of
all time." He is now dean of music at Odessa University in Texas.

Word was around in the realm of professional gospel singing that
Hovie Lister of Greenville, South Carolina, was an up-and-coming pianist who could play with the best of them.

In 1945 Connor Hall, who also had grown up in Greenville, and
now managed the Homeland Harmony Quartet, telephoned Hovie and
offered him a job playing for his quartet in Atlanta. Though only eighteen years old, Hovie moved to Atlanta and for the next two or three
years played variously for the Homeland Harmony, the LeFevre Trio
while some of the LeFevres were still in service, and finally for the
Rangers Quartet. There he became friends with Denver Crumpler, the
Arkansas tenor who was to play such a great role with the Statesmen in
later years. Soon after Hovie joined the Rangers in 1946, they moved to
Charlotte to sing on Radio Station WBT.

During those years immediately following World War II, Hovie
became acquainted with most of the people who sang gospel songs for
a living. And they took note of him. Whether his genius was recognized
then is a question whose answer is lost in time, but he had genius.
Hovie Lister had what it took to be a leader, not only of his own quartet
but of the entire industry of gospel music.

Sometime during those immediate post-war years, the idea struck
Hovie of organizing his own quartet. He did not want an ordinary
quartet. He wanted a different quartet with the finest voices in the
business. He had quality in mind, real music men. He wanted trained
voices in his quartet, not those whose training had been singing while
milking the cow or shoveling out the barn.

There were hundreds of great gospel voices around during those
days, and most of them were already singing with quartets. Almost

every radio station, especially in the South, had its own quartet. If a person was a good singer and had what it took to be a good quartet man, he could find a job. If he couldn't sing, he had best forget it and look for something else to do. Poor singing surfaced rather quickly, and not even local quartets would stand for it. There were too many good singers around.

Hovie played for the Rangers in Charlotte for about nine months, then accepted an offer from Urias LeFevre to return to Atlanta and play again for the LeFevre Trio, who had the legendary Big Jim Waits singing bass.

Atlanta was the center of the quartet-singing world at that time, and Hovie knew that was where he wanted to settle. He wanted to be in on the action, and Atlanta was the place.

Not only were the LeFevres headquartered there, but so was the Homeland Harmony Quartet; and the Sunshine Boys, who were gaining in popularity. The Sunshine Boys sang on Radio Station WSB, and the LeFevres and Homeland Harmony, on WGST. There were other groups in Atlanta, too, some up and coming.

Hovie made friends with a young man of his own age named Barry Howell, whose father, Major Howell, was chief stockholder in *The Atlanta Constitution*, the morning competition of the powerful *Atlanta Journal*.

The *Constitution* was constructing a new building in downtown Atlanta, diagonally across the street from Rich's Department Store.

One evening, Hovie mentioned to Barry Howell that he had plans to start a new and different quartet in gospel music, and Barry immediately picked up the ball and began to run with it.

He said, "Papa's fixing to put in a new 5,000-watt radio station soon as they get that building finished."

"Is that right?" Hovie said. "When will that be?"

"I don't know exactly," Barry said, "but it's almost finished now. He's already hired a station manager."

"Well, well!" Hovie mused.

"Why don't we go see Papa?" Barry asked.

"I can't talk to your dad," Hovie said.

"Yes, you can," said Barry. "He's not that big."

The two went to the building that then housed the *Constitution* and made their way past a half-dozen secretaries to the inner sanctum of Major Howell, who had the wherewithal to give Hovie and his dreamed-of quartet a start.

When Barry told Major Howell that Hovie was planning to start a great new quartet, Howell showed immediate interest. He did not question Hovie's age because he must have recognized something there beyond years.

What he said was, "When do you want to start?"

"Well, sir," Hovie hedged, "I don't even have the quartet put together yet."

"Our station," Major Howell said, "will be known as WCON, after the *Constitution,* of course. We'll want a quartet, a good one, when we go on the air."

"I don't know if I can get it together that fast," Hovie said.

"If you don't have your group together by then," Major Howell said, "you can just play records until you do get it organized."

At that time—1947—Hovie was playing gospel records on a regular show on WEAS in Decatur, which probably made him the first gospel disk jockey.

Denver Crumpler was Hovie's choice for a first tenor, but Denver had been singing with the Rangers all those years and showed no indication of wanting to change. Hovie wanted Harley Lester to sing the lead, and a finer voice could not be found. He had also picked out Aycel Soward for the bass, but Aycel was singing with Lee Roy Abernathy.

The men Hovie chose were his idols, and he made overtures to all three, but none accepted his offer. Hovie suspected that his age had something to do with it. "I was so young," he said later, "that when I approached them they probably thought, 'Well, what's this kid think he's doing?' I don't know that they thought that, but I suspect they did. What they didn't know and what I didn't tell them was that *The Atlanta Constitution* was behind me."

Hovie wanted to be able to form his quartet by his own persuasion, not by that of the Atlanta newspaper.

WCON went on the air, and Hovie didn't have his group together, but Major Howell was true to his word and put Hovie to work playing records while he formed his quartet.

Mosie Lister, the gospel songwriter who was no relation to Hovie, was tuning pianos across the street at Rich's. He listened to Hovie's program every day. Hovie knew Mosie could sing, and offered him the job of singing lead with his new quartet. He telephoned Bobby Strickland, who was singing with the Harmoneers, and offered him the first tenor. Bobby accepted and added, "Do you have a baritone? I could bring Bervin Kendrick with me."

"Bring him," Hovie said. "He's a good baritone."

Hovie and Bobby Strickland had been friends for a long time. Hovie had played for the Sand Mountain Quartet on a radio station in Chattanooga when the quartet was composed of Strickland on the tenor; Alton Jolley, lead; Erman Slater, baritone; and Ward Hurt, bass.

Bobby said to Hovie, "Have you got a bass? There's a boy over here named Gordon Hill. He sings bass and he'll come."

"Bring him, too," Hovie said. "We'll try him out."

Hovie had been toying with names for his quartet. He wanted a name that denoted greatness, and the first name he thought of was Congressmen. He vetoed that and began thinking of Senators.

But both of those names, he argued with himself, denoted an elective office.

Then the name *Statesmen* occurred to him and he mulled it over. "The only way you can become a statesman," he reasoned, "is when you've gone through the electoral process and have proven yourself to be the kind of person who can be revered as a statesman—a man of state."

He liked the name and settled on it. But an obstacle remained. Georgia Governor Herman Talmadge published a small newspaper he called *The Statesman*. Hovie was a subscriber. He went to Talmadge and told him what he had in mind, and Talmadge replied, "I think that's a wonderful idea. Get me a picture of your group and I'll run it in the paper and say that you named the quartet after our paper."

Talmadge became a fan of the Statesmen Quartet and later honored the group by naming it "Ambassadors of Good Will for the State of Georgia," which the Statesmen remain to this day.

So Hovie organized and commissioned the Statesmen Quartet in October of 1948 with Bobby Strickland singing first tenor, Mosie Lister singing the lead, Bervin Kendrick singing baritone, and Gordon Hill singing bass. Hovie himself accompanied.

They went on WCON and drew an immediate favorable response. But Hovie knew deep down that he did not have the quartet he wanted. He had not yet achieved his dream quartet. What he was looking for was a quartet that was a cut above any other, a quartet that could sing any arrangement. He needed just the right combination of voices—and he was a patient man. He had youth on his side—he was twenty-one years old—and he could afford to wait, searching all the time for the people he needed.

"To be perfectly honest with you," Hovie said forty years later, "I thought the Melody Masters Quartet was just about the epitome of anything you'd want to hear. They harmonized, they had rhythm, they could sing modern harmony, they could sing straight gospel, southern gospel, they could do anything you wanted them to do—just name it. They could do pop music, country songs, western tunes. They had in their repertoire at least five different programs they could do at any given moment. They appealed strongly to me, though I was thinking only of a gospel quartet."

The Melody Masters, having come out of the Florida gospel singing wars with the Sunny South and other quartets, were then based in Lincoln, Nebraska, singing on staff over Station KFAV of Omaha. All the staff musicians worked out of Lincoln.

The Melody Masters had a quartet of trained voices, Cat Freeman singing first tenor, Jake Hess singing lead, Alvin Toodle on the baritone, James S. Wetherington singing bass, and the great Wally Varner on the piano.

Hovie had known the Melody Masters when they sang around Greenville during the war. At one time, the quartet was starving, and Jake and Wetherington resorted to stealing peaches out of orchards to keep from starving to death.

But they kept on singing!

The Melody Masters had great flair. Hovie didn't want that, at least not as much as the Melody Masters generated. He later changed his mind and the Statesmen came on stage with a flourish and sang with as much or more flair than the Melody Masters ever did.

Personnel changes came quickly in the Statesmen as Hovie sought what he wanted and some of the others decided to take employment elsewhere—for various reasons, not any of which was because the five men did not get along with each other. They did.

But Mosie was a songwriter who did not relish long trips on the road, singing concerts. He was at his peak in songwriting, and in this period when the Statesmen were developing, he wrote some of his finest numbers, "When No One Stands Alone," "How Long Has It Been?" "When You Travel All Alone." Mosie's input to the Statesmen from the standpoint of music and arrangements and suggestions of how this part or that one should be stacked, was a fantastic help to Hovie.

He went back to tuning pianos at Rich's and concentrated on his writing, while Hovie looked around for another lead singer. Mosie continued to write for the Statesmen, and they paid him for his songs and for others he arranged into their developing style. He worked with and for the Statesmen for a long while.

Gordon Hill left the Statesmen also, moving to Asheville, North Carolina, to take a job, and eventually to Phoenix, Arizona, where he drove a truck for a living.

WCON had made a financial arrangement with the Statesmen. When Hovie informed Major Howell that he had his quartet together and they were ready to sing, Howell asked, "Hovie, how are you going to function with this quartet? You're going to have to have some sort of money. What kind of salaries are we talking about?"

"Well, sir," Hovie said, truthfully, "I don't know." He wasn't thinking of money; he was thinking of singing.

"What about fifty dollars a week per man?" Howell offered. That was good money in 1948.

But the Melody Masters, working on that huge Omaha station that employed thirty-two staff musicians, were in high cotton, making considerably more money than the Statesmen.

Money, however, isn't everything. Sometimes the call of home is stronger than money.

Early in 1949, when it was certain that Mosie Lister and Gordon Hill would leave, Hovie called Jake Hess of the Melody Masters in Nebraska and offered him the job singing lead for the Statesmen.

Jake didn't know what to do. He knew Hovie's daddy, W. Hermon Lister, in Greenville, whom he considered one of the finest men he knew; so he telephoned him for advice.

"Hovie just called me," Jake said to Hovie's dad, "and said he wanted me to join his quartet. What do you think I should do? I'm making a lot more money here."

"Son," Hermon said, "you drop whatever you're doing and get to Atlanta as quick as you can."

Hovie realized one of his dreams after Gordon Hill left. He asked Aycel Soward to sing bass for the Statesmen and Aycel accepted.

"Aycel was without a doubt one of the great voices of all time in gospel music," Hovie said later. "He always had proper pronunciation, and he wasn't a growling low bass singer but was low enough for anybody's quartet. He had a wonderful personality—but even though I had dreamed of having him sing with us, he still wasn't the bass I was looking for, and I realized that. Maybe it was the age difference, I don't know." Soward was older than Hovie and the other Statesmen.

When it became apparent that Aycel Soward would not stay with the Statesmen, Jake Hess suggested James S. Wetherington as bass singer. Wetherington was a Georgia boy from Ty Ty, who could sing bass with anyone. While Soward was not a rhythm singer, Wetherington was the personification of rhythm.

Wetherington accepted Hovie's offer, after Jake told him that the future of the Statesmen Quartet appeared to be just about as big as that of any quartet in the business. The day he joined the Statesmen in 1949, the quartet was singing in Atlanta's baseball park, Ponce de Leon Park, and Soward insisted on introducing Wetherington to the crowd. Thus, Soward bowed out gracefully and eased the way for Wetherington to slip into the group.

Lee Roy Abernathy worked a lot with the Statesmen during that time, helping with their music, and it was he who dubbed Wetherington "Big Chief."

"You don't want to call this guy James S. Wetherington," Lee Roy said to Hovie. "Nobody will ever remember that. Call him Big Chief. He's an Indian, isn't he?"

The name stuck. And those today who do not remember James S. Wetherington certainly remember the Big Chief.

One other personnel change was made before the Statesmen really hit their stride, and this one was not dictated by the quartet's style. Bobby Strickland left. He, like Hovie, had dreamed of organizing his own quartet; and when he saw the chance, he took it. He moved back to Birmingham and organized the Crusaders Quartet.

The third Melody Master to join the Statesmen was Cat Freeman, who had grown up near Bobby Strickland on Sand Mountain in Alabama. He readily accepted the job when Hovie offered it. Cat had been singing with the Blackwood Brothers in Iowa, having gone with them from the Melody Masters.

Thus, before the decade changed to the 1950s, the Statesmen had these members: Cat Freeman on first tenor, Jake Hess on lead, Bervin Kendrick on baritone, Big Chief on bass, and Hovie at the piano.

They were off and running—and the sky was their limit.

"If we had anything over other quartets in those days," Jake Hess said later, "it was that we loved what we were doing so much that we lived it. We'd go into a place and set up our records, then gather around a piano and sing. If Hovie had to go collect our money after a concert, we didn't go to the car and relax: We found a piano and sang while he was gone. We loved to sing, and I've always said that if we had anything over other groups, it was desire."

When the Statesmen began to sing over WCON, they had a tremendous advantage over other quartets. All the major groups sang on radio, not necessarily for the salaries, but for the opportunity to advertise their concerts on the air. But the Statesmen also had *The Atlanta Constitution* behind them, and the power of the press was nothing to laugh at. The Statesmen sang live on WCON at 6 a.m. and 12 noon, and their picture appeared in the *Constitution* almost every day, advertising their radio shows. Not only did their singing become well known to Atlantans, so did their faces. People who had never seen them in person knew them by sight.

The Statesmen settled into a routine. They met at the station to sing their 6 a.m. show, then walked up the street to the S&W Cafeteria for breakfast. They returned immediately to the station, and by that time Mosie Lister was usually there to help with rehearsals and arrangements, and they rehearsed hard until noon.

There was nothing easy about singing with the Statesmen during those days, and any fame they achieved was not accidental. They earned it by the sweat of their brows.

Because those radio shows kept them confined daily to Atlanta, the Statesmen did not travel far out of the state of Georgia at first. They sang concerts in Alabama, South Carolina, and Western North Carolina. They always returned to Atlanta to sing on the radio the next morning.

On days when the Statesmen had no concerts, they usually met back at the station at night and rehearsed again.

The Statesmen rehearsed rhythm, blend, chord structure, breathing, and harmony. They paid particular attention to timing and enunciation, making sure each man pronounced each word exactly the same and at exactly the same split second. Then they rehearsed choreography—movements on stage, taking bows together. They even rehearsed their entrance on stage. They left nothing to chance; they rehearsed everything. And they did this for years, even after the quartet achieved its greatness.

"We rehearsed new material every day," Hovie said. "We never went back to a place without having new songs to sing, and people looked forward to hearing what new songs we had each time they heard us."

Ed Hill, baritone with the Stamps Quartet today, said when he was growing up in St. Louis, the reason he looked forward to the Statesmen coming to town was to hear the three or four new songs he knew they would have ready.

There was never an excuse great enough for any member of the

Statesmen to miss rehearsal, unless he was ill. The Statesmen put up with no pitty-patty stuff. This was business; their livelihood depended on it; and rehearsals were considered to be as important as concerts. Attendance was required.

When the Statesmen began making sufficient money to support all the members with good salaries, with enough left over to operate the company, they began to acquire music companies, and then leased office space in the Briarcliff Hotel in downtown Atlanta. They equipped a music room with piano and other paraphernalia and rehearsed there every day.

They hired a youngster named Eldridge Fox from Asheville to operate their music companies. Eldridge also had formation of his own quartet in mind and later acquired the Kingsmen Quartet and made it number one in the nation.

Mosie Lister moved to Florida, and the Statesmen began calling in people like Larry Taylor, Larri Goss, and Lee Roy Abernathy to help with arrangements. Gradually, however, after Doy Ott came over to the Statesmen from the Homeland Harmony in 1951, Doy and the Big Chief began doing most of the arranging, and Big Chief wrote some outstanding songs.

Ott's arrival was timed with Hovie's being taken into the army in 1951. The Korean War was on and Hovie answered the draft in January of 1951. He turned over management of the Statesmen to the Big Chief, who immediately hired Doy from the Homeland Harmony to play the piano. He knew of Doy's vast talents.

Hovie was in the army only nine months, and when he returned in October of 1951, Bervin Kendrick decided to return to Birmingham and sing with his old friend, Bobby Strickland, and the Crusaders Quartet. Hovie returned to the Statesmen piano, and Doy, who had a beautiful, mellow voice, took over the baritone.

To achieve what he had started out to build, Hovie had only one more move to make. Cat Freeman was singing a creditable first tenor, but Hovie knew that Cat was not planning to stay with the quartet, and rather than sit waiting for Cat to leave, Hovie wanted to replace him with a man who would consider the position permanent.

He wanted Denver Crumpler.

The Rangers had been involved in the automobile accident in 1951, two years before this, which killed Erman Slater and crippled Arnold Hyles, and Hovie thought the time might be right to approach Denver again.

The Statesmen were one of the most popular quartets in America at this time, and were ranging far afield, transcribing their radio shows in Atlanta so they could make long road trips and sing in many parts of the country.

They were traveling to Fort Worth, Texas, almost every month to sing on W. B. Nowlin's concerts, and on one of those trips Hovie and Doy Ott visited Denver Crumpler and his wife, Frankie, at their home.

Hovie told Denver again how much he had always admired his singing and emphasized that *all* the Statesmen wanted him to become a member of the group.

"We don't want to fool around," Hovie said. "We want you to come soon."

The Statesmen had some big things up their sleeves. Hovie had worked out a deal with the National Biscuit Company (NABISCO) to sponsor the Statesmen not only on radio but in the relatively new entertainment medium of television.

"Denver," Hovie said, "to be perfectly frank, we need you, and I'm going back to Atlanta and rent a place for you to live."

"Well, all right," Denver said, not fully committing himself, but leaving Hovie and Doy with no doubt that he was interested.

Returning to Atlanta, Hovie found a house and rented it. He paid a month's rent in Denver's name, then telephoned Denver and said, "I've got you a house and have paid the first month's rent. How soon can you get here?"

Denver laughed. "You meant business, didn't you?"

"Just pack up and come on," Hovie said.

A week later, Denver rolled into Atlanta with his family and all their belongings. He was ready to sing.

That was in the fall of 1953, and the addition of Denver Crumpler's voice to those of Jake Hess, Doy Ott, and the Big Chief, plus Hovie's unique style at the piano, made the Statesmen Quartet dynamite on anybody's stage.

Denver Crumpler owned an unusually great voice. He was high and clear, with no hint of false tones. He stood up to the mike in Rangers style, unmoving except for his mouth, his arms rigid at his sides, his back straight, singing from the heart.

"He was a great singer," Hovie said, "and a great man. He had a marvelous personality and was a gentleman of the first rank."

Crump sang with great ease. He was a stylist, and anyone could see class all over him. He was that kind of a guy.

So was Jake Hess. He was a tremendous stylist who gave the Statesmen a flair no one else had. And he, too, was a gentleman, a fine personality, an extremely kind and friendly man.

Doy's talents seemed to have no end, and his personality and style matched the other Statesmen. He was a great baritone singer.

Hovie always said the Big Chief was "class personified," and no one disagreed.

"Never a performer ever walked on stage," Hovie said, "who could touch the hem of the Big Chief's garment. No one could say anything against him. He was a gentleman, a great individual. And could he ever sing bass!"

That was it. That was what Hovie Lister had been looking for—the right personnel.

There was nothing this quartet could not sing, no crowd it could not entertain. There was nothing it couldn't achieve.

You see, when Hovie added Denver Crumpler to the Statesmen Quartet, he completed the first and only perfect quartet. There had never been one before; there has not been one since.

The Statesmen had it all!

CHAPTER TWELVE

Wally Changes the World

Ideas have changed the world. In late 1948 an idea of Wally Fowler's changed the world of gospel singing. Actually, Wally had had the idea for years, but he didn't put it in motion until November of 1948 when he held his first All-Night Singing in Ryman Auditorium in Nashville, Tennessee, home of the Grand Ole Opry.

The date was Friday, November 5, and the promotion was so successful that it caught on all across the South. Quartet singing then emerged from churches and schoolhouses and courtrooms and entered the big-time realm of huge auditoriums where crowds of five thousand and sometimes many more could enjoy the music.

The idea was simple enough; to rent a large hall, hire a half-dozen or more quartets to sing, and charge admission to those attending. Gate receipts would pay the quartets, pay all expenses, and hopefully furnish the promoter a profit.

The All-Night Singing heralded a new day for quartets and soon provided many of them with the means of making a real living while singing. This was gospel music's most innovative idea since Dwight Brock revolutionized piano-playing in 1927.

Where did Wally's idea come from? What prompted him to promote a singing that big?

"The inspiration came from V. O. Stamps," Wally said. "During the eight years I sang with the John Daniel Quartet, I drove V. O.'s car for him when we were in Texas. He liked me. I took care of him. He'd go to sleep in the back seat of his car and drop a cigarette in his lap. I always kept an eye on him and stopped the car many times to get his lighted cigarettes out of his lap before they set him on fire.

"He worked so hard," Wally said, "that he would doze off with a cigarette in his hand. He was only five feet, nine inches tall, nice looking man, but he weighed two hundred and eighty-five pounds most of the time. He was a heavy man! He knew how to assert himself; he was a great personality.

"He inspired me every way he turned, and I think he felt my admiration. He seemed to love to communicate with me. I think he had a revelation that his life was going to be short on this earth, and there were some things he wanted to do—or have done. He told me of plans that I know he didn't tell anyone else. One was that he was going to be flying in an airplane all over the United States and maybe all over the world, putting on his All-Night Broadcasts. That's what he called the All-Night Singings he held in the Sportatorium at the end of each Stamps School of Music."

When V. O. Stamps ordered a steak, Wally recalled, he ordered a two-pound steak. "One night he ate all of his and part of mine," Wally said. "Then he ate three pieces of pie. At one of his All-Night Broadcasts I counted forty-six soda pops he drank, most of them Coca-Colas. He'd say, 'Son, I'm a little thirsty now. Would you get old V. O. something else to drink?' He had diabetes. His sugar was up to goodness knows what, five hundred or maybe a thousand. But he was working hard and his sugar would get low and he kept feeding it in."

Years later, after the war had passed and after Wally had made the rounds of entertaining in Knoxville and Nashville, the idea of the All-Night Singing gradually began to dawn on him.

Many churches sponsored All-Day Singings with dinner-on-the-ground, and some Southern states promoted an annual state singing convention. These were huge events. The one in Birmingham was held in a six-thousand-seat auditorium.

The traditional passing of the hat was still the way conventions such as these made the money to pay the talent, but when the hat came by most of the folks felt obliged to toss in only a coin or two. Wally Fowler took his Oak Ridge Quartet to Birmingham for the Alabama State Singing Convention and remembers that the contributions of six thousand people amounted to three hundred dollars.

"Folks, we sure are short," the man presiding said to the singers. "I don't know why we didn't get more money out of this—but it'll pay for your gas anyway."

Wally was incensed. "Go back out there," he said to the man, "and tell those people that they don't mind paying so much to go to ball games, or for theater tickets. Ask them what's wrong with them here today."

The man did exactly that, passed the hat again, and came back with three thousand dollars, Wally said, to divide among the quartets.

"I think that incident was what made up my mind," Wally recalled. "With the inspiration of V. O. Stamps in the back of my mind, and thinking why people shouldn't pay to hear their favorite music when they paid for everything else, I thought I might be able to change things enough so folks wouldn't deadhead till the Lord came back. I decided I was going to have an All-Night Gospel Singing similar to what V. O. had thought of, and the idea came to me at that time to see if WSM would broadcast an hour of it at eleven o'clock."

Wally's Oak Ridge Quartet was a fixture on WSM.

When he got back to Nashville from that Alabama convention, Wally put the wheels in motion. He talked to Jack Stapp, program director of WSM, and Jack Bullait, the artist-service manager, who was actually talent coordinator and manager of the Grand Ole Opry.

They agreed to broadcast an hour of the show, from 11 p.m. till midnight.

Bullait called Wally aside later and said, "Wally, if you don't have at least a third of a house that night, enough people to make a racket, me and Harry Stone are gonna skin you alive."

Wally rented Ryman Auditorium for Friday night, November 5, contracted a multitude of talent, and turned his attention to selling tickets. He put the Oak Ridge Boys on the streets selling tickets. They sold one-dollar reserved seat tickets in supermarkets, to businessmen, in residential sections—anywhere they could.

On the morning of the singing, the guys finished their ticket-selling; and they had peddled 1,836 tickets, more than half of Ryman's 3,214 seats.

All that day, the skies opened and rain poured down in bucketsful. Five major automobile accidents, attributable to rain, were reported in Nashville that afternoon.

At 4 p.m. Jack Stapp dashed into Ryman, soaking wet, and collared Wally.

"I'm glad to get hold of you, Wally," he said. "I've talked to Harry Stone and we can't broadcast with an empty house. We just can't do it."

"Don't worry, Jack," Wally said. "The house will be full."

"Come on," Jack said. "Are you kidding me? We don't have but two hundred and eighty-nine tickets sold for the Grand Ole Opry tomorrow night."

"I wouldn't kid you, Jack," Wally said, "not about this. Take my word: We'll be sold out."

"You're kidding, all right?"

"No, Jack," Wally put emphasis on his next words. "Eighteen hundred and thirty-six people have bought tickets in advance!"

"They what?"

"Yes, sir. We've worked hard on this, harder than you'll ever know."

"Well, I don't care how many you've sold," Jack said. "Have you looked outside? They won't come in this weather."

"They'll come," Wally said.

He really believed the house would be filled. He had faith enough to believe that.

His faith was upheld. People crowded into Ryman that evening in droves, filling every seat, taking three hundred seats set up on stage, leaving barely enough room for the quartets to come on, and more than a thousand people were turned away because Ryman couldn't hold them.

Jack Stapp and Harry Stone were overjoyed. They even ushered, helping people find their seats.

The program had been billed as "Wally Fowler's Gospel and Spiritual All-Night Singing." Advance advertising promised a hundred singers on stage and twenty-five quartets.

No wonder people came by the thousands in the rain. Look what talent Wally had that evening:

Wally Fowler and the Oak Ridge Quartet; Frank Stamps and the Stamps Quartet; the Stamps All-Star Quartet; the Blackwood Brothers Quartet; G. E. (Kieffer) Vaughan and the Vaughan Radio Quartet; Deacon Utley and the Smile-A-While Quartet of Macon, Georgia; The Speer Family; Milton Estes and the Musical Millers Quartet; the Gospelaires Quartet; and the Sunshine Boys.

Milton Estes was a country singer who also had a gospel quartet; and the Gospelaires Quartet was a local group that included Virginia Nell Cook, who helped Wally put words to his song, "Jesus Is Mine."

The singing began at 8 o'clock, and the quartets really turned it on. They sang their best songs, and all were in great voice. The people responded, clapping and cheering, and thoroughly enjoyed themselves.

At the start of WSM's one-hour broadcast at 11 o'clock, Grant Turner, the dean of WSM's announcers who emceed the show, told the people in radioland that they could send telegrams. "And," Turner said, "we'll read a few of them."

The WSM telephones began to ring, and soon all lines were swamped with calls.

At a quarter to midnight, Turner said over the air, "Ladies and gentlemen, we are swamped with telephone calls. All the lines to Ryman Auditorium and all lines to WSM are tied up, and we apologize to the rest of you who are trying to call. We don't have people to answer the phones, this program has made such an impact. We're hearing from all over the United States and Canada."

Western Union boys were busy. By that time, 11:45, more than four hundred telegrams had been taken to Ryman Auditorium.

Harry Stone was amazed. He cornered Wally. "If we get another hundred telegrams during this hour, we'll broadcast another hour," he said. By midnight, two hundred thirteen more telegrams came in and the broadcast went on until one in the morning.

WSM's signal carried all over the East Coast, the South, the Midwest, into many parts of Canada, and all the way to the Rocky Mountains. Only those beyond the Rockies were out of range.

When the radio portion of the program ended at 1 a.m., the singers continued to sing to the huge crowd until 3 o'clock when Wally called a halt. The crowd was reluctant to leave; it still wanted more singing.

Wally's next All-Night Singing in Ryman was on New Year's Eve, and Harry Stone was so excited that he got NBC to carry an hour of it coast to coast. More than six thousand pieces of mail came in as a result of the nationwide broadcast.

People everywhere loved the quartets!

That did it! Wally Fowler had started something that couldn't be stopped. The All-Night Singing idea snowballed rapidly across the South and before long such extravaganzas were being promoted—not all by Wally—from Oklahoma City to Miami, and as far up as St. Louis and Detroit. Atlanta, Birmingham, Nashville, and a few other cities of similar size were gold mines for gospel promoters—and for gospel quartets.

For the first time, big-time quartets did not have to worry about having places to sing.

W. B. Nowlin had promoted his first All-Day Singing and dinner-on-the-ground with Eddy Arnold, the Stamps Quartet, and the Stamps-Ozark Quartet on July 18, 1948. He picked up Wally's All-Night Singing idea and really opened up the Southwest with it. Lloyd Orrell took advantage of the idea to promote northern and midwestern metropolises, and before long Wally Fowler's idea was making money for thousands of people.

Everyone called Wally the "All-Night Singing Man."

Everything didn't come up roses, however. Greed soon reared its ugly head. "Show me enough greed and jealousy," Wally said, "and I'll show you something that can destroy the world."

Wally went into certain areas to help others promote the All-Night Singing idea. Promoters were only too happy to go into a partnership with Wally—until they learned how to run the singings themselves.

In one city, Wally helped a promoter with his first All-Night Singing. Wally brought in the Chuck Wagon Gang and the Blackwood Brothers, two sure-fire drawing cards, but only 4,600 of the 6,000 seats were occupied for the singing.

"The promoter," Wally said, "told me he would handle all the churches and we could fill the house from them. But I found out later that he had told a number of preachers that I was a sot drunkard and that their people should not have anything to do with my singings. He told some others that one of the Chuck Wagon Gang even smoked cigarettes! He wanted the territory for himself, and that was his way of cutting me out. I never thought people in gospel music would play dirty pool—but money was involved! I found that people would cut my throat, stick me in the back, hang me to the nearest limb for enough money."

For years, Wally promoted Nashville, Birmingham, and Atlanta regularly, and occasionally he promoted other towns.

Wally wound up owing some of the quartets money, but he also paid the quartets more than anyone in history. He brought them out of the schoolhouses and churches and put them on the map, in the big-time, where they could make a decent living singing.

"Do you know what happened to my profit from Birmingham, Atlanta, and Nashville?" Wally asked. "I used it for chopping down trees and blazing trails for everybody in the business."

Wally was an entrepreneur. He knew how to get things done—and he knew how to get around certain things, too.

When his All-Night Singings from Ryman continued to be broadcast over WSM from 11 to midnight, the station forbade him to announce any other engagements on the air. He could say nothing by way of announcing an upcoming All-Night Singing in Atlanta or Birmingham.

He pondered for weeks and finally found a solution. He always closed the radio hour with a prayer, and one night he prayed fervently:

"Well, dear Lord, we thank you tonight for this good singing here in Ryman Auditorium. Thanks for how you blessed us, and we pray that you'll bless us tomorrow night as we all go down to Atlanta, Georgia, to City Auditorium where the Blackwood Brothers and the Statesmen and the Oak Ridge Quartet, the LeFevres, and the Harmoneers will appear to sing Your praises. Bless us there, Dear Lord, and bless those who want to come and hear us sing. May they have the dollar and a quarter necessary to buy reserved seats. Thanks again, Lord. Amen!"

Stories of how Wally promoted towns and burgs across Southern America are legend. He promoted many groups, many singings, but first and foremost, Wally Fowler loved to sing.

Eldridge Fox remembers a singing with the Chuck Wagon Gang, the Kingsmen Quartet, and the Oak Ridge Boys when word came before the singing began that a tornado was imminent.

"It wasn't a tornado watch," Eldridge said. "It was a warning. The tornado was coming! Wally came running over and told us we would sing one song each and give the people their money back and send them home. The Chuck Wagon Gang sang one song, the Kingsmen sang one—and Wally and the Oaks did a forty-five minute stand. Then Wally gave 'em back their money. We were all scared to death—but, thank goodness, the tornado missed us."

No wonder Wally loved to sing. Singing was his salvation, as it was for so many others of his day. He was born February 15, 1917, near Adairsville, Georgia, northwest of Atlanta. His father was cotton king of Bartow County, raising 125 bales, but the depression broke his spirit as well as his wealth, and at a tender age Wally, then known as Wallace, wound up supporting his parents on $7.20 he made per week working for a florist. He learned to sing in a singing school and had a quartet called the Harmony Quartet. Singing in Gadsden, Alabama, on a Sunday in 1936, John Daniel heard Wallace sing and hired him to sing lead for the Daniel Quartet, which he later renamed the John Daniel Quartet. For a while, the John Daniel Quartet represented the James D. Vaughan Music Company and switched over to the Stamps-

Baxter Company when J. R. Baxter, Jr., made them a better offer in Chattanooga one evening.

With the John Daniel Quartet, Wallace did solos like "New San Antonio Rose," copping a trick from Bob Wills and the Texas Playboys. The quartet did a mixture of gospel and variety songs. Carl Raines, the red-headed bass singer, was a good rube comedian. He handled that until he left, and Troy Daniel became the comedian when Big Jim Waits replaced Raines. The quartet called Wallace its "secular solo singer."

When it signed with Stamps, the Daniel Quartet moved its headquarters to Lubbock, Texas. Wallace wrote country or pop songs as well as gospel. The second year the Daniel Quartet sang on the All-Night Broadcast in the Sportatorium in Dallas, V. O. Stamps requested that Wallace sing one of his own compositions called "I'm Sending You Red Roses." V. O. loved the song so much he said to the crowd, "I think this song borders on being sacred. I know it is sacred to the young man who wrote it and I wanted to see how you people liked it." The crowd made Wallace take a triple encore.

Soon after that, V. O. Stamps died.

The year that V. O. died—1940—the Daniel Quartet moved to Nashville to sing on WSM from 5 to 5:15 each morning, and after a couple of years went on the Grand Ole Opry. Wallace met a lot of people in almost three years there.

But in April of 1944 he had decided to form his own show, and he gave John Daniel six months' notice in April. Lowell Blanchard of Knoxville had asked Wallace to form a group and come to work on WNOX on the Mid-day Merry-Go-Round. Wallace told John Daniel of the Blanchard offer, and John scoffed, "Aw, you ain't got no business doing that."

"Well, Lowell thinks I can make it," Fowler told him.

Wallace put together a group in Columbus, Georgia, and all the guys agreed to meet him in Knoxville on Sunday, October 15, 1944, so they could start work on the Mid-day Merry-Go-Round on Monday at noon. Blanchard had told him that he was "but a springboard for the people." Accordingly, Archie Campbell and Roy Acuff had sprung off his show to greater heights.

At noon on Sunday, John Daniel and the other members of his quartet let Wallace Fowler out of their car about a hundred miles from Knoxville, and Wallace caught the next bus to Knoxville. He carried a little suitcase, and was dressed in a black suit with pearl buttons, black shoes, and black belt with a shiny silver buckle. On the bus, Wallace surveyed himself, and said, "This is not me. This is not Wallace Fowler. I'm going to call myself Wally," and from that moment on he has been known as Wally.

Reaching Knoxville, Wally Fowler walked to WNOX and began looking for his band. He saw no one familiar, and when he asked, no one had seen any strange musicians.

Panic time came and Wally saw a fellow walking through the station with a guitar in his hand.

"Hey," Wally stopped him, "my name's Wally Fowler. What's yours?"

"Tommy Trent," the fellow said.

"Do you sing any?"

"Oh, I sing a little harmony."

"Are you working now?"

"No, I'm not doing a thing. Wish I was."

"You want a job?"

"Yeah."

"I've got a contract to go on here tomorrow at noon, and I need some help."

"Oh, you're the new man; you're Wallace Fowler. I'd love to work with you."

"Okay, you're hired," Wally said, and just like that he had the beginnings of his band, the Georgia Clodhoppers. He told Trent that he had put together a band but no one had showed up.

"I need some people," Wally said.

"My Lord," Trent said, "let's get busy here. Don't worry. We can put together a full band right here. Let's see," he mused, "there's a guy named John Gallahar who plays bass. He don't sing, but he plays a good bass. He'll be up here pretty soon."

Thirty minutes later, Gallahar walked in, listened to Wally's proposition, and agreed. "I'll be glad to join you," he said.

They found an accordion player, an Italian kid named Tony Cinciola, who agreed to join the Clodhoppers. They needed only one more man, a lead guitarist.

"There's a guy here who's real sharp," Trent said, "He practices a lot. Never misses. Comes in at four-thirty and . . . hey, here he comes now."

A tall, slender young man walked up with a guitar case in his hand.

"Chet," Trent said, "meet Wally Fowler. Wally, this is Chet Atkins."

"How are you, Mr. Fowler?" Atkins offered his hand and Wally shook it.

"Well, I'm feeling better than I did a couple hours ago," Wally said. "I'm putting a band together." He told Atkins the story. "I've got three people here for my band and I need a good lead guitar player. I hear you're good."

Chet laughed. "I don't know about that," he said.

"Can you play that thing?" Wally asked.

"Some," Chet said.

"Then you'll do," Wally said, and when Chet Atkins agreed, Wally had hired his band without an audition. That's a dangerous thing to do under most circumstances, but for Wally, shot through at that time with luck, it worked well. The four musicians he hired played together marvelously, and from the first they had a great sound.

Wally then wanted to build a gospel quartet out of his band, but didn't have the voices.

He had a good band, though, one that even got better as time went on. Lowell Blanchard liked the Georgia Clodhoppers. Atkins was great on the lead guitar, and he played for the Clodhoppers for eleven months. Trent played rhythm guitar, Cinciola the accordion, Gallahar the stand-up bass, and Wally sawed the fiddle. With Wally's great voice leading, they sang rather well, too.

Wally immediately began promoting personal appearances. Blanchard announced them on the air, and Trent and Cinciola helped Wally put up posters and handbills advertising their shows. Some of the posters read simply, "WALLY FOWLER'S COMING WITH THE GEORGIA CLODHOPPERS."

Two months later, Wally also had a quartet going. He called it the Harmony Quartet, like the one he'd had before in Rome, Georgia.

"The Four Tones" had just broken up in Raleigh, North Carolina, where they had sung pop songs through the war on WPTF. They had had Lee Roy Abernathy playing piano and managing, Johnny New singing first tenor, Shorty Bradford on the lead, and Curley Kinsey singing bass. When the group disbanded, Lee Roy and Shorty went back to Georgia to sing together, and New and Kinsey came to Knoxville to sing with the Harmony Quartet. Wally hired Lon (Deacon) Freeman to sing baritone. They sang sometimes with the Georgia Clodhoppers backing them musically, and sometimes took along a piano player.

Every Saturday morning, Wally took the quartet to nearby Oak Ridge, Tennessee, to sing for fifteen hundred school children. The quartet sang those Saturday dates free for almost a year, entertaining the kids of the men and women who built the atomic bomb. The kids loved the quartet.

"They had all kinds of entertainment for those kids," Wally said, "from the big bands on down. We had to pass through six security gates to get to the auditorium. Those kids loved us. We'd do 'Dry Bones' and they would clap their hands and stomp their feet and laugh their heads off. They loved us so much that the day we did our last performance for them, I told them, 'Kids, you've been so good to us that I'm gong to re-name my quartet for you. From now on, we're the Oak Ridge Quartet.'"

Two months later, the Bomb fell on Hiroshima, and Wally had a winner!

It was Red Foley who changed the quartet's name from Oak Ridge Quartet to Oak Ridge Boys. Wally moved the quartet to Nashville soon after re-naming it the Oak Ridge Quartet and became a part of the Prince Albert Show with Foley on the Grand Ole Opry. The quartet sang on the show from 1946 to 1950.

Foley would introduce the quartet by saying, "Now, here come Wally Fowler and his Oak Ridge Boys"—and the name stuck.

The Oak Ridge Boys became one of the stalwart quartets of gospel music. In the 1970s, long after Wally left, they switched to country music and became a great country music group.

And through his years in the Nashville spotlight, during which he wrote many beautiful country songs and hundreds of gospel numbers, including some of gospel's classics, Wally developed much talent. He discovered a lot of stars, including Patsy Cline who became a country star before she was killed in a 1963 airplane crash, along with Cowboy Copas, Hawkshaw Hawkins, and Randy Hughes.

In recent years Wally has slipped into relative obscurity, promoting gospel and variety shows around North Carolina.

CHAPTER THIRTEEN

ℐℎe ℐeam

By 1952, a year before Denver Crumpler joined the Statesmen, Hovie Lister's quartet was drawing big crowds everywhere it went. So were the Blackwood Brothers, who had been back in Memphis two years and were making the rounds of the South steadily.

The quartets were of different styles. The Blackwood Brothers had Dan Huskey at first tenor (who would be replaced later in 1952 by Bill Shaw of the All-American Quartet), James singing lead, R. W. on baritone, Bill Lyles at bass, and Jackie Marshall playing piano. They were not nearly as showy as the Statesmen; so they concentrated on quality singing. Pretty singing, James called it.

Both quartets had their following and their own particular fans. The Blackwood fans thought the Blackwood Brothers were the best, and, of course, Statesmen fans thought the Statesmen were best. These fans enjoyed hearing both quartets sing. Their loyalty was such that if a family had a previous engagement and couldn't come to the concert, they would drive downtown in the afternoon just to see the bus roll in.

Both quartets stayed busy. Wally Fowler had promoted the first All-Night Singing in Nashville four years before that, and most of the larger cities—and many smaller ones—were gospel crazy all over the South.

Usually, $275 on the barrelhead insured a promoter of the services of one of the nation's best quartets for an evening. Talent was relatively inexpensive and ticket prices in most areas were only a dollar or so.

One evening the Statesmen and Blackwood Brothers sang together in an auditorium long since lost from memory, but James remembers that it was a large auditorium in a good-sized town, and the auditorium overflowed an hour before the singing began. Hundreds of people were turned away for lack of seats.

Hovie and James were sharp businessmen and keen observers of the passing scene. That night they came to a joint realization that they had an opportunity no quartets had ever had before.

"We saw that both sets of fans enjoyed both groups," James said later. "We got to talking about what it would be like if the two quartets teamed up and worked together. Both sets of fans would fill most buildings, we thought."

They tried out the team idea at Birmingham Central High School later in 1952, and it worked. The place packed out, all standing room was sold, and folks were turned away by the fire department.

"James," Hovie said when they passed each other in a backstage hallway, "we've got something here."

The same thing happened in the big auditoriums in Nashville and Atlanta. Will Rogers Auditorium in Fort Worth, Texas, was a huge hall, and W. B. Nowlin booked the Statesmen-Blackwood team and filled the place. He immediately booked the team again for the following month and filled the auditorium again. For five years, the Blackwood Brothers and Statesmen, with other groups, sang every other month in Fort Worth and never failed to fill the house.

They still hold the attendance record for drawing more people than any other event of any type in Will Rogers Auditorium.

Because of their popularity and drawing power, the Statesmen-Blackwood team commanded higher prices, and most promoters were willing to pay because of the drawing power of the team. While other quartets sang for $225 to $275 per night, the team commanded $1,000 to $1,500 for an evening of gospel entertainment.

They sang every month in Atlanta, Birmingham, Nashville, and many other major cities across the South. Many of these cities were promoted by Wally Fowler, who knew exactly who buttered his bread, and regardless of what other quartets sang on the program, the Statesmen and Blackwood Brothers were featured.

With their increasing popularity came power. That is the normal result in the scheme of business matters: Popularity commands money, and money brings power.

The Blackwood Brothers and Statesmen were the most powerful groups in the gospel singing business.

"We didn't really have it in mind to corner the market," Hovie said. "It was simply that no one else was doing the things we were doing. We found that our combination would draw people. Promoters liked that. They began to look to us for information and sometimes for advice."

"I suppose, to an extent," James Blackwood said, carefully choosing his words, "that we did kinda control the market. We became headline groups for promoters like Lloyd Orrell, who promoted all through the North—Detroit, Chicago, Indianapolis, Grand Rapids—and we usually sang in all of his cities four times a year."

Orrell and Nowlin especially worked closely with the team. If James Blackwood called Orrell and said, "We'd like you to book this group," Orrell booked it. A lot of promoters booked a lot of new groups on the word of James Blackwood and Hovie Lister.

"I suppose the fate of some groups like the Kingsmen did rest in our hands," James mused. "Very much, very much."

Once when the team was booked in Dayton, Ohio, by Lloyd Orrell, the Oak Ridge Boys called James Blackwood and asked if he would ask Orrell to let them sing a couple of songs on the program that night. "We wouldn't charge him," the Oak Ridger said, "We'd sing for free."

James called Lloyd who said, "Okay, let 'em come on." The Oaks sang before a capacity crowd and Orrell liked their singing so much that he booked them for later dates.

The LeFevre Trio moved to Philadelphia and worked with a preacher in the North for some time, and when they returned to Atlanta they had lost most of their contacts. Urias LeFevre telephoned Hovie Lister and asked Hovie if he could get the LeFevres some bookings. Hovie called W. B. Nowlin, who booked the LeFevres on Hovie's word, and W. B. worked them for years after that.

At the peak of their popularity, the Statesmen grossed a half-million dollars a year and those who owned the quartet did extremely well. The Blackwood Brothers were in the same position.

Not all members shared in the ownership; some were salaried. Hovie, Denver, Jake, Doy, and Big Chief had joint ownership of the Statesmen. When Denver died, the other four purchased his part of the quartet from his widow. When Jake left in 1963 to form the Imperials, they purchased his part. Chief died in 1973, leaving Hovie and Doy the owners, and when Doy died, Hovie became sole owner of the quartet. Hovie had retained copyright of the name "Statesmen Quartet" in his own name from the first, and also of subsidiary names like "Hovie

Lister and the Statemen," "The Statesmen," "Statesmen Productions," and others.

Rosie Rozell was never a partner in the ownership of the Statesmen. He sang for a salary.

The Blackwood Brothers had the same arrangement in which all members shared in the ownership. When J. D. Sumner and Cecil Blackwood joined that quartet in 1954, Cecil came aboard as a salaried singer and J. D. took his partnership, but about six months later Cecil accepted a partnership, and James, Bill Shaw, Cecil, J. D., and Jackie Marshall owned the quartet.

Perhaps "cornering the market" is too strong a phrase to describe the power of the Statesmen and Blackwood Brothers for years, but no one will question their dominance. They had tremendous influence on the whole industry of gospel music, more than anyone else at that time.

Their's was a powerful team.

CHAPTER FOURTEEN

Dignity Takes a Back Seat

"Dignity," Jim Hamill said, "that's what the Blackwood Brothers had. They were always so dignified—especially James."

Hamill remembers the Blackwood Brothers coming to his father's church in Memphis, the First Assembly of God, in 1951. They had sung the night before in Birmingham and after a late Saturday night finish had driven to Memphis in their car.

"Hide Me, Rock of Ages" was one of the Blackwood Brothers' big songs then, and they saved it for the second round, after intermission.

"You could tell they were tired," Hamill said. "It was about a five-hour drive, and they had sung late in Birmingham, and had to travel most of the night to get to Memphis, cramped up in that limousine trying to sleep."

The quartet did very well through the first stand. Then the church took the offering and made announcements, and Dr. Hamill called the Blackwood Brothers back for their second stand.

"And now, ladies and gentlemen," James began, "here's our bass singer, Bill Lyles, singing 'Hide Me, Rock of Ages.'"

They started singing, "Oh, thou blessed Rock of Ages. . . ." At that point, the bass was supposed to come in on the underlay with "Rock of Ages, I am. . . ." But Lyles uttered not a word. He was sound asleep on the front bench.

Poor James was flabbergasted.

The Blackwoods experienced another incident years later in Dr.

Hamill's church. This was after 1958 when Wally Varner came to play the piano for them. He was a flamboyant artist at the keyboard, bouncing around on the bench, running easily up and down the scales. He would scoot the bench back and do all those ripples and rills on the high keys.

On this Sunday night, James introduced him to play "How Great Thou Art," and Wally scooted the bench back and tipped it off the platform. He plunged to the floor on his back with his cowboy boots sticking straight up and his pants legs over his knees. Folks crowded around him, fearing that he was really hurt, but he bounced to his feet, replaced the bench and gave that piano a real going over.

Such was life in the Blackwood Brothers Quartet.

Low-down London Parris, one of several great bass singers to come out of Asheville, went with the Blackwood Brothers in January of 1968, replacing Big John Hall. Soon after he joined the quartet, the Blackwood Brothers sang in a rather dignified First Baptist Church in West Texas, and London felt moved to give his most heartfelt testimony. While doing so he mentioned his coming to the Blackwood Brothers.

What he meant to say was, "When you come to the Blackwood Brothers, you don't have any seniority and they put your *bunk* in the back of the bus."

But what he said that broke up the crowd was: "When you come to the Blackwood Brothers . . . they put your *butt* in the back of the bus."

The Statesmen also had that great dignity, but sometimes things came apart for them, too.

It is easy to get your tongue tangled up when you're trying to be master of ceremonies on stage. Once as the Statesmen sang to a tremendous crowd in California, Hovie Lister leaped from the bench and started to quote Scripture.

"And Jeezley said. . . ." he thundered. Quickly, Jake Hess said, "Hovie, His name is Jesus." He so angered Hovie that Hovie sat down and began thumping the piano and refused to say another word.

The Statesmen once worked a postal convention in Atlanta, and Hovie had his men wear black suits, white shirts, and red ties. They sang the first song and when Hovie leaped up from the piano, the audience began to laugh. Hovie looked around suspiciously at the other fellows, thinking they were clowning behind his back, and said softly, "Cut it out back there, fellows."

He sat down and played another song, and when he stood up the audience laughed again. Hovie turned to Jake and Big Chief, sure that they were the culprits, and said "Now you guys shut up. I'm trying to be serious."

He played another song and when he stood up that time, laughter rippled through the crowd for the third time. Certain that his men were cutting up, Hovie said, "I'm serious. Knock it off!"

"Hovie," Chief said, "your pants are unzipped."

"Yeah, yeah," Hovie said. "I said to cool it."

The Statesmen did another song, the quartet almost breaking apart with suppressed laughter, and when Hovie stood again, the crowd hee-hawed.

"No kidding, Hovie," Chief said, "your pants are unzipped." Hovie refused to check his zipper, knowing that would be giving in to Chief's little joke. He said, "If you say that again, Chief, I'm gonna give you this mike."

"Say it, Chief," Jake urged.

"Hovie," Chief deadpanned, "your pants are unzipped."

Hovie backed away from the mike about a foot and said to the audience, "Big Chief and Jake are telling me my pants are unzipped."

He looked down and to his consternation, his pants were unzipped and gaping open.

The crowd laughed for ten minutes.

When the Statesmen got a crowd going right, Hovie became a taskmaster—perhaps the best stage general ever.

"On stage," Rosie Rozell, who became the first tenor for the Statesmen in 1958, once described Hovie's generalship, "if Hovie decided to encore fifteen times and we needed a pump to get some air, we got the pump and used the air."

In Birmingham one night, the Statesmen sang "Get Away, Jordan," on which Hovie sang an exciting run, and at the end of the song Hovie was standing up pulling "Amens" from the audience. The quartet did about five encores and on the last one Rosie jumped up on the piano stool—and felt his pants rip from crotch to knee.

He didn't know how to gracefully climb down from that piano stool, let alone extract himself from the stage, but when he finally got himself behind the curtains, he heard Hovie, still on stage, say, "Come on, Fat Boy, and sing that again!"

Rosie shook his head vigorously and said, "I'm not coming out there again."

Hovie froze. Could he believe his ears? Had Rosie actually refused an order? He looked at Rosie with one eye going up and the other coming down and said, "I said to come back out here."

"I'm not coming back out there," Rosie said, and turned around to show Hovie his ripped pants.

Hovie walked over and dragged Rosie back on stage. "Now," he said, "sing that song one more time."

Rosie's sense of humor was rather dry, and he exerted it occasionally. Once when the Statesmen and Lester Family went on tour in Canada, Rosie had to return to the United States before the Statesmen came back. He hitched a ride with the Lesters, and to make himself handy, offered to help drive the bus. He was at the wheel when the bus rolled up to the border late at night.

"How many people on the bus?" the border guard asked.

"I don't know," Rosie said.

"Any children on there?"

"I think so."

"How many adults you got on there?"

"No adults at all," Rosie said. "They're all grown-ups."

The man shook his head in bewilderment.

"Go ahead," he said, and backed off the bus.

CHAPTER FIFTEEN

The World Comes Tumbling Down

No question, the Blackwood Brothers and Statesmen had the world by the tail. Their companies were solvent; they were making good money; and more importantly, they were entertaining the public in a way that was completely satisfying. Their only problem was time—time to do all the things they wanted to do. Time was limited because of the snail's-pace of travel. This was before the interstate highway system began. Great cities like Los Angeles were just perfecting their systems of freeways on the drawing boards.

James Blackwood reasoned, rightly so, that if the Blackwood Brothers could cut down on their road time, they could accomplish so much more than they were currently doing.

He had some irons in the fire that would command fast travel, some things of national scope. He hit upon the idea of flying to their engagements. Most of the cities and towns in which the Blackwood Brothers sang had airports; so why not fly?

When Bill Shaw replaced Dan Huskey as the Blackwood Brothers first tenor in the fall of 1952, James implemented his idea of flight. The Blackwood Brothers bought two airplanes, an eight-seat, twin-engine Cessna for their primary transportation, and a slightly smaller aircraft for a backup plane. With the airplanes, James reasoned again, they could broaden their scope, covering more territory than they ever had before. Even the West Coast began to beckon him.

The Blackwood Brothers hired a pilot to fly them until R. W. got his license and was checked out in twin-engined aircraft. Bill Lyles also learned to fly. R. W. became the aircraft's captain and Lyles was his co-pilot. The Blackwood Brothers felt safe in their hands.

When Bobby Strickland died in an automobile wreck on September 24, 1953, the Blackwood Brothers also remembered Erman Slater's death on January 12, 1951, in a speeding car belonging to the Rangers Quartet—and they were glad they were flying.

"Flying," they were told until they convinced themselves, "is safer than driving any time."

The summer of 1954 rolled around, and for the Blackwood Brothers it was to be their most eventful season ever. In it they were lifted to the tremendous heights of national television stardom, and then they were quickly dropped into the pits of despair.

It all began when James was notified that the Blackwood Brothers had been chosen to audition for Arthur Godfrey's "Talent Scouts" on CBS television in New York. What a break! Godfrey and Ed Sullivan had the two most-watched shows on television for entertainment talent. Both scouted the nation to bring to their shows the best acts they could find.

Appearance of the Blackwood Brothers on Godfrey's show was scheduled for Monday evening, June 11, 1954. James cast about for a song to sing, perhaps a new number that the Blackwood Brothers had not done before.

James was a connoisseur of good music. He enjoyed all kinds of music, particularly Hawaiian (the Blackwood Brothers later recorded a Hawaiian gospel album), and he especially enjoyed some of the leading pop stars of the day. Kay Starr was one of them. Her big recording was "Wheel of Fortune."

James heard Kay Starr sing a song entitled "Have You Talked To The Man Upstairs?" and he thought it was great. It had been written by Miss Starr's manager and seemed suited to the Blackwood Brothers' style.

They took the song straight off Miss Starr's recording and learned it. James thought it would be a winner.

When the Blackwoods did the song on Godfrey's show, the applause meter, which indicated the act that drew the highest response from the audience, went all the way over and pegged.

The Blackwood Brothers were thrilled. The song was a big, big hit. Godfrey quickly recognized that and did the remainder of the show in rhythm to match "The Man Upstairs."

The McGuire Sisters were regulars on the Godfrey show. From Dayton, Ohio, where their mother was a preacher, they had attended a Blackwood Brothers' concert one evening and had come backstage to get the Blackwood Brothers' autographs. Later, when they won the Talent Scouts, Godfrey liked the McGuire Sisters so well that he gave them a regular job on his show.

Winners of the Godfrey Talent Scouts got to appear on his network radio show all week, and the Blackwood Brothers sang several songs nationwide that week, each receiving proper response and special accolades from Godfrey himself.

The McGuire Sisters invited the Blackwood Brothers to Christine McGuire's apartment one evening for dinner, and had their manager come over to hear them sing. That evening, they worked up a number together, "Lead Me To That Rock," and sang it jointly on Godfrey's show the next morning.

All week when the Blackwood Brothers walked down Broadway, or up Fifth Avenue, they heard people say, "There go the Godfrey winners!"

While in New York, at RCA Victor's insistence, they recorded "Have You Talked To The Man Upstairs?" and the record became one of RCA's top ten that summer.

Figuratively walking on air, the Blackwood Brothers flew back to Memphis after that week's work in New York and resumed their concert schedule. Everywhere they went, people turned out in record numbers to hear them, packing auditoriums and ball parks.

Never before had a quartet been on such a high. Never had a quartet reached such heights.

Almost three weeks later, on Saturday night, June 30, 1954, the Blackwood Brothers were booked with the Statesmen to perform at the Chilton County Peach Festival in Clanton, Alabama. They were to sing in the Old Airport Hangar.

R. W. flew the quartet in from Gulfport, Mississippi, where they had sung on Friday night, and had a bit of difficulty getting the airplane on the short Clanton runway.

The plane arrived in the morning and the Blackwood Brothers sang at a civic club luncheon at noon. They were driven around the town that afternoon, seeing the sights, and in late afternoon returned to the airport.

People gathered early for the singing, and R. W. told James he wanted to take the airplane up before dark to see how much room he had for a takeoff after dark.

The Clanton airfield was not lighted and the runway w
it concerned R. W. It did not worry him, but there were lines or concern on his face. Flying out of an unlighted field at night was nothing
new to the Blackwood Brothers. Many times they had had their fans
line the runway with automobiles and R. W. took to the air by the light
of the cars' headlights. They planned to do it that night.

R. W. and Bill Lyles strapped themselves in the cockpit of the
airplane. Behind them sat an eighteen-year-old local youngster, Johnny
Ogburn, son of a Clanton banker who founded the Peach Festival.
Johnny went along for the ride.

From the time the Blackwood Brothers had landed, the wind had
shifted. It had done an about-face; so R. W. made allowances for this
and took off in the opposite direction, into the wind.

He got the plane off the ground easily and circled the runway. On
final approach to land, he had to clear a small hill at the end of the
runway, and drop the airplane in on the sod field.

He had trouble dropping in after clearing the hill. On the first
pass, he didn't let the wheels touch the ground, but gunned the engines
and rose into the air again.

He brought the Cessna in a second time and still had trouble getting it down. About a third of the way up the runway, the wheels still
hadn't touched down when suddenly the plane dropped onto the turf
and bounced tremendously high.

Newspaper reports the following day said the landing gear caught
in the soft turf and caused the plane to crash, but that was not what
happened. When the plane bounced, R. W. shoved the throttle forward to wide open and quickly lifted the landing gear, hoping to regain flying speed and get the craft back in the air.

Suddenly the airplane turned nose up and rose high in the air. It
stalled, and then plunged to earth in a terrifying crash.

In the intervening years, James said he has talked to many experienced pilots about the cause of the crash and they generally agree that
R. W. failed to retrim his tabs from the landing position to takeoff, and
thrusting full power with the tabs in landing position carried the plane
straight up.

"In all the excitement and anxiety of getting the plane down,"
James said, "we think he simply failed to trim the tabs—and that was a
fatal mistake."

Several hundred people standing at the hangar watched in horror
as the plane hit the ground and exploded into flames.

The cabin door burst open and James began to run for it, hoping against hope to see three figures emerge. But none did, and when he reached the plane's door, he heard someone at the front of the aircraft yell, "Here they are!"

Thinking the three had been thrown clear, James raced to the front of the plane. The plexiglas canopy was shattered, and through the flames he saw R. W. still strapped in the pilot's seat, his head dangling at an odd angle to one side. He could not see Bill, and learned later that Bill's seatbelt had broken and he had been thrown under the instrument panel.

Autopsies showed that all three men had been instantly killed, their necks broken by the violent impact of the crash.

In a state of shock, James started through the flames to get to his beloved nephew, but Jake Hess grabbed him in a bear hug and wrestled him away. James fought so hard that Jake had to manhandle him.

The singing was cancelled, of course, and the Statesmen put James in their limousine and drove him back to Memphis.

James's first reaction was that he would never sing again.

"We had reached the heights three weeks before when we won the Godfrey show," he said, "and we were sitting on top of the world. But it all came crashing down with that airplane."

The funerals of R. W. Blackwood and Bill Lyles were held in the spacious City Auditorium in Memphis, and fans packed the auditorium full. Members of twenty-seven professional quartets formed a choir and sang for their fallen comrades. Gov. Frank Clement attended.

Bill Lyles was thirty-three years old, R. W. thirty-two. Their lives were snuffed out so quickly that the Blackwood Brothers gave no further thought to flying. They sold the other airplane and bought a limousine.

A few days after the crash, James, Bill Shaw, and Jackie Marshall drove to Fort Worth, Texas, where the Blackwood Brothers had been scheduled to sing, and made their first appearance since the crash. They worked with the Statesmen, and Big Chief filled in on the bass and Doyle Blackwood sang baritone.

James decided to go ahead with the quartet, and gave R. W.'s younger brother, Cecil, the baritone job. He looked over several bass singers and finally settled on J. D. Sumner, the low bass of the Sunshine Boys.

Lyles had been a smooth, mellow bass whose depth of voice was sufficient for the Blackwood Brothers. He suited their style. He had also been a lively fellow whose humor kept the quartet laughing.

When a group of men work together as closely as a quartet, and spend most of their time on the road away from home and family, they often resort to a rough sort of humor to keep things on an even keel.

Early in Bill Lyles's stint with the Blackwood Brothers, they had Calvin Newton singing first tenor, and Calvin was the butt of some of Bill's jokes. Driving through the countryside in a big DeSoto Suburban that had all their belongings tied onto a rack on top, James Blackwood needed something from the rack, and Calvin, knowing they were running late to their next engagement, said, "Here, I'll climb up and get it." He was a small fellow who easily squirmed out the window and climbed onto the top of the car—and Bill Lyles rolled up the window. At sixty miles an hour, Calvin Newton held on for dear life and rode several miles on top of the DeSoto, repeating over and over, "I'll kill him! I'll kill him! I'll kill him!"

Pianist Jackie Marshall succeeded Newton as fall guy for Lyles. Marshall loved to pull jokes, too, and he often pulled them on Bill Lyles; so the two became rather accomplished in their joking.

Once the Blackwood Brothers checked into a motel in Fort Worth, Texas, taking two rooms which were separated by a little landing at the top of a set of outside stairs. Lyles, who had been the butt of a Marshall joke that day, cooked up a scheme to get even with Jackie, and had to bring in the rest of the guys to make it work.

Lyles was in the room across the landing from Marshall, and timing it right with the help of another member of the quartet, called for Jackie to come over to his room to see something just as Jackie undressed to take a shower.

"I can't come," Jackie yelled. "I don't have any clothes on."

"Just jump across here," Bill yelled back, "Nobody will see you."

Jackie jumped—and Bill shut the door in Jackie's face. Jackie wheeled around to return to his own room, and someone slammed that door, too. And there stood Jackie Marshall, naked, on the landing at the top of the outside stairs.

"He couldn't scream for help," James Blackwood said, "because he would attract attention. But he did some of the most desperate whispering I've ever heard."

Another time in Oklahoma City, the Blackwood Brothers stayed in one room of a motel, for economic reasons. The motel moved some foldaway beds into the room, and Jackie slept in one of them. During the night, Lyles got up and folded Jackie up in his bed with only his head and hands and feet sticking out.

*   *   *

Addition of J. D. Sumner's deep, powerful voice gave the Blackwood Brothers a wonderful flexibility they had never had. His voice was so low that the rest of the quartet, who sang a high harmony anyway, could sing as high as they wanted to. J. D. could balance it on the other end.

The first time the Blackwood Brothers sang together publicly with Cecil and J. D. was at the Old Airport Hangar in Clanton, within sight of the crash scene.

Arthur Godfrey knew of the crash, and had his staff contact James to see if the Blackwood Brothers would appear again on the Talent Scouts when they reorganized.

They did—and won it again. Ironically, they won the second time with another of Kay Starr's songs, "The Good Book."

James Blackwood was the 1985 recipient of an award for excellence in the field of arts and communications given by Memphis State University. In 1988, he learned that Kay Starr was to receive the same award. When James told the people at Memphis State that the Blackwood Brothers had won Arthur Godfrey's Talent Scouts twice using Miss Starr's songs, they insisted that he sing both songs at the awards banquet. When he sang "Have You Talked To The Man Upstairs?" Miss Starr joined him in the singing, producing one of the big thrills of James's life.

That the Blackwood Brothers could bounce back from the brink of disaster without losing their position of prominence in the world of gospel music, was a tribute both to the fabric and texture of the men involved and to the type of music they sang.

They and the Statesmen continued their dominance for a few more years, and then a sort of parity crept back into the business as other groups emerged as leaders and the tastes of the fans began to change.

Gospel music with the Statesmen and Blackwood Brothers was a sort of happy rhythm, best expressed by a couple of statements made by Hovie Lister.

He once said, "God didn't intend for religion to wear a long face."

And again, when criticized for his flamboyant piano style, his flashy dress, oversized rings, and upbeat entertainmnet style, he defended them by saying, "If it takes shaking my hair down and beating a piano like Liberace or Piano Red to keep those young people out of beer joints and the rear seats of automobiles, I'll do it.

The Devil's got his kind of entertainment—and we have ours."

Furman Bisher, sports editor of *The Atlanta Journal*, once wrote an article for *The Saturday Evening Post* about Hovie Lister and the Statesmen Quartet, and in it he wrote, "He (Hovie) put rhythm into religion."

That he did—and in doing so, his quartet, the Statesmen, sang on NBC, ABC, and CBS television networks; they, too, won Arthur Godfrey's Talent Scouts; they sang on the Tennessee Ernie Ford Show, Dave Garroway's Wide Wide World, and Jimmy Dean's Show, among others; and they were featured in major publications such as *Look, Life, Billboard, Cashbox, The Saturday Evening Post*, and many others.

They were perhaps the busiest quartet in America—the busiest in history, even. Early in their career they were the first quartet to have their own nationwide television show. They sang at the premiers of two motion pictures: *A Man Called Peter* and *God Is My Partner*, and then they recorded the title songs from those movies for RCA.

The year 1964 was one of the Statesmen's busiest years. They worked 287 one-nighters, helped produce 51 hours of syndicated television shows, cut three record albums, did a pilot film for one of the television networks, and sang two days at the New York World's Fair.

With various personnel changes, the Blackwood Brothers and Statesmen sang on into the 1980s, but not with the prominence they held in the 1950s and 1960s.

All of the fifties-sixties vintage Blackwood Brothers still live—those who sang after the plane crash—and at old-timers conventions Bill Shaw, James, Cecil, and J. D. get together to sing a few songs with Wally Varner or Jackie Marshall at the piano.

But death wrecked the Statesmen.

Denver Crumpler was the first to go. He sang with the Statesmen four years in poor physical condition, suffering primarily from diabetes.

The Statesmen worked a revival in Detroit in March of 1957 and came home to Atlanta on Monday morning, March 18. Denver's church was also in revival, and he asked the Statesmen if they would sing with him at his church on Wednesday night.

Denver sang well. He was in good voice, and his pride in the other members of the quartet showed through that evening. They were proud of him, too.

The next morning, Thursday, March 21, Frankie Crumpler telephoned Hovie and said, "Denver is very ill. He has been up all night vomiting."

That was bad, Hovie knew. Doctors had told Denver that such strain on his heart and blood vessels could be dangerous. He had taken insulin for thirty-five of his forty-four years.

Hovie told Frankie he would call an ambulance for Denver and that he, Hovie, would meet them at Emory University Hospital.

When Hovie saw the ambulance attendants bring Denver into the hospital, he seemed to be unconscious, but actually he was dead. An autopsy showed he had died of a heart attack.

Cat Freeman returned to take Denver's place for a short time while Hovie went after Rosie Rozell, who sang with the Tulsa Trumpeteers, a gospel group in Oklahoma. Hovie thought Rosie would fit the Statesmen well, and again his judgment was unerring. Rosie had a soul sound that was different than Denver's voice, and certainly different than Cat's, and the Statesmen felt that something different was what they wanted.

Rosie had joined the Tulsa Police Department, but when Hovie called he quit the police and came to Atlanta to sing with the Statesmen. He helped the quartet carry on its great tradition through the years.

Jake Hess left the Statesmen in 1963 and formed the Imperials with Sherrill Nielson, Gary McSpadden, Armond Morales, Henry Slaughter, and himself. Jake said he wanted a quartet that could stand flat-footed and sing all night without an encore, and he had it in that crew.

Jake was replaced by a succession of good lead singers, not any of whom reached the prominence Jake enjoyed. Jake Hess had become synonymous with the Statesmen. Over the years Jake has been wracked with a variety of ailments that would have killed many healthy mules, but he survived to keep on singing.

Big Chief died at the National Quartet Convention in October of 1973. His death was sudden—but not totally unexpected.

A year before his death, Big Chief went with the Statesmen on a tour of the West Coast. Just after they sang in Phoenix, Arizona, Chief became ill with an abscessed tooth. Hovie begged him to fly home, but Chief, who was the epitome of what quartet people call "a real quartet man," wouldn't go. He was a trouper.

From Phoenix, the Statesmen sang their way up to Oregon. Passing though San Francisco, Hovie noted that Chief was no better and urged him to fly home from there, but Chief went on.

They reached Eugene, Oregon, and sang at the University of Oregon. Before the quartet went on that night, Big Chief came to Hovie and said, "Don't say anything until we've sung our last song, and then you might ask if there's a doctor in the house and have him come backstage."

No doctors were there, but the head nurse of the University Medical Center was. She talked to Big Chief a while, and then said she would make a doctor's appointment for him for the next morning.

He was admitted to the University Hospital and a blood clot was discovered on his lung. He was hospitalized a month and then flew back to Atlanta and spent another week in Georgia Baptist Hospital. Doctors put him on blood-thinning medication.

At the quartet convention in 1973, Big Chief brought Liz, his wife, for the first time. The Statesmen sang one night, were off the next, and were scheduled to sing the following night. Hovie was having coffee in the coffee shop of the Ramada Inn near the auditorium and heard the desk paging him. When he responded, he saw medics rolling Big Chief from the elevator on a gurney. The Statesmen's great bass singer of twenty-four years was dead. He had collapsed in his room and Liz summoned Doy Ott from his room across the hall. Big Chief died in Doy's arms.

Liz said she was relaxing, dozing on the bed, and Chief was beside her, working a crossword puzzle. She felt Chief get up and asked, "What are you doing?"

"It's time to shave," Chief said. "We're singing tonight."

He walked toward the bathroom and fell in the floor.

"He was one of the greatest quartet men I've ever worked with," Hovie said of Big Chief. "Didn't matter to him, he was ready to go any day of the week, any hour of the day. He would rehearse as long as you wanted to rehearse. If we had a new song and rehearsed it today and this was the first time Chief had seen the song, he would know his part and everybody else's tomorrow—words and music. He was some kind of guy."

Doy died November 6, 1986, at age sixty-seven, long after his retirement from singing. He realized his dream of becoming a chiropractor and opened a clinic in Ardmore, Oklahoma. He was in the clinic on November 27, 1982, when he suffered a stroke. In January his condition was complicated by meningitis, and though he lingered, he never recovered.

CHAPTER SIXTEEN

Soft
Harmony

The Swanee River Boys were different from the start. They intended to be, singing a soft harmony that fell somewhere between black gospel and white gospel. The way they sang was appealing.

They began the gospel style of soft harmony, and others followed: the Jordanaires, the Foggy River Boys, and more locally Freddy Rose and the Dixie Knights of Knoxville.

The Swanee River Boys originated soft harmony in 1939 when quartets were hard-singing groups, accustomed to hammering out their songs without benefit of sound equipment.

Ironically, though they started the soft-harmony format in gospel, the Swanee River Boys were primarily secular singers who made their living singing popular, country, and spiritual numbers, and only occasionally dipped into the gospel quartet field. Still, they exerted heavy influence on gospel.

The Swanee River Boys sang for more than thirty years—from 1939 into the early 1970s—and it was only the last three or four years that they sang almost all gospel.

"We made our living in radio and television," said Buford Abner, who helped originate the quartet and sang with it thirty years. "We made some personal appearances, too, and we preferred to sing in hotel lounges, state fairs, and radio and television to singing the night club circuit. When we turned down the club circuit, it was a huge financial mistake—but money is not everything, and we were satisfied with our decision.

"The gospel circuit was only a minor part of our work," Buford said, "until the last three years of our quartet's existence. We had a reasonable amount of success in gospel. I love gospel; I was raised in it. I have written gospel songs all my working life. And when our schedule permitted us to sing gospel, we did. We sang it when we could."

Today's generations have trouble understanding the structure of music when the Swanee River Boys started singing. No one had even dreamed of rock 'n roll; country music was still hillbilly; gospel was only a fledgling babe on the horizon that few people recognized or even knew about. THE music was popular. Big Bands abounded and people danced the jitterbug and thrilled to the renditions of the Dorsey brothers, Benny Goodman, Glenn Miller, Kay Kiser, and dozens of other bandleaders.

That was the age that spawned Sinatra and Dick Haymes and Margaret Whiting—and the Mills Brothers, who had a tremendous influence on the Abner brothers, Buford and Merle, who with Billy Carrier organized the Swanee River Boys.

The Abners were from Wedowee, Alabama. They had begun to sing about 1935 with the Pepperell Quartet of the Pepperell Manufacturing Company in Columbus, Georgia. That quartet sang on Columbus radio for a couple of years.

Apparently, their musical ability was recognized, for in 1937 Stacy Abner, Buford and Merle's uncle, called them to Knoxville to sing with him and Billy Carrier of Brownsville, Kentucky, in the Vaughan Five Quartet over Radio Station WNOX.

A year later, the idea of forming their own quartet entered the minds of the Abner brothers and Billy Carrier, and in 1939 they did it.

They got George Hughes of Texarkana, a town that straddles the Texas-Arkansas line, who had been the original first tenor with the Texas Rangers Quartet. Hughes sang first tenor in this new quartet; Buford sang the lead; Carrier sang baritone and played guitar; and Merle sang a tremendously harmonizing bass.

They began singing on WDOD in Chattanooga.

Merle Abner named the quartet after Stephen Foster's song, "Way Down Upon the Suwanee River," but thought the 'u' should be dropped because Swanee was easier to recognize and remember.

Buford, as the quartet's arranger, dictated the style.

"I always liked the Mills Brothers," Buford said, "and they influenced my thinking when I was setting our style. What I tried to do was split the difference between black and white gospel. We had a little of each sound. We were trying to be distinctive, and thought our style sounded better than the hard-driving gospel style. The rhythm and accents came out better.

"If you heard us sing, we wanted you to know who we were—that was the general idea."

The Swanee River Boys sang almost constantly on network radio during their early days and on into the post-World War II era. They sang for a year with Grady Cole on the CBS network from Radio Station WBT in Charlotte. Then they went to WSB in Atlanta and had a variety network show.

When the Mills Brothers left WLW in Cincinnati to devote full time to the night club circuit, the Swanee River Boys replaced them. They were sponsored by Western Auto Stores on a network show.

Television was in its infancy, and local shows were telecast live. The Swanee River Boys did two or three shows daily on WLW-TV.

They recorded on the MGM label, and later with King. After they became primarily a gospel group, they recorded with Zondervan and Skylite.

"We had the opportunity to perform with many famous people over the years," Buford said. "We worked with Bob Hope, Bing Crosby, Martin and Lewis. We knew the Mills Brothers, met them in California, but never worked with them. They were good people. When they went on the night club circuit, we were offered a contract to do the same, but we turned it down. We were engrossed with television and were doing well for a bunch of country boys."

When the Swanee River Boys played the gospel circuit, fans loved them. They sang spirituals and regular gospel songs and put them across in a most soothing manner. It was inevitable that someone else would start a soft-harmony gospel group.

The Jordanaires were the second quartet to sing soft-harmony gospel. They toured for a while after the war, then took a job at the Grand Ole Opry with Red Foley on the *Prince Albert Show*, and went on staff at WSM. They were excellent singers—Gordon Stoker, Monty and Bill Matthews, Curly Holt, and Bob Hubbard.

Once they got in the Nashville swing and began singing backup for country and popular singers, they didn't have time to come back on the gospel circuit. They enjoyed a long and successful run as a backup group.

They also showed some of the nation's biggest singers how much a good-harmonizing gospel group could add to a show, and paved the way for groups like the Imperials, the Oak Ridge Boys, and the Stamps

Quartet to back singers like Jimmy Dean and Elvis Presley in later years.

The Swanee River Boys sang twelve years without a personnel change. Then Billy Carrier decided to leave and Floridian Horace Floyd took his place, singing high tenor. George Hughes moved from high tenor to baritone. Don Stringfellow replaced Hughes, who sang with some other quartets. Bill Nelson took Stringfellow's place years later, and Bill Carter became the tenor, replacing Horace Floyd.

"We were quite fortunate," Buford said, "that we had to make no more changes than we did."

Age crept up on the Swanee River Boys, and in 1970, after thirty solid years on the road, Buford left the group and began to tune pianos. He also ran a piano-tuner's school.

The quartet sang a year or two longer, then folded up.

Buford wrote many good gospel songs through his long career. His work was recorded by most of the leading quartets.

The University of Florida recognized his long years of work with the Swanee River Boys by presenting Buford with a copy of Stephen Foster's handwritten manuscript of his song, "Way Down Upon The Suwanee River."

"I'm proud of that," Buford said. "And in it I noticed that Stephen Foster had to work at writing his stuff, too. He originally wrote it 'Way Down Upon The Pee Dee River,' but crossed out Pee Dee and wrote Suwanee above it.

"That's the way with songwriters," Buford concluded. "I guess even the best have to work hard at it."

CHAPTER SEVENTEEN

The Innovators

The earliest customized buses, which revolutionized travel throughout the entertainment world, were equipped only with the bare necessities—and sometimes not with those.

They contained bunks, closet space for clothing, and comfortable chairs in which the singers could relax—and not much else.

No one thought of putting a shower in those early buses, and that created a problem for the Blackwood Brothers once.

They sang in Pennsylvania one night and were scheduled to sing in Nebraska the next, and then in Texas on the third night.

On the long ride from Pennsylvania to Nebraska, the air-conditioning unit on the bus went haywire and the interior became stifling hot.

Sweat rolled.

They managed to reach Nebraska just in time to sing; so the members of the quartet applied talcum powder sufficiently to suppress the stench of unwashed bodies, did their stand, then piled back on the bus and headed for Texas.

"What do we do now?" Bill Shaw asked. "We haven't been to a motel and we're all beginning to smell like horses."

"We'll do something," James said, but he didn't know what. He wasn't sure they would make their date in Texas on time.

As Bundy Brewster rolled the bus along in the middle of the night, rain began to fall, at first gently, then harder, and finally in a downpour. Suddenly, Bundy whipped the bus off the road.

"Ain't been a car passed us in thirty minutes," Bundy said.

"Let's take a shower!" shouted pianist Tommy Fairchild, ripping off his clothes.

In a moment, all the Blackwood Brothers and their driver were out in the rain, soaping themselves in the downpour, and laughing gleefully.

Just when everyone was covered with soap, the headlights of a car appeared in the distance. The whole naked quartet ran to the rear of the bus and huddled beside it, out of sight as the car passed.

When that one was gone, before the quartet could resume its collective shower, another car came along, then another, and another. The road suddenly resembled a thoroughfare.

Finally, blessed darkness descended again, and the quartet moved back out in the rain and soaped up again.

Then the rain stopped. Just like that, the downpour ended. James looked through soapy eyes at the others. "What do we do now?" he asked.

"Wait a minute," someone said, hopefully. "Surely it'll start again."

But it didn't. The rain was over. Not another drop fell that night. Swiftly, the winds aloft blew the clouds away and the moon came out. Everybody looked around, but there wasn't a creek, nor even a small branch, in sight where they could rinse off the soap.

Slowly, they climbed back on the bus, toweled off the soap as well as they could, and dressed.

Fairchild said they smelled like Palmolive for hours.

But Bill Shaw thought that was better than smelling like horses.

Had it not been for J. D. Sumner, the Blackwood Brothers might not have been riding that bus at all. They might still have been cramped in a limousine.

J. D. built the first customized bus in 1955 and changed the world of quartet singing.

Were it not for far-sighted men and women—people of vision, if you will—neither gospel music nor any other type of music would be what it is today.

These people are the innovators, the ones who think up new ideas and put them in motion. Some of the ideas simply make for better promotion—but others have great impact.

Lee Roy Abernathy was such an innovator. So, too, was J. D. Sumner.

Named John Daniel Sumner long before anybody ever heard of

the John Daniel Quartet. J. D. came out of Lakeland, Florida, to succeed Pappy Jim Waits, Aycel Soward, Arnold Hyles, Frank Stamps, and those other fine bass singers of the 1930s and 1940s as the King of Bass Singers.

Though he sang with several quartets in Florida through most of the 1940s—the Stamps Sunny South Quartet and the Dixie Lily Harmoneers, to name a couple—J. D.'s star did not really ascend until he came to Atlanta in 1949 to take a singing job with the Sunshine Boys.

Just as Atlanta was then moving toward its position as the "Hub of the South" in air transportation, the burgeoning city was also becoming known as the center of quartet music.

"Getting a singing job in Atlanta," J. D. said, "was about the same thing as dying and going to heaven. Everybody wanted to come to Atlanta to sing."

Ace Richman and Eddie Wallace had returned from the West Coast where the Sunshine Boys were making Western movies, but the Smith brothers, Tennessee and Smitty, chose to remain out west.

Ace telephoned Horace Floyd, a tenor singer who lived in Orlando, and asked if he would take the job as tenor with the Sunshine Boys. Horace agreed to terms, and when Ace asked him if he knew of an available bass singer, Horace suggested J. D. Sumner.

Thus, J. D. made his way to Atlanta and began putting low notes into the Sunshine Boys' programs. He was also quickly recognized as a bass singer who could stay on pitch. He split every note down the middle. Before long, J. D. was known as one of the lowest and most popular bass singers in the business.

J. D. stayed five years with the Sunshine Boys, filled with ideas but unable to implement them because he didn't have the money; and the Sunshine Boys weren't interested in spending money on any innovations except those in their songs—and there were plenty of those.

J. D. tried to interest the Sunshine Boys in traveling by bus rather than limousine; and in starting a national convention for professional quartets that would bring all the pros together once a year; and in some other new ideas. Actually, the Sunshine Boys were not in financial position to pick up on J. D.'s brainstorms and do anything with them.

But when Bill Lyles and R. W. Blackwood died in that 1954 airplane crash, and James Blackwood hired J. D. as the Blackwood Brothers Quartet's bass singer, things began to happen.

J. D. soon gauged the Blackwood Brothers, James in particular, as being more progressive—aggressive, too—in business than the Sunshine Boys, and he immediately began talking up his idea of buying a bus for the quartet's travel.

He talked at length with any of the Blackwood Brothers who would listen, telling them how he envisioned quartets traveling in comfortable, custom-built buses, complete with bunks for sleeping, easy chairs up front for relaxing, a rest room, television, and as many of the comforts of home as they could pack in a bus.

What he received from all the members of the group except James was uproarious laughter.

"Haw, haw," one member laughed. "Well, we ought to get us a boat, since we live on the Mississippi (in Memphis), and when we go to St. Louis or New Orleans to sing, why we can just get in our boat and go."

"That's right," another said. "And we ought to get us a train, so when we go somewhere that's not on the river and we can't ride our boat, we can ride our train. Haw, haw!"

Finally, in 1955, James said to J. D., "I like the idea. If you think you can sell our limousine and trailer and put us on the road in a bus for that money—go ahead and do it."

The Blackwood Brothers had a new Cadillac limousine and a good trailer for hauling records and other paraphernalia, and when J. D. offered them to Lee Roy Abernathy, Lee Roy bought them for $3,700.

J. D. had been shopping for buses and had one spotted. It was a 1937 model Aerocoach owned by Trailways. He bought the eighteen-year-old bus for $2,400.

He bought several sheets of three-quarter-inch plywood and with hammer and saw made four bunks, two sets of double-deckers, which he fastened into the back of the bus. He bought mattresses and bedsprings for each. Then he carefully measured each man in the quartet, went to Mississippi and had reclining chairs made to fit each man. These he installed in the front of the bus, behind the driver.

He partitioned the bus into relaxing quarters up front and sleeping quarters in the rear.

The chairs and plywood and other supplies cost J. D. $1,200, and when he finished customizing the old bus, he had used $3,600 of the $3,700 he got from Lee Roy, and had $100 left over.

J. D. hired a bus driver named Buddy Darvis to drive the bus, and he was at the wheel when the day came on which the Blackwood Brothers ventured out for their first trip in the new conveyance. Certainly they rode in more comfort than cramped in a limousine, and the kidding soon died down. Even the more skeptical members of the group began to feel that J. D. might not be as crazy as they thought.

After the first night's singing, the quartet piled on the bus, and four of them went to sleep in the bunks. The fifth slept in one of the chairs, and Darvis headed for the next town.

Out in the country, sailing along, Darvis hit a bump in the road— and bodies suddenly flew all over the back of the bus. The Blackwood Brothers were rudely awakened flying out of their bunks and bumping into each other, landing in a tangle of arms and legs on the floor of the bus.

They crawled back in the bunks again, and when Darvis hit another bump, out they flew again.

Sheepishly, the four crept up front to sleep in their chairs. They simply couldn't stay in the bunks when the bus hit a bump in the road, but they slept much better in the reclining chairs than they had ever slept in a limousine.

J. D. tried to interest other quartets into going into the bus business, but no one would listen to him. All reserved opinion until they saw how the Blackwood Brothers' bus worked out.

One day, J. D. chanced upon an old friend, country singer Hawkshaw Hawkins, with whom the Sunshine Boys had sung on the WWVA Jamboree in Wheeling, West Virginia. Hawkshaw saw J. D. with the Blackwood Brothers' bus, and went through it. Before he left, J. D. talked Hawkshaw into getting a bus. He bought an airport bus and had it customized, and became the first country singer to venture out in a custom bus.

Less than eight years later, on March 5, 1963, Hawkshaw died in an airplane crash in Camden, Tennessee, along with Patsy Cline, Cowboy Copas, and Randy Hughes.

J. D. tried to talk the Statesmen into buying a bus, but they refused. Every conversation deteriorated into a kidding session.

"They made so much fun of me," J. D. said, "that I was determined to put them in a bus."

One night when the Blackwood Brothers and Statesmen sang in Little Rock and were scheduled to sing in Fort Worth the next night, J. D. took Jake Hess of the Statesmen aboard the Blackwood Brothers' bus, ostensibly to talk to him about "something important."

But when the bus got underway, J. D. said, "Okay, Jake, I don't want to talk. Get in my chair and go to sleep." Jake protested, fussing about being tricked, but the bus was well on its way; so he sat down and soon went to sleep. He slept all the way to Fort Worth, and when he woke up, he jumped out of the chair and said, "We're gonna get a bus! Let's go see Hovie."

That afternoon, J. D. made a deal with Greyhound in Dallas for two identical Silversides. He undertook the job of fixing them up for quartet travel.

He also sold the old Aerocoach to the Rebels Quartet in Tampa. London Parris, who sang bass for the Rebels, remembers the purchase.

He said, "J. D. said to me in that low, rumbling voice 'Now, Sarge, when that little red light comes on, it may need a little oil.' Sure enough, when the light came on, it needed a little oil. There wasn't a drop left in it. That bus was an oil-drinker."

But it served its purpose. It's air-conditioning unit always worked well—but some other parts didn't.

The first three months the Blackwood Brothers rode that first old Aerocoach, their repair bill was $3,300.

"We just can't afford that," James said. "We can't afford a bus."

"Oh, yes, we can afford a bus," J. D. said, and he quickly took corrective action: He fired Buddy Darvis.

"Buddy," J. D. told him, "you're the best bus driver we've ever had, but we just can't afford you." Actually, J. D. thought Darvis was a rough driver and that many of the repair bills could have been avoided with more skilled handling of the wheel. J. D. paid Darvis too weeks salary and let him go.

When the Blackwood Brothers started to the television station the next day to do their show, J. D. sat at the bus's wheel.

"We don't have a bus driver," he announced.

"What do you mean?" James asked. "What are we going to do?"

"I'm going to drive," J. D. said.

"Can you drive a bus?" James asked.

"Never have," J. D. said, "but I drove a semi-truck. I ought to be able to drive this."

"Let me out," Bill Shaw said. "I'm not riding with you."

"Then you'll have to hitch-hike," J. D. said, "because I am going to drive the bus."

Riding proved more attractive than walking, and for the next six months J. D. drove the bus to all engagements, and the repair bill came to $18.

Then he hired Bundy Brewster, who drove the Blackwood Brothers' bus for the next fourteen years.

J. D. accidentally discovered why the beds didn't work in that first bus. He took the mattresses off the old bus and threw them on the floor of the new bus. When the Blackwood Brothers slept on them that night, they slept like babies. The bus's springs were enough for the beds. When J. D. put the mattresses *and* bedsprings in the old bus, the springs created too much spring and flung the occupants out of bed. So J. D. built simple bunks in the new buses with three-quarter-inch plywood bottoms and six-inch airfoam mattresses. He hung curtains on each bunk to give its occupant privacy, and the beds were like Pullman berths on a train.

Next thing he knew, everybody in music—from gospel to country to rock to Broadway—rode customized buses.

"I always thought the bus would be the most dependable transportation of all for entertainment groups," J. D. said. "When you fly, you leave later. If we were flying to Detroit to perform tonight, we would leave Nashville at three or four o'clock in the afternoon, and if bad weather set in we would have to try to get on through because we're under contract. So we take a chance we don't like to take.

"But if we're in a bus," he said, "we're already on the way. If the bus happens to break down, we can rent a car and still make our date. And when we encounter bad weather, we don't have to stop; we just drive on through it. It can be clear in Nashville and storming like crazy in Detroit, and dangerous for flying. So the bus is the best form of travel we could have—unless we went back to the horse and buggy like Brock Speer used to travel."

Sometimes great ideas are born of necessity—or accident. The Speer Family was gospel music's first group to use two microphones on stage, putting two singers on each mike. J. D. was the first to use four—one for each singer.

"That was after I took over the Stamps Quartet in 1965," J. D. said. "I had Jimmy Blackwood in the quartet, and he hadn't learned to sing. He's a good singer now, but he couldn't sing a lick then. Mostly we could cover up for him, but sometimes we came to a part in a song on which his voice stood out like a sore thumb. The only solution I could think of was to use four mikes, and when we came to one of those parts, I could just reach over and cut his mike off."

Actually, moving Jimmy Blackwood to the Stamps Quartet was one of the reasons J. D. moved from the Blackwood Brothers to the Stamps. James Blackwood and J. D. bought the Stamps Quartet Music Company from Frank Stamps in 1964 and inherited the Stamps Quartet. The Little Blackwood Brothers broke up about that time and James said he wanted Jimmy to sing with the Stamps.

"The only way I'm gonna agree with that," J. D. said, "is if I move over there and run the Stamps. If you want to do it that way, all right."

James agreed. J. D. went to the Stamps Quartet and Big John Hall came from the Stamps to sing bass for the Blackwood Brothers. After four or five years, Jimmy Blackwood got the hang of singing and soon moved over to take a spot with the Blackwood Brothers.

"So using four microphones was a necessity for us," J. D. said, "not a luxury. I didn't have any idea we could do with them what we do today. You can balance a quartet perfectly using four mikes. We discovered that by accident."

The National Quartet Convention was J. D.'s baby. He had thought for years about starting a convention for quartets based on the old campmeetings he attended as a boy in Wimauma, Florida.

"You could go to campmeeting," J. D. said, "and see people you hadn't seen all year—all the big preachers, and a lot of good singers like the Rangers Quartet, the Stamps Quartet, and the Church of God Bible School Quartet, which later became the Homeland Harmony. I thought if we had a convention for quartets, folks could come there and see all the quartets, and those of us who seldom got to see each other would have two or three days to renew acquaintances."

That was the idea J. D. had tried to sell the Sunshine Boys, but they wouldn't go for it. Then he braced Wally Fowler, who considered it, but apparently thought it was too much a gamble to risk the money it would involve. After he went with the Blackwood Brothers, as soon as he was satisfied they were in the bus business for keeps, J. D. turned his attention to that big convention.

He sold James on the idea and the Blackwood Brothers underwrote the convention's expense. When they were discussing the idea, they thought of promoting several state conventions at which professional quartets would sing, and nonprofessional groups would compete. All the professional groups and the nonprofessional contest winners from each convention would then come to a yearly meeting where the amateur groups would compete for a huge national prize.

"We also talked to different groups who thought it was a good idea," James Blackwood said, "but we didn't get any help on backing it financially, so we just took it on ourselves."

They called it the National Quartet Convention, and the first two were held in Memphis, home of the Blackwood Brothers, in 1956 and 1957.

"We chose Memphis," J. D. said, "because that's where we lived and it seemed as central a point as any other. Too, it had good facilities."

The first two conventions were successes. The 1958 convention was moved to Birmingham and the 1959 convention to Atlanta. The thought was that by moving the convention around, more people from various areas would be able to attend. But in Birmingham attendance dropped off, and in Atlanta it was even worse. So the 1960 convention went back to Memphis and from that time the convention enjoyed steady growth.

After a few years, J. D. became sole operator of the convention— and he ran it with an iron hand. He made it a true quartet convention, and only quartets could sing on the program. He turned down Bill Gaither, the Rambos, and other outstanding groups and acts that were not quartets.

The convention also grew to such proportions that J. D. eliminated all amateur and part-time groups.

It was about that time that Ace Richman and the Sunshine Boys came to the convention. They were no longer singing full time because Ace had had back surgery and could no longer travel like he once had, and all the guys were content with part-time singing.

Ace went to J. D. as soon as they got to Memphis, and asked when the Sunshine Boys were scheduled to sing.

"Gee, I'm sorry Ace, old buddy, but you can't sing," J. D. said. "I'd put you on in a minute, but if I did every part-time group in the country would be down my throat."

"Part-time!" Ace snorted. "Why, you lame-brained idiot, you know we can sing as good as anybody you'll have on that stage."

"I'm not questioning that," J. D. said, and round and round they went. As usual, J. D. won—temporarily.

Ace stomped off in disgust.

About ten o'clock that night, when the house was fullest, and the show at its prime—the lights suddenly went off.

Not just the stage lights went out, but every light in the house, including even those small lights imbedded in the stairways to illuminate footing when the house lights are down.

The darkness was stygian.

Everyone who knew anything about lighting, including J. D.,

rushed around, tripping over things, trying to locate the problem. After five minutes, someone found the box and discovered the master switch had been pulled.

"Huh oh!" J. D. exclaimed, and slammed the switch home.

The lights flashed back on, and there on stage, poised at the microphones, stood Ace Richman with a rakish grin on his face and the Sunshine Boys. Eddie Wallace's fingers were poised above the keyboard.

"Good evening, ladies and gentlemen," Ace said, and Eddie played a run for background. "We are the Sunshine Boys, and we're here to entertain you. . . ."

Anybody else would have had a hissy, but J. D. Sumner's craggy face crinkled into a smile of admiration.

"That old so-and-so," he said, and he sat down to listen.

The convention remained in Memphis until J. D. moved the Stamps Quartet to Nashville in 1971. He took the convention with him because Nashville had bigger facilities.

Soon, however, the convention became too big for one man to run, and J. D. had to decide between singing and operating the convention. He chose singing, and people from several other quartets bought the convention and operate it today.

From the beginning, the National Quartet Convention was the ultimate for most quartets in the business.

"It was the end of the world," said Eldridge Fox, whose Kingsmen Quartet was just beginning to sing the first few years of the convention. "It was the epitome of all gospel music. For groups like us who were just getting into the business, the aura of all that talent was overwhelming."

Back then, everything happened at the convention. The early conventions were before talent agencies, before most record labels. Promoters like W. B. Nowlin and Lloyd Orrell booked their entire year there.

"They never had to spend a nickel on the phone," Eldridge said. "They just came to the convention and set up a room and contacted every group they wanted to use and arranged dates."

Orrell carried a legal pad on which he wrote down his dates and places, and under each date he wrote the names of the groups he booked. No questions asked; no contracts signed. He booked them on their word; he recorded the agreements in his book; and the quartets put the agreements in their date books.

That was that. On the given date, the quartets showed up. Business was simple in those days; many men ran quartets out of their shirt pockets.

"The quartet convention," Eldridge Fox said unequivocally, "was the greatest thing that ever happened in our business. The amount of togetherness it generated among the groups had never before been equalled, and never has since."

The convention opened doors for a lot of groups, doors that might otherwise never have been opened.

"It made you belong," Eldridge continued. "Once the convention was so big and so powerful that singing on the quartet convention one time was just like singing one time on the Grand Ole Opry. It carried the same amount of prestige. You got better bookings, more money for your dates, record labels could easily become interested in you there. You had a cross section of people from all across the country, and if Marvin Norcross was there and you hit a home run on stage, that opened the door. Marvin would sit down and talk to you."

For years, Marvin Norcross headed Canaan Records and was a powerful man in gospel music. He had so many friends in the far-flung industry that a word from him would indeed open almost any door.

The quartet barrier finally came down and all gospel groups— trios, duets, whatever—were allowed to sing. Some groups were shoved into the big time by appearing on the convention—like the Rambos, the Happy Goodman Family, and a few others who got their first big breaks at the convention. They made big hits and were suddenly flooded with bookings.

The first recording company set up strictly for Southern gospel music was Skylite Recording Company. The idea for the company came from J. D. Sumner and Jake Hess.

J. D. wrote more than seven hundred gospel songs, most of them written when he was singing with the Blackwood Brothers. He had a publishing company called Gospel Quartet Music Company. Jake started a publishing company called Faith Music Company. Before that, quartets were not in the publishing business; but once they got going, Jake bought the Henson Publishing Company, and James and J. D. bought the Stamps Quartet Music Company.

The only record labels then were the major labels—RCA Victor, Decca, Columbia—and a lot of quartets couldn't get on a label. J. D. and Jake came up with the idea of starting a recording company that would record only the songs they had written and the others they held in their publishing companies.

So the Skylite Recording Company was born, and it did a land-office business from the start. The Harvesters, Speer Family, the Rangers, Blue Ridge, Oak Ridge all signed with Skylite. So did others. Business boomed.

The question naturally arose as to the legality of the Blackwood Brothers and Statesmen recording on the Skylite label. The Blackwoods were under contract to RCA Victor, and Victor told them that they could record on Skylite anything in the public domain that they had not recorded for RCA. The songs they recorded for Skylite, then, all had to be old songs in the public domain, nothing new. So both the Blackwood Brothers and Statesmen recorded some on Skylite while maintaining their major labels, too.

The second gospel music recording company was Heartwarming, and the third was Canaan. Canaan is still going; so is Heartwarming, but it's under the RiverSong label now. And Skylite is still recording gospel groups. Joel Gentry bought the company and still runs it. There are many other gospel recording companies in the business today.

Thinking back to his original publishing company, the Gospel Quartet Music Company, J. D. said, "I organized the company because I was a songwriter, and I was forced to either publish my own songs or let somebody else publish them."

Necessity had struck again!

CHAPTER EIGHTEEN

The Recording Business

World War II, with its rationing of gasoline and ban on civilian use of certain materials needed for the military, shut down much of the professional gospel singing industry. Many quartets disbanded and their members went into the armed forces of the United States for the duration of the war.

Those who loved quartet singing had to be satisfied with what they heard in their own churches, or else they simply hungered for it. Those old 78s made by the Vaughan and Stamps quartets, the Chuck Wagon Gang, and other quartets in the 1930s became precious; and most were played over and over on the home Victrola until they wore out. Few of them survive today.

When the war came to an end in 1945, the record industry began to flourish immediately. Gospel quartets gathered in makeshift studios with recording machines and cranked out as many songs as they could afford to record. Almost anywhere would do for a studio. The Hopper Brothers and Connie cut their first recording in a carport.

There was no question but that the Blackwood Brothers were the immediate postwar champions of the record-selling business. From the end of the war, when the Blackwood Brothers regrouped in Shenandoah, Iowa, they sold hundreds of thousands of recordings.

Roy Blackwood, at the age of forty-five, still sang tenor for the quartet. James sang the lead. He had spent the war in San Diego, working in the aircraft industry and singing on weekends. R. W. came back from service to sing baritone, and the bass singer was a Texan named Don Smith, who had sung in the 1930s for some of the Stamps quartets. Doyle Blackwood, the quartet's bass until the war, had returned to Mississippi in poor health. Hilton Griswold was the Blackwood Brothers' pianist. James had met Don Smith in California during the war, and the two sang together some on the West Coast.

Terry Moss, program director at Radio Station KMA in Shenandoah, owned a recording machine that cut a "mother" recording, and from that a "master" recording was made. The master was used to stamp the records.

Recording tape did not exist at that time. Any portable recording was done on a wire recorder, and the quality was not good enough for professional recordings. Neither was the quality of some of the mothers the quartets cranked out, but that was rather the fault of the quartet and not the recording.

Those who sang the gospel in 1946 and made the 78 rpm recordings would have marveled at the way recordings were made four decades later. But we tend to make do with what we have, and quartets were thankful for any opportunity to cut their singing voices on records.

Terry Moss set up his recording machine in the small control room off the main studio of KMA. Through a window he could see into the studio, and in that way he controlled things as well as he could during the recording sessions.

The Blackwood Brothers sang into a microphone in the studio, and Moss twisted his dials and watched his gauges in the control room.

"We made all decisions," James Blackwood said. "We were our own producers and everything else. We just hired Terry to record for us with his machine. We paid him one hundred dollars for every master he made for us, and that included the master, the mother, and the stampers. We sent these to a record-pressing plant where the records were pressed. The plant even made the labels and shipped the finished product to us.

"As I remember," James added, "we paid about thirty-five cents each for the records and sold them for a dollar apiece."

Every time they released a recording, the Blackwood Brothers sold them in bulk. Because of advertising on the radio, they would already have large orders awaiting the release of a record.

The Blackwood Brothers' label was black and white, with the words "Blackwood Bros. Quartet, Shenandoah, Iowa" printed above a picture of the quartet.

The Rangers recorded on their own label, called "Rangers Record of the Month." But even though the Rangers were the widest-ranging quartet, and perhaps the most popular and best-known in those immediate postwar years, even they didn't sell records like the Blackwood Brothers.

James Blackwood was a marketing genius. He knew how to control costs and sell records.

Sometimes quartets had to resort to devious means to sell its records. Once, the Blackwood Brothers, J. D. Sumner and the Stamps Quartet, and the Sego Brothers and Naomi played the Illinois State Fair together, and the fair manager forbade them to plug records from the stage.

"I do not want anyone saying a word about records," the manager said. "In no way can you make an announcement that you have records for sale."

They took the man at his word. No one *said* a word about records, but James Sego made up a song which included a good plug for his records and sang it at each performance.

The song was funny; the fair manager thought it hilarious. He laughed so hard that he requested James sing the song each night.

Every time the Blackwoods brought out a record, in a year's time it would sell five to ten thousand copies, and each year the quartet released fifteen to twenty records. When they had a recording session, they recorded up to a dozen songs, enough for a half-dozen records.

Later, when the Blackwood Brothers recorded for RCA Victor, that company pressed many more copies of each record. A good seller like "Keys to the Kingdom" sold forty to fifty thousand copies. The Blackwoods drew a six percent royalty on the wholesale price of the records, which amounted to good money.

When they recorded with Terry Moss on their own label, the Blackwoods rehearsed a song for a while, then cut it, and that was it. They went on to the next song. Later, with RCA Victor, they might cut a song over and over to get it exactly right, sometimes spending hours working on one song.

At Shenandoah, the Blackwoods advertised their records on the air, and orders poured in. They shipped records all over the country.

After Lyles joined the Blackwood Brothers, they began recording on the White Church label, owned by two Kansas City businessmen. White Church also recorded the Homeland Harmony Quartet with Connor Hall, Lee Roy Abernathy, Shorty Bradford, James McCoy, and

A. D. Soward. James Blackwood advertised the Blackwood Brothers' White Church records in various religious publications like *Sunday School Times* and *Christian Herald,* and found many new customers there.

At the same time, the Blackwood Brothers continued to record on their own label.

By 1950 the Blackwood Brothers wanted to return to the South. They chose Memphis as an alighting place and signed a contract to sing over Radio Station WMPS. The quartet that moved to Memphis had Alden Toney singing tenor, James and R. W. and Bill Lyles. Griswold stayed in Iowa and James hired Jackie Marshall to play the piano.

James signed a contract with RCA Victor in 1951. It was a five-year, non-exclusive contract that contained a provision allowing the Blackwood Brothers to continue to record on their own label as long as they didn't record the same songs they cut for RCA.

RCA assigned its chief A&R man, Steve Sholes, to produce the Blackwood records. Sholes had a good ear and a particular mind. He insisted that the quartet re-cut a song if he heard the slightest flaw. "Let's get it right," he would say.

Late in 1951 the Blackwoods cut their first album for RCA Victor. This was a ten-inch album, cut before the twelve-inch albums came along. Today, that ten-inch album is a valuable collector's item. It was recorded upstairs in a room at the old Fox Theater in Atlanta.

The Blackwoods recorded most of their songs in little studios around Nashville, and at one session backed Hank Snow singing "Invisible Hands" and "God's Lighting Little Candles." That was also in 1951, the same year in which the Blackwoods recorded "Keys to the Kingdom," a big winner for RCA. It was recorded in a small Nashville studio, before RCA built its own studios there.

Steve Sholes was a sharp man. He was the one who signed Elvis Presley after buying Sun Records' contract. He recorded Elvis. Steve Sholes loved gospel and country music. He was one of those who signed the Billy Graham Team to record for RCA—George Beverly Shea, Paul Nicholson, Tedd Smith, and Cliff Barrows. Sholes also recorded some of Graham's crusade sermons for RCA.

The fastest recording session the Blackwood Brothers ever did for RCA Victor was for an album entitled "Stranger of Galilee." They cut twelve songs in three hours in the RCA studio in Nashville, and the album remains to this day one of the best the Blackwood Brothers ever made. The Blackwood Brothers sang with perfection.

"Many of the songs on that album we did in one take," James said. "We did it in RCA's old Studio B in which many stars like Elvis, Eddy Arnold, and Hank Snow were recorded."

Across the country, quartets made their own deals with record companies. The Bibletone label had many of the best quartets of the day, like the Homeland Harmony and the Harmoneers. The Sunshine Boys and Blue Ridge Quartet recorded on Decca, and the Statesmen on Capitol. Others made records on their own labels, but the problem there was distribution. Quartets had trouble distributing their own records; so the only place one could buy some of the quartet records was from the quartet itself.

James Blackwood opened a record shop in Memphis, selling Blackwood Brothers records on both their own and the RCA labels. He furnished those on his own label himself, but he had to buy his own RCA records from a distributor and pay the full wholesale price.

When the Blackwood contract with RCA Victor was up in 1956, Sholes wanted to sign the quartet to another five-year contract. He said this contract would have to be exclusive, that the RCA people in New York would have it no other way.

James reasoned it out. "Steve," he said, "we can't afford to pay what we're having to pay the distributor. If there is some way we can get a better price on our RCA records, I'll sign an exclusive."

Sholes mulled that over, then said, "What if I set you up as a distributor for RCA religious products? Then you can get them at distributor price direct from the factory.

"Fine," James said, "then I'll sign."

Sholes kept his word. He set James up as a distributor of all RCA religious products; so James distributed all the early Billy Graham, Paul Nicholson, Tedd Smith, Bev Shea records to Bible book stores across the country.

"I was the first all-religious distributor in the United States," James said. "I had no restrictions on territory. I shipped records all over the United States. This was before Word, before Benson, before Zondervan had records. But as each company came on the scene, I took on their products to distribute, and until 1979 I had a wholesale distributorship for records, tapes, printed music, choir books, cantatas, everything."

He finally gave up the business because it became too competitive.

"In the early beginnings of these companies," he said, "they were glad to have distributors handling their products, but as they got larger and larger they started selling directly to stores. They could sell to stores at less cost than I could. All I had to offer was service. So this gradually squeezed me out of business, and I closed up shop."

Each quartet had its own recording story to tell, few of them as elaborate as that one, because James Blackwood was the greatest record-seller of the day.

Sometimes that fact created a bit of tension in the Statesmen-Blackwood Brothers team.

"There was a lot of competition between the Statesmen and Blackwoods," said Eldridge Fox, who worked for the Statesmen in the early 1950s. "I don't care if they were a team, they were still in competition in certain areas."

One of those areas was selling records.

"The Statesmen were always my heroes," Eldridge said, "but they never could sell records like the Blackwood Brothers. The Blackwoods would burn 'em; I mean, just eat 'em up! The Blackwoods could sell records better than any quartet I ever saw in those early days. I saw the Statesmen sit in meetings and talk about selling records. They'd say, 'What *are* we going to do?' And it never changed. The Blackwoods would kill them every night."

Rex Nelon remembers when James Blackwood's distributorship was also a thorn in the side of the team.

The Statesmen had to buy products from James, and occasionally singers from other groups stirred up trouble within the team. Rex once saw Doy Ott of the Statesmen buying Bibles from Cecil Blackwood at a singing in Chicago. Maneuvering to Doy, Rex casually said, "Say, Doy, do you know what Cecil pays for these Bibles?"

"No," Doy said, and when Rex told him, the figure was less than what Doy paid Cecil for them wholesale.

Doy jumped Cecil that night and after they went round and round, Cecil came to Rex. "Boy, do you know what you've done?" he asked.

"No," Rex said. "What?"

Cecil said, "You've just about torn up the team."

"Hallelujah!" Rex shouted.

"Nothing would have suited me better," Rex said years later. "That team wasn't very good for the rest of us."

CHAPTER NINETEEN

The
Songwriters

Gospel singing has always been blessed with good songwriters. There was a saying in World War II that a convoy was no faster than its slowest ship; by something of the same token, quartet singing can never be better than its songwriters.

More groups today have their own built-in songwriters, quartet members who write primarily for their own quartets; in bygone days there were more writers who wrote for all because they wrote for publishing houses. Instead of selling a song to a group, writers in the days of Stamps and Vaughan and Hartford and Tennessee sold songs to the publishing houses, and quartets got them from the songbooks.

However they get them, most quartets find themselves, even today when there are hundreds of professional groups singing, with sufficient material. On occasion, a quartet will come up with a lack of material—the Inspirations have complained of it on occasion, but for the most part, the groups that sing generalized songs have plenty of material available.

Most of the old-timers in quartet singing today—George Younce, Glen Payne, J. D. Sumner, James Blackwood, Les Beasley, Glen Allred, and so on—grew up singing such songs as James Cleveland Moore's "Where We'll Never Grow Old" (1914); Emmett S. Dean's "Just Over In The Glory Land" (1906); Homer Morris's "Won't It Be Wonderful There"; M. D. McWhorter's "Just A Little While To Stay Here"; "In The Sweet Bye And Bye" (1935) by W. S. Tidwell; "I Feel Like Traveling On," by James D. Vaughan; and that all-time favorite

"If I Could Hear My Mother Pray Again," written in 1922 by John W. Vaughan.

Men like that were prolific writers, but even in that age some were more prolific than others. Curtis Taylor, for instance, born in 1879, wrote more than 3,800 songs. He survived the sinking of the Titanic and lived to become the writer of beautiful love songs in New York City. Charlie D. Tillman, who penned "Life's Railway to Heaven," was the author of thousands of songs.

Some songs failed to gain popularity with the public, as every songwriter knows, and there are good reasons why some don't. "In The Closet With Jesus," by Charles Q. Counts, never quite made it. Neither did the first song J. D. Sumner wrote, "Working In The Sawmill For Jesus." Some wrote specialty songs that didn't really stand a chance, like James V. Reid's "Over The Top For Jesus," a World War I song written at the height of the war in 1917.

By and large, gospel songwriters have adherred to the accepted subject matter—writing about salvation, a better day, things to make people feel better, death, the Great Beyond, and walking in step with Jesus.

Among the more popular songs ever written for the gospel field were "Give The World A Smile," which M. L. Yandell and Otis Deaton fashioned in 1925; Albert E. Brumley's "I'll Fly Away" of 1932; Brantley C. George's "Hide Me, Rock of Ages," perhaps the most recorded song ever written; and Lee Roy Abernathy's "Gospel Boogie," which became "A Wonderful Time Up There" when folks objected to the word "boogie." Pat Boone's recording of it sold three million records.

Hundreds of songwriters worked in the teens and twenties, and especially during the depressed thirties.

The music of the 1940s began to change, not because of World War II, but because songwriters began to figure ways of making their songs more tuneful. Some of the greatest gospel songs—for quartets and small mixed groups—came out of the late 1940s and 1950s.

The year 1948 was a good one, for example. Marvin P. Dalton wrote a song entitled "Oh, What A Savior" that year, and Vep Ellis followed with "I'm Free Again," and then Bob Prather came along with "Roll On, Jordan." Any quartet that sang those three songs on any program was an immediate hit.

Songwriters got away from a lot of the norms set in the 1920s and 1930s, and distinctive writing styles began to be recognized. Folks could usually tell the songs of Albert E. Brumley, Vep Ellis, Mosie Lister, Lee Roy Abernathy, and some others of that age, because these men had different styles of writing.

Several writers of that era wrote more than five hundred songs each.

Albert E. Brumley was one of those. His songs were so popular that both the Chuck Wagon Gang and the Statesmen Quartet recorded albums of Brumley songs.

He did not confine his songwriting talents to gospel, but also wrote of other things. Besides gospel groups, his songs were recorded by Red Foley, Jim Reeves, Elvis Presley, the Louvin Brothers, Roy Acuff, Webb Pierce, and others in the country and pop fields.

Born in Indian Territory, at Spiro, now Oklahoma, October 29, 1905, Albert learned to play an old-fashioned organ; and his musical talents blossomed early. At nineteen, he attended the old Hartford Musical Institute at Hartford, Arkansas, and sang with one of the early Hartford Quartets.

In 1931, when Brumley married Goldie Edith Schell, he had begun writing songs mostly for his and his family's pleasure. Goldie encouraged him to publish some of his songs; so he mailed one entitled "I'll Fly Away" to the Hartford Music Company. The song was published in the Hartford book, *The Wonderful Message*, and the company asked for more songs.

Through the years, Brumley wrote many classics that were published by Hartford, Stamps-Baxter, the Stamps Quartet Music Company, and others. All the quartets sang Brumley's songs and looked for more.

He wrote "Jesus Hold My Hand," "I'll Meet You In The Morning," "Turn Your Radio On," "Did You Ever Go Sailing?" "He Set Me Free," "The Sweetest Song I know," "Go Right Out," "Heaven's Radio Station Is On The Air," "Twill Be Glory There For Me," "Little Pine Log Cabin," "Bound For That City," "If We Never Meet Again," "God's Gentle People," and a long list of others. He turned out hit song after hit song. His songs seemed to say just a little more than those of some of the other writers, or perhaps it was simply that he said it differently.

Albert Brumley wound up owning the Hartford Music Company.

Vep Ellis was of slightly later vintage than Brumley. He was born March 11, 1917, in Oneonta, Alabama, and christened Vesphew Benton Ellis. Unlike Brumley, whose songwriting and music teaching were his livelihood, Vep Ellis was a preacher. He was a pastor, evangelist, songwriter, and soloist.

He began writing songs about ten years later than Brumley, but when quartets began to receive Vep's contributions, they waited breathlessly for his next ones. He never disappointed them. His writing was always of the finest quality.

Although he considered his preaching ministry to be his primary function, Vep Ellis still wrote more than five hundred songs and hymns. He was published through the Lillenas Publishing Company and the Tennessee Music and Printing Company.

As a singer, he recorded five long-play albums and a large number of 78s and 45s; and he also published several songbooks filled with his songs.

One of his songs, "Heaven's Joy Awaits," published in 1942, became one of the Statesmen Quartet's early hits. The Harmoneers recorded his "There Is A Change," and found it to be a hit. The Statesmen did "When I Got Saved," and scored big. Then everyone recorded "I'm Free Again" when it came out in 1948, and the world loved it.

He also wrote "My God Can Do Anything," "The Love of God," "Let Me Touch Him," "Do You Know My Jesus?" "Heavenly Love," and "Over The Moon." "At The End Of The Trail" was a gospel hit song of the year.

"I met Vep Ellis in the forties," Lee Roy Abernathy said. "That's when he was writing great songs. He was a great preacher, but his songs and his singing were especially outstanding."

When Ellis wrote "Over The Moon," he tried to give it to Lee Roy, apparently thinking that it was a different song from those he wrote normally.

"He felt backward about it," Lee Roy said. "He thought someone might take offense at it. But he wanted people to sing it; so he tried to give it to me. I told him I would feel bad about taking it, and that he would feel bad about giving it to me when it became a hit. He finally published it, and it was an immediate hit. What a beautiful song! One of the prettiest he ever wrote."

Ellis and Abernathy did collaborate on one song, "I'm Riding The Range For Jesus," which the Harmoneers rode to hit status.

"Vep whistled the song for me," Lee Roy said, "and he could even whistle pretty. I was publishing sheet music and needed enough of a song to fill two pages. He only had four parts written; so I bought the song from him and wrote a fifth part to it—the part that pianist Charles Key sang for the Harmoneers." Wherever the Harmoneers went, that song was one of the requests they received.

Vep was a minister for forty-nine years in the Church of God. He had amazing energy, and was seldom satisfied doing nothing. He was associated with Evangelist Oral Roberts for six years, working under Oral's big tent as music director and soloist.

His great smile and mellow voice had a way of charming people, and his ministry, whether in word or song, was always successful.

Lee Roy himself wrote many great songs during the 1940s and 1950s. He wrote some of the classics of that period, and his songs were always recognizable. Lee Roy had a touch that made music and words mesh in his mind.

But he also had a knack for the unusual, and he loved to seize upon current events and write about them. Two of those songs that stand out in the memories of those who followed gospel singing in the 1940s were "The Burning of the Wynecoff Hotel" in 1946, and "Television," written a couple of years later when television was becoming big in America.

The Wynecoff Hotel burned in Atlanta on the night of December 7, 1946, and 119 people lost their lives. Lee Roy wrote about the tragedy so poignantly that those who heard the song could almost hear the screams of the victims. Lee Roy even had an ambulance siren in the Homeland Harmony Quartet's recording of the song.

In "Television," the medium was so new that folks still thought of it as radio with pictures, and that's the idea that Lee Roy captured. It was really a tremendous song.

Many of the singers were good songwriters. J. D. Sumner was among the best. He wrote more than seven hundred songs, and some are still often heard. J. D. had a drive that many singers did not have. Even though he sang full time with the Blackwood Brothers, he still had time to invent the customized bus and write songs one after the other. All he required sometimes was a word from James Blackwood. James would say, "I think we need a new song about the Jordan River," and a half-hour later J. D. would have written four or five new songs about the Jordan.

"Big Chief" Jim Wetherington was a talented songwriter. The Statesmen recorded a lot of his songs, and so did other quartets.

Some of the songwriters in gospel music were talented enough to write country and popular songs, and some few writers did, but it is a tribute to the type of music quartets sing that so many of the most talented writers held their talents to gospel music, especially when some of them could have made fortunes writing something else.

And it was also worth noting that just when gospel music needed good, solid songwriters, they suddenly appeared on the scene, ready to work.

That speaks for itself.

CHAPTER TWENTY

Stalwart Men

At the end of World War II, singers began coming back from military service, and the big quartets geared themselves up for whatever lay ahead. That's the way it always was in the early days. Men who had music in their voices and wanted to sing more than they wanted to eat regularly, did so on a one-day-at-a-time basis, always hoping for the big break that would put them into better times.

Jack Pittman, who has now been with the Palmetto State Quartet in Greenville, South Carolina, for more than forty years, was ready for the good years that followed a victorious war effort. He had attended the Vaughan School of Music in Lawrenceburg, Tennessee, in 1941 and 1942, and wanted to sing. He had grown up with Hovie Lister in Greenville and sought nothing more than a good life of singing. He sang with the Vaughan Quartet at the 1945 National Singing Convention in Charleston, West Virginia, and Frank Stamps offered him a job singing for the Stamps Quartet Music Company. Frank was in the process of breaking his ties with J. R. Baxter, Jr., and the Stamps-Baxter Music Company.

Frank pulled a hundred-dollar bill out of his pocket and offered it to Jack if he would join the Stamps Quartet Music Company. That was the first hundred-dollar bill Jack Pittman had ever seen. He took the bill and the job.

That's the way things worked back then.

Jack's first assignment for Frank Stamps was in West Texas to sing first tenor for the Great Plains Stamps Quartet, but after a short while

Frank Stamps pulled him back to Dallas, then sent him to Raleigh to sing with Carl Raines and Clarence Turbyfill in the Lone Star Quartet. But after a short time there, Raines, Turbyfill, and Pittman moved to Winston-Salem and organized the Stamps-Carl Raines All-Star Quartet on Radio Station WSJS. They were sponsored by Bicks Bakery.

Pittman moved once again, to Little Rock, Arkansas, to sing with the Stamps Melody Boys, and remained there until he went into military service in 1950. When he came out in 1952, he sang with Cat Freeman and Aycel Soward in the Church of God Quartet in Greenville, but before the year ended Cat left to rejoin the Statesmen and the Church of God Quartet broke up. That's when Pittman went with the Palmetto State Quartet, where he has remained all these years.

For years the Palmetto State was made up of Claude Hunter singing first tenor—and a fine one he was—Jack Bagwell on the lead, Jack Pittman singing baritone, and Ken Turner on the bass. Jamie Dill played piano for more than forty years.

Jack Pittman went into business in Greenville, organizing Pittman Textile Machinery Company, which bought up shut-down textile mills and re-sold the textile machinery all over the world. He shipped machinery into Africa, Mexico, Honduras, and many other places and sent crews to set it up.

He became a wealthy man, but he never forgot his buddies in the gospel singing world, and in 1988 Pittman footed the bill—more than $70,000—to bring back all the old-timers he could locate for a reunion in Greenville. More than six thousand people turned out to hear them sing.

Pittman paid for the old-timers' airplane tickets, put them up in the Hyatt-Regency Hotel, fed them, and showed them a genuine good time.

Charlie Waller did the legwork and organizational chores for Pittman and produced some outstanding video work on the Grand Ole Gospel Reunion.

The convention was so popular that Pittman and Waller made it an annual thing, reuniting such groups as the Sunshine Boys, the old Blackwood Brothers, the Rebels, the original Dixie Echoes, the Rangers Trio, the Blue Ridge Quartet, the Statesmen, and even the Lee Roy Abernathy Quartet to the delight of the people. This convention gives the public, especially the younger segments, a glimpse of what fun and harmony gospel singing was in the early days. It is held the second Saturday in August.

* * *

Two of the big quartets that geared up for the post-war boom were the Harmoneers of Knoxville, Tennessee, and the Homeland Harmony of Atlanta, Georgia.

Fred C. Maples was a handsome man with a fine voice. He was one of the real pioneers of quartet singing. Having grown up in Cleveland, Tennessee, in the center of quartet country, he first sang with the Cleveland Quartet in 1932, then with some other groups, including the early Homeland Harmony Quartet and some of the Blackwood family of Mississippi.

In 1940 he organized the Harmoneers, his own quartet. They weathered the war, singing whenever they could, when they could scrape up enough gas-rationing stamps to get them to a place to sing.

When the war ended, Maples was itching to broaden the horizon of the Harmoneers. He did it by hiring Bobby Strickland to sing first tenor, Erman Slater to sing baritone, and Seals Hilton, who became known as "Low Note," to sing bass. All three were from Sand Mountain, Alabama. Charles Key played the Harmoneers' piano.

The Harmoneers made famous such gospel songs as "Way Out Yonder," the great Mosie Lister song; "When He Calls I'll Fly Away," "There Is A Change," "I'm Winging My Way Back Home," and "Riding The Range For Jesus."

Soon after the war's end, this quartet was in great demand. The Harmoneers were headline singers. Promoters could build programs around them. And any promoter who contracted the Harmoneers and the Homeland Harmony for the same night had a winner.

After the war, the Homeland Harmony regrouped with Connor B. Hall as its leader. Connor got Hovie Lister to play piano and Big Jim Waits to sing bass. That was the start of the Homeland Harmony Quartet that so many people came to know and love.

The quartet affiliated with the Chattanooga Medicine Company, which sponsored it on a network of fifty-five radio stations. That exposure brought in hundreds of requests for concert dates, and the Homeland Harmony was off and running.

The Homeland Harmony developed a style all its own. On stage, it had a different sound, mostly because of its high harmony and its selection of songs. Many of its songs were fast, tinkling songs like "Bells of Joy Keep Ringing," some of which can be attributed to the fact that Connor hired Wally Varner to play piano, when Hovie left after a few months. Wally could play those fast, ringing little songs better than anyone else and with no appreciable effort. In fact, Wally wrote "Bells of Joy Keep Ringing."

Through the years, the Homeland Harmony Quartet sang with a harmony unsurpassed. With pure singing, it could entertain a crowd as well as any group. Most of this was due to Connor's fetish for perfection. He had such a super ear that he could detect the slightest variance from the proper key, and he was perhaps the best harmony first tenor who ever walked on stage.

The Homeland Harmony went through various personnel changes and came into the middle 1950s with Connor singing tenor, James McCoy and Wayne Groce singing the middle parts, and a string of men singing bass, including variously Johnny Atkinson, Jim Waits, Aycel Soward, and finally George Younce.

In 1955 Younce left because he was starving to death and Connor gave the bass job to Rex Nelon, a youngster from Asheville who was still wet behind the ears.

Connor made some other quick changes and wound up with himself singing tenor, Jim Cole of West Virginia singing lead, James McCoy singing baritone, Rex singing bass, and Jack Clark, also a West Virginian, playing great licks on the piano.

As soon as Rex joined the Homeland Harmony, Connor told him he was singing sharp.

"I don't believe it," Rex said. "Nobody has ever accused me of singing off pitch."

"Let's just record one and see," Connor said. They were rehearsing in a small recording studio. They recorded "I Am A Pilgrim," and when the song was played back Rex was so sharp he wanted to cry.

"Well, I didn't know," he said to Connor. "What do I do now?"

Connor showed him how to bring his singing back on pitch.

Connor Hall was a caring man who had little toughness about him. He was one who really believed what he sang. If a promoter wished not to pay him, Connor was easy pickings, Rex said; he adopted a Christian attitude toward all men and everything, and if a promoter said he couldn't pay him, Connor said, "That's all right. We'll make it up later."

He was honest as the day was long, and he was a worrier. If one of the guys was thirty minutes late to leave on tour, Connor became a nervous wreck.

Rex only saw Connor mad once in the two years he worked with him. The Homeland Harmony sang in the old Labor Union building for a union celebration in Atlanta.

"They had a piano that was so low," Rex said, "that I found it hard to even think that low."

They prepared to sing "He's A Personal Savior," a song that Connor had always done in the key of F, which pushed the bass down on a low C. At the time, Rex was struggling to reach a low C; so he got Connor to raise the song to G. Connor then had to struggle to hit his own notes.

When they got on that low piano in the union hall, Rex told Jack Clark to raise it again. Unfortunately, Clark couldn't play the song in the next highest key; so he went on to the key above that—a B flat.

"When I came in on the line 'For He's a friend . . .'" Rex said, "I was almost singing tenor, and the rest came in like three little mice playing on a window pane. When Connor had to sing his lead—'He's a personal savior . . . He's mine, I know . . . I love him so,' he had to drop it a notch and sounded like he was trying to sing bass."

Connor was boiling mad when the quartet came off stage. He began to chew Jack Clark.

"It wasn't my fault," Jack said.

"Whose fault was it?" Connor asked.

"Rex told me to raise it."

Connor glared at Rex. "Don't you ever raise another song without asking me," he snapped.

"He was so mad," Rex said later, "that he wouldn't speak to me for two days. Oh, he was hot! That was a *high* song."

Rex learned part of his stagemanship the hard way, much to the consternation of Connor Hall.

"The first or second night after I joined the Homeland Harmony," Rex said, "we went to Elkin, North Carolina, to sing. Jack Clark and Jim Cole were also new. We were on the program with the Harmoneers and Seals Hilton had already scared me to death just by being there.

"We were going to do a song entitled 'In My Father's House,' and we were supposed to do a verse and chorus and then Jim Cole was to do a solo verse. As Connor started introducing the song, Jim said he didn't know it well enough and he was going to take the mike to Jack Clark, who knew the song, and let Jack sing it. We only had two mikes; James McCoy and I shared a mike, and Jim and Connor shared the other one.

"Since I stood nearest the piano, Jim was going to take my mike and stick it over to Jack. About halfway through the first verse—we hadn't even started the chorus—Jim took my mike and pulled it about two feet over toward Jack, and I grabbed it and pulled it back. He pulled it toward him and I pulled it back toward me. Right in front of the audience, we wrestled over that mike and I said, 'We gotta do my chorus first!'

"By then the song was gone, we were gone, Connor was gone, and James McCoy was doubled over laughing. I lived at Connor's house at that time, and when we got back home, Connor's wife asked him how we did, and Connor said, 'Well . . . well . . .' and big tears welled up in his eyes. Our act was so bad, he cried. I guess he thought his singing career was ruined forever."

At that time, a typical Homeland Harmony program would consist of songs like "He's A Personal Savior," "Sing Your Blues Away," "Bells of Joy Keep Ringing," "He's Not Disappointed In Me," "Hide Me, Rock of Ages," and James McCoy would recite every book in the Bible in ten seconds. The Homeland Harmony had the first arrangement of Jim Hill's great song, "What A Day That Will Be." They sang "When We All Get Together," a special arrangement of "What A Friend We Have In Jesus," and James McCoy's big song, "Take A Little Time To Pray."

Most of their arrangements were written out on paper, and Harold Lane, who left the Homeland Harmony just before Rex came, did the arranging and mailed the songs to Connor.

Some groups just got together and started to sing and developed their special arrangements that way, but the Homeland Harmony left nothing to chance; their special arrangements were put on paper.

The Homeland Harmony never did any hard comedy routines on stage; they were more intent on singing. Connor wasn't a funny man. He was one of the greatest singers; his voice had a fine edge and not a trace of falsetto. Like Denver Crumpler's, Connor's voice rang like a clear bell, a true tenor. Connor appreciated a funny story, but there was little humor about him on stage. He was all business.

Anyone who never heard Connor sing "The Love of God" missed a wonderful experience. No one every sang that song like Connor, perhaps because he, more than any other, really felt the love of God when he sang it.

Sometimes, when something happened to quartets like the Homeland Harmony, it appeared to be even funnier than it really was.

Once, soon after Bob Shaw joined the Homeland Harmony, the pastor's wife—Mrs. Tidwell, rest her soul—of an Atlanta Church of God, died. Most of the Homeland Harmony boys were members of that church. They were asked to sing at the funeral, along with the Statesmen and the LeFevres.

Wally Varner, the Homeland Harmony's pianist, was supposed to play the organ at the funeral; but he was late, and everyone was growing more nervous by the minute.

Hovie Lister was there, but he wasn't about to be saddled with playing the organ. He hid in the bus and sent Jake Hess in to suggest that Bob Shaw be the organist.

Bob reluctantly agreed, but recently said, "I play the piano about like Derrell Stewart sings, and I had never played an organ before. I said I would try, though, if somebody would set it for me. I didn't even know how to set an organ."

James McCoy volunteered. "I'll set it for you," said he.

He set the organ, and whether by accident or design, he left the volume turned up full bore.

The first song was "In The Garden," and Bob Shaw, trying to appear as much like an organist as possible, poised his hands momentarily above the keys, glanced at the funeral director, got the nod, and bent into his work with a fervor.

The first blast from the organ almost lifted the roof. Hovie heard it all the way out on the bus. It rattled windows and shook people in their seats.

"It sounded like thunder in the garden," Shaw said later. "People told me that poor Mrs. Tidwell actually sat upright in the casket when I hit those first notes.

"I've never forgiven any of the three," Shaw said. "I've never forgiven Hovie for suggesting that I play the organ, or Wally Varner for being late, or James McCoy for setting the organ that way.

"I learned that day," he concluded, "that if you don't want to make an utter fool of yourself, don't try to do anything that you know from the start you can't do."

That funeral is one of Bob Shaw's fondest memories—and one that Connor Hall is probably still trying to forget.

There were other giants in the business in those immediate postwar days. Big Jim Waits was one. He came from Atlanta and sang in Vaudeville in the 1920s. One of the songs he sang was "Oh, ho, ho, ho, gee whiz! I got the rhumatiz! I got the rhumatiz all over me!" He sang on Broadway in Vaudeville with the Policeman's Quartet.

He sang with the Morris-Henson Quartet, the John Daniel Quartet, the Electrical Workers Quartet, the Vaughan Radio Quartet, the Stamps Quartet, the LeFevres, the Homeland Harmony, the Rebels Quartet, and with any other that happened to need a bass singer at the moment. Often a group needing a strong bass for a recording hired Waits. The Speer Family once hired both Waits and Connor Hall to record "Rainbow of Love" with them.

Waits was a trouper until the last. Jim Hamill recalls Waits, whom everyone affectionately called "Pappy," singing with the Rebels at the end of his career.

"We had already hired London Parris to sing bass," Hamill said, "because Pappy's health was failing. We got a job singing on a nation-wide show sponsored by Minute Maid Orange Juice on a Sunday morning in 1960, and we sang "A Beautiful Life." Old Pappy sang, 'Life's evening sun . . .' and he nailed that low note like a buzz saw. I heard one of the orange juice people say, 'Boy, he sure is loud!'

"Pappy never went anywhere without a suit and tie," Hamill said. "He didn't think he was dressed without them. And every time he left his suitcase, he locked it. I guess that was the result of playing Vaudeville. What I remember most about Pappy, besides his singing, was that his shoes were always shined, his tie knotted perfectly, and his suitcase was always locked."

Pappy could sell himself to an audience. He earned the title of "Dean of the Bass Singers."

J. D. Sumner admired Pappy as much as he admired Arnold Hyles. "I took the Dixie Lily Harmoneers to Jacksonville to the Duvall County Singing Convention," J. D. said. "This was soon after the end of the war, and the Homeland Harmony Quartet was there with Big Jim. I had never seen anybody like him.

"They sang 'Lead Me To That Rock,' and Big Jim left the stage and went all over the auditorium, and singing without a mike in that booming bass voice, you could hear him from any part of the building. He kissed all the babies and most of the women and tore that place apart.

"He had pride," J. D. said, echoing the words of Jim Hamill. "You could use his shoes for a mirror. He could wear a suit a month without getting it wrinkled. He always had a Ford automobile and you could eat lunch on the motor."

Waits sang with the Electrical Workers Quartet in Atlanta about the time of the rise of the early Stamps Quartet.

He had had a taste of the bright lights of New York when performing in Vaudeville, and perhaps something rubbed off on him from the Vaudeville stars of the era. Big Jim became a star in gospel music who liked to have his way, or he would go elsewhere and sing. That was one reason he never stayed too long with any quartet. Despite that idiosyncrasy, he was widely respected in the business. After all, a man had to have some eccentricities, especially if he could sing like Big Jim Waits.

"The biggest thing I ever did," said J. D. Sumner, "was conquer the fear of singing bass. At times, every bass singer is afraid he can't hit the low note. There seemed to be a little man inside of me who kept telling me I couldn't hit that lower note, and I never could—until I told that little man to go jump. If Big Jim could have done the same thing—which he never did—he would have been greater still, and lower. He could have sung a lot lower than he did. If he had had the confidence I found, he would have been ferocious."

There is one bass voice in gospel music today like Big Jim Waits' voice. It belongs to George Younce.

"George sings a lot like Big Jim," J. D. said, "through his nose. I kid George a lot about singing through his nose, but he can project better than I. He's the closest thing we have today to Big Jim Waits."

Waits was a genuine character on stage. He would pull up his pants legs and shake them to get the low notes to fall out. J. D. mimicked him a lot in that respect, and in 1949 when J. D. left Atlanta for Wheeling, West Virginia, with the Sunshine Boys, Big Jim breathed a sigh of relief and confided, "I'm glad that guy is gone."

He was a showman who had the ability to cover his mistakes on stage, and no doubt he learned that on the Vaudeville circuit. He'd go down low and if he missed hitting his low note squarely in the middle, he'd growl or yell and shake himself, and no one would know he hadn't hit the note.

Big Jim knew all the tricks.

He lived many years after retiring from the stage. Waits died December 28, 1974, and was buried in the Garden of Memories in Tampa, Florida.

Aycel Soward, who was often called by his initials, A. D., was a contemporary of Pappy Waits. He, too, made the rounds. When a quartet needed a bass singer to fill in until it could hire someone, Aycel Soward was the man. And when the new guy showed up, Aycel Soward would be the first to glad-hand him.

Soward's voice was big. When he sang with a quartet, the entire quartet had a big sound. To young bass singers coming into the business, Aycel sounded as if he had no bottom to his voice. His voice was so full he seemed to be able to keep going down.

He sang with too many quartets to name and was always ready to help out a group until it could find a bass singer.

Like Waits and the others, however, A. D. Soward was not the perfect bass singer. He had trouble singing rhythm. The Big Chief was the epitome of rhythm basses. In that respect, he could sing circles around the others.

Soward probably had the best bass voice in his time. He had studied voice at the Cincinnati Conservatory and knew how to get the most from his voice.

He was not a showman, not like Waits. He was not a salesman from the stage. He could sell anything but his singing. To be good, he had to be surrounded by a good quartet.

Soward stood six feet and had a full head of hair.

He was a true pioneer of quartet singing and might have become greater still had he not died young. He sang until his death on Easter Sunday, April 1, 1956, at the age of forty-two.

Ask J. D. Sumner who is the best bass singer he has ever heard and you'll get a quick answer, "I am." He neither hesitates nor equivocates—nor does he lie.

Who, then, is second best?

"I'll tell you what," J. D. said, "old London Parris, when he was right—which was about one time out of ten—could sing bass as well as anybody I've ever heard. He sounded like a bull moose coming through the woods, knocking down every tree. But he had to be right.

"Now, if you're talking about consistency, I'll have to say Big Jim Waits. He could sing anything, any time.

"Arnold Hyles could sing low, but he couldn't sing fast. He couldn't sing 'Jubilee's A-coming' because it was too fast for him. Arnold couldn't get the words out. His mouth was shaped wrong. And he had enough teeth for five men.

"If Jim Waits had had the opportunity these modern day singers have—the refined equipment and all—he would kill 'em all every night. He never really had good technical equipment. When I was with Elvis, we had enough equipment to tear a building down. I've vibrated people in their chairs. But Jim Waits didn't have that sophisticated equipment."

J. D. was listed for years in the Guinness Book of World Records as having sung the lowest note: "J. D. Sumner of Nashville, Tenn.," Guinness wrote, "in his album 'Blessed Assurance,' reaches the C below low

C (32.7 cps). He also reached this note singing on the Elvis Presley recording of 'Way Down.'"

The amazing thing about J. D. is that he can still hit the double-low C at the age of sixty-five.

"I've lasted longer than even Jim Waits, being able to sing," J. D. said. "I don't have as much breath as I used to, but I can still hold a note, and I can still sing on pitch. I know when I'm on pitch and when I'm off pitch.

"The only way I can describe my voice is saying I've been blessed of God. Equipment won't help you sing; it projects what you sing. You can have the best equipment in the world, and if you can't sing you've got a big problem.

"Take Big Jim and Big Chief both," he said, "before they died they got to the point that they really couldn't sing. But I can still register and stay on key with anybody today. Brock Speer can do that, too. Brock is a bass singer, but not a low one like me and London and Jim Waits and Arnold Hyles. I'm talking about show singers now, the ones who can get down low and dig it. Brock doesn't have that low bass register."

J. D. has a theory about singing low bass. He is convinced that he can sing so low because he convinced himself that he could. His voice has deepened considerably over the years.

"I fully believe that if you think you can sing," he said, "then you can sing. I used to do London this way: sit out in the audience and motion to him that he was off key, and he'd get off key. You can't do that to me. Psychologically, you ain't gonna bother me whatsoever."

When writing of giants in the gospel music industry, there is a place that should be called "Giant-Country"—Sand Mountain, Alabama. The list of outstanding singers who were born there and developed their talents there is as long as a grown man's arm. It includes Bobby Strickland; Erman Slater; Cat Freeman; Cat's sister, Vestal Goodman; Seals (Low-Note) Hilton; Carl Raines; Bill Hefner; Alton Jolley; Bob Prather; Bob Crews; the Goodman family; and Jack Toney. What a quartet could be formed from that group! Even J. R. Baxter, Jr., came from Sand Mountain.

Ace Richman was a giant and an anachronism: He came out of pop music to carve a niche in gospel music, one of the few to do so.

Born in Cincinnati, Ohio, August 14, 1916, Ace was a strapping fifteen-year-old boy when the nation hit the bottom of the Great Depression, feeling that he should be able to make his own way in a world turned upside down, yet too young to break away from home and hit the trail.

He had music in him, and music became his way to livelihood. He never thought of gospel music; in fact, he had never heard of it. He learned to play instruments—bass, tenor banjo, clarinet, and he could also sing. He organized his own ten-piece orchestra, "Ace Richman and the Sophisticates of Rhythm," and played clubs and colleges in and around Cincinnati and Kentucky. He envisioned himself a future Dorsey or Goodman, both of whom had gained immense popularity with their swing bands.

He organized a four-piece group in 1937, "The Hottentots," a novelty band, and took the group to Plattsburgh, New York, for four months, then to Charleston, West Virginia, for a year, playing on Radio Station WCHS. Finally, in 1938, he wound up with his band in Macon, Georgia, playing on Station WMAZ, which also had a gospel group, Deacon Utley and the Smile-A-While Stamps Quartet.

Ace had two Smith brothers, known as Smitty and Tennessee, and a young man named Frank Dituro, an Italian fellow who played the accordion. They were a string and pop band and thought their music was pretty good, but they began to notice that the Smile-A-While Quartet was doing twice as well at personal appearances.

Sophisticated Ace thought the Smile-A-While was a pretty corny group, and so was their music; but he had an eye for the dollar and a good business head, and when he figured out that the Smile-A-While was doubling the income of his own group, he decided to look closer.

He knew nothing of shaped-note music, but he knew a barber who did, and the barber agreed to teach Ace and his boys shaped notes. He taught them in a back room in his barber shop, using a small blackboard. When the barber put the first shaped notes on the board, Ace furrowed his brow and said, "Man, we can read—but what are those things?"

The four were good musicians. They learned quickly. After four lessons they got the hang of shaped-note singing. Their minds transposed the notes and they discovered they could sing the four parts.

"Since I was the lowest voice among the four," Ace said many years later, "I became the bass singer. Tennessee, the violinist and guitarist, had the highest voice because he could sing falsetto; so we made him the first tenor. Smitty was a good-looking guy, which made him a natural lead singer, we thought. He also played guitar. And Frank Dituro sang baritone and played his accordion."

At the end of their country show on radio, the group began to add a hymn for the day—and within a month their gross increased to almost half again as much as they had been making.

"Boys, this is pure corn," Ace said one day, "but it works. However," he added, "let's change it a little." So they added a bit of Western swing to their gospel songs, and people liked them even better.

They had been singing as the Red River Rangers, and when time came to cut a record disk they cut Red River Rangers Western tunes on one side, and on the other they cut gospel numbers and called themselves the Sunshine Boys. That name had been used by two brothers in Louisiana as far back as the 1920s, and Ace wrote immediately to them and got a letter of clearance to use the name.

Ace took the disk to Chattanooga to the Chattanooga Medicine Company, which marketed Black Draught. Walking into a designated office, he laid the disk on an official's desk. Ace was a rather brash northern boy who remembered that the North had whipped the South and could do it again, and when the official asked, "What's this?" Ace replied, "It's a group that can sell your products."

"Do you have an agent?" the man asked.

"No," Ace replied. "I'm the agent."

"Do you have a license?"

"I've got the group," Ace replied, evading the question. "If you want the group, you'll have to talk to me. Why don't you listen to the songs?"

The man listened to the Red River Rangers and said, "I like that. It's good Western swing."

"We're the Red River Rangers," Ace said.

He flipped the disk and played the other side.

"What is this gospel music?" the man asked. He was a northerner, too, and not really attuned to Southern gospel.

"That stuff sells down here, doesn't it?" he asked.

"It sure does," Ace said.

The man looked at the disk and mused, "Hummmm. The Sunshine Boys. Can I get both groups?"

Ace laughed. "No," he said, "but if you hire our group, you can get 'em all." He explained that the Red River Rangers and the Sunshine Boys were one and the same group. They simply laid down their instruments and did gospel with a guitar and accordion.

Ace signed a contract for thirteen weeks to sing over WGST in Atlanta for sixty dollars a week per man. That was good money in 1939.

Ace moved his group from job to job, always increasing income, and in 1943 hired Eddie Wallace, a college man who was studying electrical engineering at Georgia Tech. At the end of the war, Eddie suggested the Sunshine Boys move to California and try to get in moving pictures. "It's wide open out there," he reasoned, and as a result of that suggestion the Sunshine Boys became movie stars—actors, anyway. The group consisted of Tennessee, Smitty, Eddie, and Ace, and over the next four years they appeared in nineteen movies as singing cowboys. They made eight pictures with Eddie Dean, a former bass singer with the Stamps quartets; two with John Carradine and Martha O'Driscoll; one with the Hoosier Hot Shots; and eight with Charles Starrett as the Durango Kid, and Smiley Burnette, the famous "Frog Millhouse," former sidekick of Gene Autry.

In late 1948 Ace and Eddie moved back to Atlanta. The Smith brothers stayed in California and built a new Western band.

J. D. Sumner and Fred E. Daniel came with the Sunshine Boys in 1949, making a quartet that became one of the most harmonious in the business. They drove to California to make pictures with the Durango Kid, and they backed Red Foley on a couple of records, including "Peace in the Valley," which sold more than a million.

The Sunshine Boys believed in singing—but that's as far as they would go. Ace told preachers, "We do not testify; we are an entertaining group. You pay us to sing these songs, and we'll sing 'em. But that's all. If you want the people to come to the altar, you get 'em there and do what you wish. But we are only coming to sing." Ace did not equivocate; he leveled with everyone. The Sunshine Boys would have been uncomfortable doing it any other way.

The next big break for the Sunshine Boys came in Wheeling, West Virginia, in late 1949. They went on WWVA and Ace believes to this day that folks in and around Wheeling had never heard anything like what the Sunshine Boys did.

"We did uptown, swing stuff," he said, "good harmony, four parts, and Man! they opened the doors for us." The Sunshine Boys decided not to book any personal appearances for sixty days while they established themselves on the radio. When they opened up their schedule for personal appearances, they booked four months of dates the first day they asked.

They became a favorite entertaining group in West Virginia and stayed till 1951 when Wally Fowler coaxed them back to Atlanta to sing on his All-Night Singings around the South.

The early gospel quartets discovered a rhythm and style that they seldom slipped out of, although occasionally, even in the 1920s, you could hear a group slip some barbershopping chords into a song.

The Sons of the Pioneers actually were a quartet, not a gospel quartet, but their music was constructed in four or five parts, and they were more tuneful in the 1930s than the gospel quartets because they were not as restricted instrumentally. They not only used Western swing in the instrumentation, but in their harmony also—and that's what the Sunshine Boys added to gospel: the same type of swing that the Sons of the Pioneers had popularized.

During their glory years, the Sunshine Boys made the Statesmen, Blackwood Brothers, and Homeland Harmony live hard when they went head to head on stage.

Sumner left the Sunshine Boys in 1954 to replace the late Bill Lyles with the Blackwood Brothers, and the Sunshine Boys continued to sing for years, first with Burl Strevel singing bass and later with Johnny Atkinson.

But they didn't stick to gospel. They returned to the Western field in later years, playing Las Vegas and other cities in the West—always using a spiritual number or two in their act—and then they faded out of the picture.

Ace Richman was one of the most talented performers who ever sang a gospel song, and he was showman enough to know when to turn the talent on. He was the man who put swing into gospel.

Actually, there was as much talent in the Sunshine Boys as in any quartet ever. Their Western songs were as pleasing as those of the Sons of the Pioneers, and when they really harmonized on a gospel song, few quartets in the business could match them, and none could surpass them.

Their showmanship was unsurpassed, and showmanship counted in those days. Eddie Wallace and J. D. Sumner are funny, funny men, and Ace Richman and Fred Daniel were perfect foils.

Ace held the group together and kept its quality up. He would not stand for less. He was a showman!

Ed Hill is a quiet fellow who looks more like an old-time, bespectackled country doctor than a gospel singer, but he is one of those who

James Blackwood, above, had the pleasure of singing at the Garden Tomb in Jerusalem, which commemorates the burial of Jesus Christ. Photo at right shows James as he really is: a star surrounded by stars. Below, two old-timers, Lee Roy Abnernathy, left, and Jake Hess talk things over.

A young version of the Florida Boys, above, includes L-R: seated, Glen Allred, J. G. Whitfield, and Les Beasley; and standing, Billy Todd, Derrell Stewart, and Coy Cook. At lower left was a tuneful quartet, the Deep South Quartet, with Cat Freeman, top; Jimmy Jones, Brownie Jones, and Bob Crews, center; and pianist Wally Varner, bottom. Below is one of the greatest songwriters of all time, Albert E. Brumley, who penned hundreds of gospel, country, and pop tunes.

High-flying Freddie Daniel, top photo, hits a high note for the Blue Ridge Quartet and the photographer caught him at the exact right instant. L-R: Burl Strevel, Bill Crowe, Donnie Seabolt, and Daniel. That's J. G. Whitfield at right, bass singer, promoter, and entrepreneur. Below are the LeFevres on stage about 1957, L-R: Rex Nelon, Uncle Alf, Leonard Hollifield, Urias LeFevre, Eva Mae, and Little Rex.

Above left is Rosie Rozell, who came from the Tulsa Trumpeteers to carve a huge niche in gospel music as the first tenor soul singer with the Statesmen Quartet. Right is the Stamps Quartet which in the late 1950s became the Plainsmen Quartet. Top, L-R, are Bill Randall and Joe B. Davis, the latter one of the all-time great bass singers. Center are Rusty Goodman and Howard Welborn, and below is pianist Easmon Napier. Lower left is a quartet that has mostly stayed together for forty years, the Palmetto State Quartet of Greenville, S.C. L-R: bass Ken Turner, lead Jack Bagwell, baritone Jack Pittman, first tenor Claude Hunter, and pianist Jamie Dill. The handsome man with glasses at lower right was one of the great piano players, Jack Clark, of the Homeland Harmony and the Harvesters.

At top left is an excellent view of the piano playing of Derrell Stewart of the Florida Boys, and at top right Derrell proves he has talents other than playing the piano. Left is Marvin Norcross, head of Canaan Records until his death. Marvin was a friend to all in gospel music. Below, the Sego Brothers and Naomi pose for photographer. L-R: James Sego, his wife Naomi, his brother W. R., his other brother Lamar, and pianist Eddie Crook.

The original Dixie Echoes pose in top photo, L-R, Joe Whitfield, J. G. Whitfield, Sue Whitfield, Jack Toney, and George Forbus. Right is Dale Shelnut, one of the all-time greats who rose to fame with the Dixie Echoes. Below, the Blackwood Brothers sing with Tennessee Ernie Ford. L-R: James Blackwood, Bill Shaw, Jimmy Blackwood, Cecil Blackwood, London Parris, and Tennessee Ernie.

One of the days the Inspirations will always remember was the one they spent with Billy Graham at his home in Montreat, N.C. They sang and talked with Billy for most of the afternoon. L-R: seated, Martin Cook, Ron Hutchins, Marlin Shubert, Eddie Dietz, and Graham; and standing, Archie Watkins, Troy Burns, and Jack Laws. At right, from beneath an umbrella, Wendy Bagwell tests the weather on a rainy day. Below, four of the great bass singers from Asheville, L-R, Calvin Runion, Rex Nelon, London Parris, and Ray Dean Reese.

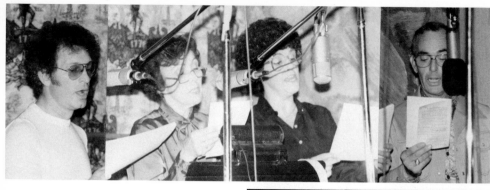

Behind a tangle of wires and microphones, the Chuck Wagon Gang, above, puts a song on record, L-R, Ronnie Page, Ruth Ellen Yates, Bettye Goodwin, and Roy Carter. At right, Dottie Rambo keeps time during chorus of a song with the choir singing behind her. Lower right, the Jordanaires back Winnie Breest of the Kerr Singers in a recording session at Goodman Sound in Madisonville, Ky., L-R, Hoyt Hawkins, Gordon Stoker, Breest, Neil Matthews, and Ray Walker. Below, James Blackwood sings a solo.

The Kingsmen Quartet was both the leading singing group and the gospel music promoters in Asheville. At left was the cover shot on a booklet the quartet printed about 1970. Singing, L-R, on the Asheville City Auditorium stage, were high tenor Jerry Redd, lead Frank Cutshall, baritone Eldridge Fox, and bass Calvin Runion. That's Ray Talley playing the piano and singing, too. At left, on that same program, between songs, the look on Eldridge's face would make you think that Calvin just did something wrong. Below, the Kingsmen sang to a full house that night. Above is another great promoter, W. B. Nowlin of Fort Worth, Texas.

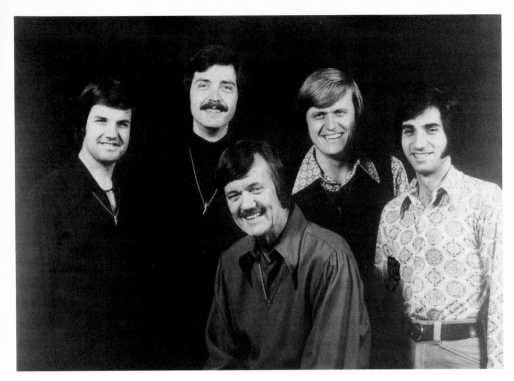

Above, the Stamps Quartet that backed Elvis Presley for the last six years of Elvis' life, L-R, standing, Bill Baize, Donnie Sumner, Ed Enoch, and Richie Sturben. That's J. D. Sumner seated. Note that they are wearing the TCB ("Take Care of Business") necklaces Elvis gave them. Below, the early Cathedral Quartet gets into a number. L-R: Roy Tremble, Danny Webster, Glen Payne, George Younce, and Lorne Matthews.

An older Connor B. Hall, left photo, smiles for camera. At right is the Prophets Quartet, clockwise from upper left, Ed Hill, Lew Garrison, Jay Simmons, Roy McNeil, and Joe Mosqueo. Below, London Parris, right, and silver-haired Coy Cook pose with London's Apostles.

THE PROPHETS

Pictured in Springfield, Missouri's Fantastic Caverns are the Thrasher Brothers of Birmingham, Ala., L-R, Jerry Goff, Jim Thrasher, Ellis (Moose) Hill, Buddy Thrasher, Joe Thrasher, and Randy McDaniel. And at left are the later Happy Goodman Family, L-R, Sam, Howard, and Rusty, with Vestal seated.

With the Inspirations, Archie Watkins, left photo, really gets into a song; and at right the sheer joy of gospel singing is reflected in Martin Cook's face. Below, 420-pound John Broome, the Kingsmen Quartet's drummer in the early 1970s, lets the quartet know what he thinks of a song.

Recreation is a mighty important thing to the Kingsmen Quartet as you can tell in top photo by their hurry to get to the first tee. Left photo, Eldridge Fox of the Kingsmen, right, poses with Maurice Templeton, owner of *The Singing News.* At right is Bill Gaither, whose songwriting turned from Southern Gospel to church standards. Choirs around the world sing his beautiful songs.

Television was once a major medium for gospel quartets. Top photo, the Kingsmen Quartet does a TV show at Asheville's WLOS-TV. Below, the Kingsmen show their ample waistlines while being weighed on the truck scales at a weighing station near Asheville. That was when they were called a "Ton of Fun." L-R: Johnny Parrack, Jim Hamill, Jim MacCauley, Leonard Hollifield, John Broome, Ray Dean Reese, Eldridge Fox, and Charles Abee.

For a quartet like the Statesmen, whom Death robbed of several members, it was hard to come back. In the late 1970s, the Statesmen above—Buddy Burton, Rosie Rozell, Hovie Lister, Tommy Thompson, and Jake Hess—had a tremendous sound, but the quartet didn't quite make the grade because too many fans remembered the "old Statesmen." Some other oldtimers are shown at left: three Turbyfill brothers, L-R, Preston, Clarence, and Paul, sing in Paul's home in Newton, N.C., with an aged Arnold Hyles of Rangers fame about 1975. Remember Clarence Turbyfill of the Lone Star Quartet in Raleigh and as a member of the original Blue Ridge Quartet? Below are Arnold Hyles and his son, Gene, both of whom died in 1979, Arnold of old age, and Gene in an automobile accident returning home from his father's funeral.

PHOTO CREDITS

Pictures in the two photo sections came largely from the collections of Riley Smith of Asheville, Paul Turbyfill of Newton, N.C., Tommy Wheeler of Texas, the files of The Singing News, the author and a scattered few came from other folks.

represent the unsung heroes of quartet singing—the harmony men, or the baritones.

Normally—for the most part, anyway—a quartet will variously feature its high tenor, its lead singer, or its bass, and the baritone stands smiling in the background, putting the harmony to all the quartet's songs and making the other fellows look good, sometimes better than they actually are. Seldom does a baritone get a lead in a song, and when he does, he often has to leave his harmony part and sing the melody line.

Like Ace Richman, Ed was something of an anachronism in quartet singing in the 1950s and 1960s, because he didn't come from the South. He was from St. Louis, Missouri.

Born February 23, 1935, Ed was the son of a Baptist minister.

Ed had two great boyhood loves, both hooked to his father. His dad loved baseball and he and Ed spent many a happy hour in old Sportsman's Park, watching the St. Louis Cardinals play.

And Ed loved to sing gospel songs. He sang them in his daddy's church. When Ed was eight years old, his dad, who played the guitar, would stand Ed in a chair in church and play the guitar while Ed sang. "I guess I was a ham then, too," Ed says today.

At fifteen, Ed and his cousins formed the Humble Hearts Quartet and Ed sang first tenor. They sang in his daddy's church, and now and then they sponsored another group to sing in the church.

Once they promoted the Blackwood Brothers Quartet in St. Louis, and another time the Humble Hearts went to Central Illinois to sing on a program sponsored by a group called the Gospelaires, giving them a taste of the road.

"Since that time," Ed said, "I've never done anything that wasn't connected to the quartet business."

After Ed finished high school in St. Louis in 1953, his father accepted a pastorate in Elizabethton, Tennessee, and moved there. Ed remained in St. Louis, planning to attend the Stamps School of Music in Dallas.

He visited his folks in Elizabethton on Mother's Day, 1953, and met a big youngster named Lew Garrison. Everybody called him "Big Lew." He and Ed Hill hit it off very well together, and soon Big Lew was urging Ed to move to Elizabethton with his parents and go to college at East Tennessee State College (now University) in nearby Johnson City. That's where Lew was studying.

The magic words came when Lew said, "We could even start a quartet." Lew had a high tenor voice.

Ed moved to Elizabethton in 1953, met Sharon Knode, and married her on August 27, 1954. In 1955 they moved back to St. Louis, and Ed began singing in a quartet there called the King's Men. The lead singer was Jay Berry, and he and Ed wanted to sing professionally, but the others in the quartet were older and did not wish for a life on the road.

Ed and Jay fell in love with the Statesmen, and every time the Statesmen came to St. Louis or anywhere nearby, they managed to get Jake Hess and Big Chief Jim Wetherington aside to talk about singing. Jake and Chief spent a lot of time with them, telling about the business.

Ed telephoned Big Lew and talked with him about forming a quartet. Big Chief recommended his cousin, R. C. (Randy) Taylor, a Georgian, as bass singer, and Jake thought Gary Trussler of Knoxville would be a good piano player for a new quartet. Gary had played for the Harvesters.

On Thanksgiving of 1958, Jay Berry and Ed and Sharon Hill went to Sharon's parents' home in Elizabethton for the holiday. Randy Taylor came up from Georgia and Gary Trussler from Knoxville, and all of them gathered around the Knodes' piano and began singing.

The Prophets Quartet was born that day. All the guys became excited; they thought they sounded good enough to sing professionally.

Before Christmas Ed and Jay talked to Chief and Jake again and they recommended that the Prophets headquarter in Knoxville or Birmingham since there was not a quartet operating out of either town at that time.

Since Gary lived in Knoxville, the Prophets chose that city and all the fellows moved there soon after the first of the year of 1959. They rehearsed for three months until they had a large enough repertoire of songs and good stagemanship, and in March of 1959 they hit the road singing. With some personnel changes, they sang as the Prophets Quartet until June of 1972 when the quartet finally broke up.

Randy was first to leave, and Fred Rose of Maryville, Tennessee, replaced him. Then came bass singers Jim Boatman, Jay Simmons, and Dave Rodgers.

Jay Berry got an offer from the Rebels Quartet in Tampa, Florida, and moved there, then came back to the Prophets for a short while, got married, and quit the road. He was succeeded by Jack Toney, Roy McNeil, and Jim Wesson.

Big Lew sang tenor until 1971, but Ed Hill quit for nine months in 1965 and was replaced by Duane Allen. When Duane thought he was going to be drafted in 1966, Ed went back to the Prophets. Duane hit it big with the Oak Ridge Boys, with whom he now sings in the country music field.

Grady (Chico) Nix replaced Big Lew in 1971 as first tenor.

David Young followed Trussler as the quartet's pianist, and then Joe Moscheo came along and played piano for five years until he went with the Imperials.

When they disbanded, the Prophets had only Ed Hill left of the original personnel. There were Chico Nix, and Carl and Butch Sanders, with Bob McCollum playing the piano.

At first, the Prophets didn't make enough money to live on, but they stuck with it. Sometimes they had nothing left after expenses for a weekend. Within a few months, however, they were earning $50 to $75 per week per man, and finally when J. Bazzel Mull began booking them for weekend singings in Knoxville, Chattanooga, and Asheville, he paid them $200 a date, and the $600 income, plus whatever they made off record sales, boosted them to salaries of about $100 a week. They added to their income when they began to sing on the television show, *Gospel Caravan.*

When Ed Hill folded up the Prophets, he went to work for J. D. Sumner in J. D.'s *Sumar Talent Agency* in Nashville. One day, J. D. called Ed and said, "I need you to fill in with the Stamps Quartet while I audition some people." Ed filled in—for five years.

The Stamps Quartet had been working as back-up singers for Elvis Presley for two years when Ed joined them, and he remained with the Stamps through their next four years with Elvis.

"I was scared," Ed said, "not knowing anything about Elvis, but he had a way of making you feel comfortable. The first program I did with the Stamps with Elvis was in San Bernardino, California, and I hadn't seen Elvis yet when he came on stage.

"We sang on the first half of the program, then had intermission, and when Elvis came on to sing the second half of the show, the Stamps Quartet was on stage with him. He kept looking at me and grinning, and when we were about halfway through, he walked over and stuck his hand out and said, 'Welcome to the show.' That made me feel good, that he would even care.

"Being around him the next four years," Ed continued, "I came to look on him as a friend. We sat and talked like friends. He liked to talk about gospel music, and he knew everything about it. He loved it. This was an exciting time for me, a highlight of my life."

After a couple of years, Ed Hill became Elvis's announcer. Al

Devorin, the regular announcer, was also head of concessions with the Elvis Presley Show. He worked for John Denver, too, and once when Denver and Elvis had tours scheduled simultaneously, Devorin found himself committed to Denver. Colonel Tom Parker was Elvis's manager, and his office called J. D. and asked if he had anyone in the group who could announce. J. D. recommended Ed. "Okay," J. D. was told, "he'll have to do the show tonight."

Ed agreed, provided he could announce from the side of the stage where he stood with the Stamps. "I don't want to be out front," Ed said, "for when I introduced the Stamps, they'd have to come to me." So he did it his way, and the Colonel liked his announcing so well he gave him the job permanently. For two years, then, it was Ed Hill who spoke those final words, "Ladies and gentlemen, Elvis has left the building. Goodbye, and God bless you."

"Those were great days," Ed said. "That was an experience, especially when you figure you've been on stage with the greatest superstar the entertainment world has ever known."

After Elvis's death and the breakup of the Stamps Quartet in 1980, Ed went with the Singing Americans as manager and baritone. Then J. D. needed a baritone to replace Jake Hess with the Masters V, and brought Ed back. When J. D. changed the Masters V back to the Stamps Quartet at the 1987 National Quartet Convention, Ed Hill became baritone singer with the Stamps Quartet once again.

"I look at young guys today," said Ed, a thirty-year veteran now, "and I try to take a little time with those in our business who are just starting out. I remember how Jake and Chief used to sit for hours with me, and I remember how much those talks helped me. So if I can do or say anything to help the young guys now, it makes me feel good. I feel I'm putting something back. I feel that you have to give as well as receive."

The inspiration to become gospel singers comes from many different things—sometimes from the music itself. Cases in point are Herman Harper, who sang bass for the Oak Ridge Boys for thirteen years, and Eddie Crook, the excellent pianist for the Happy Goodman Family for many years.

Both were inspired by the singing itself, and both, ironically, received their inspiration in the same place, Ryman Auditorium in Nashville.

In each case the Statesmen Quartet was involved.

Eddie Crook said a classmate took him to one of Wally Fowler's Friday night All-Night Singings in Nashville. "I saw all those singing groups," he said, "the Statesmen, the Blackwood Brothers, and so on, and I liked the singing. I got involved in it and have been in it ever since."

Eddie played first with the Tennesseans Quartet of Dale Shelnut, Noel Fox, Dean Basham, and Wally Laxon, graduating then to the Happy Goodman Family for several years before he went into the production end of gospel music and guided his Eddie Crook Company to an exalted place in the business.

Harper preceded Crook by several years, starting in the early 1950s. He, too, went to Nashville to a Wally Fowler All-Night Singing. He saw Hovie Lister wave his red bandana that evening and his life was forever changed—not by the bandana but by the music.

"I fell in love with the music," Herman said. He went back to his home in Portland, Tennessee, and immediately organized the Portlandaires. That was in 1952. Next he sang with a group called the Big Hope Quartet, then with the Southlanders, and finally, in 1957, he became the bass singer with the Oak Ridge Boys, who included Smitty Gatlin, Ronnie Page, Hobart Evans, and Powell Hassell.

He sang with the Oak Ridge until the first Friday of December, 1968, and his departure from the ranks of singers may still be something of a record.

Herman was married and had three growing sons by that time. He missed his wife and kids and knew they missed him. He came to the conclusion that his kids needed him more than the Oak Ridge Boys did.

The Oaks were coming off a six-weeks tour of the West Coast and Canada, and Herman knew he was burned out on the road. The bus rolled out of Vancouver and down through Washington.

Suddenly, Herman saw the Seattle Airport by the side of the road. On impulse, he said to Charlie Carr, the driver, "Pull this thing over, Charlie, and when the other boys wake up tell them I'll be home."

He boarded an airplane, flew to Nashville, and was home before the Oaks reached California. He never went on the road again.

Today, Herman and his three sons, Ed, Clay, and Jeff, operate one of Nashville's leading gospel agencies, Harper & Associates.

When a gospel singer really decides to come off the road, the best time is now.

CHAPTER TWENTY-ONE

This Crazy Life

Here was a man who saw humor in everything. His name was David Reece. He was a North Carolinian from Elkin who played piano for a number of quartets and could milk laughs out of a rock.

He didn't have to have an audience to be funny. He was his own audience. Once he and his wife moved to Nashville and found a house on a corner lot. The house had a clothesline outside, in clear view of the street.

David went downtown to buy some things and when he went in Woolworth's he saw a sale table piled high with women's bras of every size. He didn't know why, but he bought two of the biggest bras, took them home, cut them apart, and sewed a cup from one between the two cups of the other, making a three-cup bra.

Then he went outside and hung the bra on the clothesline. Neighbors said there were three collisions and four near misses at that corner in the next hour.

Reece and James Blackwood walked up the street in Charlotte one morning. At a bus stop a man stood engrossed in the morning newspaper, holding it open in front of himself, reading with great intent. David walked by the man, struck a match, and lit the newspaper. Twenty yards up the street, James got up the nerve to look back—and saw this frantic man stomping his burning newspaper on the sidewalk with a bewildered look on his face.

* * *

David got up one morning in a hotel and put his shoes on the wrong feet, a stunt he often pulled. He met George Younce in the hallway and together they walked downstairs and got up on the shoeshine stand. The shine boy had trouble getting his rag popping like he usually did, and he paused, stepped back, and surveyed David's feet.

"Heh, heh, heh," he laughed softly. "Kinda got yo' shoes on the wrong foots there, ain't you?"

"No," David said, seriously. "My feet were shot off in the war."

"Is?"

"Yeah," David said, "they sewed 'em back on the wrong legs."

Younce had a newspaper in front of his face, and he was almost choking, wanting to laugh. He dropped the paper a bit and looked at the shine boy's face, and the boy was in such pain that it tightened his expression. He tried to put his rag on the shoes tenderly, and finally stopped and looked up at David, and in a low tone, asked, "Do they hurt?"

Reece joked about his boyhood in the hills of North Carolina. He said his father taught him to swim by throwing him in the lake and letting him swim to shore. "The swimming part wasn't so hard," David said. "The most trouble I had was getting out of the sack."

He liked to tell audiences that there were sixteen brothers and sisters in his family. "There were so many of us," he said, "that we had to sleep five and six to the bed, and every night five or six kids wet the beds. Many a morning I woke up with a rainbow in the room.

"Finally," he said, "we put Mama up on a pedestal where Daddy couldn't get to her."

David would do anything for a laugh.

He said to J. D. Sumner, "I heard you had a heart operation."

"Yeah," J. D. said, "I had a triple by-pass."

David said, "Well, I did, too."

J. D. said, "So did Jake Hess and Connor Hall."

"We ought to get together and form a quartet," David said. "We could call it the Artery Brothers."

It takes all kinds of people to make up the gospel singing world, and most are people of humor. Strange and funny things happen to them.

J. D. Sumner learned once that if he didn't know exactly what he was talking about it was better to keep his mouth shut.

J. D. was a young man, married, not highly educated. He grew up in Florida under a stern father and said he thought when a man died he went to Atlanta to sing in a major quartet.

J. D. finally got a job singing with the Sunshine Boys in Atlanta and moved his small family there. He began to rub elbows with Jim Waits and Mosie Lister and folks like that, and he liked it.

One day, J. D. and Mary decided to invite Mosie Lister to dinner at their home. Mary was a good cook, and she really fixed things up that evening with all the trimmings.

At that time, J. D.'s vocabulary wasn't the widest in Atlanta, and he particularly had no knowledge of words that ended in "rhoids" or "roids."

"We were raised Pentecostal," J. D. said, "and we thought words like that were cuss words."

J. D.'s throat had been a bit sore and during the meal he rubbed it repeatedly and once caught Mosie watching him. He wanted to explain his problem to Mosie but couldn't think of the word the doctor had used, "thyroids." He blundered on anyway.

"I been having some trouble," he explained to Mosie. "My hemorrhoids have been killing me."

Mosie looked shocked. "Man, if they're up that high," he said, "I can understand why."

When Ken Turner sang bass for the Palmetto State Quartet, an IRS man showed up at Ken's house.

"Do you have any records?" the man asked.

"Oh, yes," Ken said. "We've got 'Down on Bended Knees' and a couple more."

"How many of 'em have you sold?" the man asked.

Scenting a sale, and thinking he might impress the man into buying a lot of records if he told him an astronomical number, Ken said, "Oh, we've sold seven or eight hundred thousand of them things."

Jack Pittman said it took five years to get straightened out with the IRS.

Alphus LeFevre was reared in the Church of God when it was very strict. "Young people in the church didn't go around smooching and hugging and everything like that," Alphus said.

"I was pretty naive," he said, "and I guess pretty shy, and I fell in love with a pretty girl. I went with her for several weeks and made no attempt to kiss her, and one night she decided she was gonna do something she had never done before.

"As I started to tell her good night," he said, "I was standing on the top step with my back toward the steps, and she planted a kiss on my cheek. I mean she really planted one on me—and I fell backward down the steps."

"They never could take Uncle Alphus to a funeral," Jay Simmons said. "He grinned all the time."

It has been fun, singing in quartets down through the years— actually, it's been more than fun. It has been a blessing to hundreds of thousands of people—and the men who sing the gospel know it.

They would never knowingly hurt anyone with a prank or a joke. But they can't avoid humor, because theirs is a business that lends itself to humor.

CHAPTER TWENTY-TWO

The Lighter Side

No question about it, those who sing gospel music today are more serious about what they do than singers were forty years ago. One reason is because more performers consider themselves to be a part of a ministry than a business, and another reason is that there simply aren't as many funny people in the business today. Too, because there were more pure entertainers in the business back then, hilarious things just naturally happened.

Like the time a well-to-do professor at the Bible college in Winona Lake, Indiana, hired the Weatherfords to sing in a special project for him. The Weatherfords then consisted of Earl and Lily Fern Weatherford, Jim Hamill, Danny Coker, and George Younce.

The professor was a great admirer of the group, and he took care of all members. He arranged for them to live in cabins on Lake Winona, saw that they had their favorite foods, and put a speedboat at their disposal. They had never had it so good!

Then the professor brought in a fleet of bulldozers and scraped out a long, flat airplane runway alongside the lake, and as soon as it was finished, a pilot few a twin-engined airplane in and landed on the runway. The airplane was to be the heart of the Weatherfords' work for the next few weeks, for the professor had an idea for an unusual radio show called "Wings of the Morning" on which the Weatherfords would sing a thirty-minute gospel show from the airplane as it circled the town. The professor had visions of being able to sell all the commercial time on the show because it was such an unusual idea.

He fitted a piano, like a Wurlitzer, into the aisle of the airplane, and had seats for all members of the Weatherfords to gather around a microphone and sing. There was room for the pilot and the professor in the flying seats, those occupied by the pilot and co-pilot under normal circumstances.

The Weatherfords did a daily show from the cramped quarters of the airplane for several weeks while the plane sat on the runway. On each program the professor announced that on May 18 the airplane would take off, the Weatherfords would do their first broadcast from the air, and "Wings of the Morning" would be born.

The professor sold the show to local business people. The spots went so quickly that he began to envision syndicating the show, and eventually he thought it might become a radio network show. It would be billed as the most unusual show of its kind—actually, it was the *only* show of its kind—and would be an eventual big money-maker. The professor spent all kinds of money to get the show off the ground— literally speaking.

The Weatherfords were tickled to death to be a part of such an enormous and promising undertaking. They did a thirty-minute program at ten o'clock each morning, and had the rest of the day off to splash in the lake or do whatever they pleased.

On May 18, the prescribed day for the first flying "Wings of the Morning" show, the quartet gathered early, loaded aboard the plane, and as the professor and the pilot buckled themselves into the flying seats, the Weatherfords prepared to make history.

The pilot warmed up the engines, moved the craft into takeoff position, and at the professor's signal, shoved the throttles full forward, and the airplane roared down the runway on its maiden broadcasting flight.

As the wheels left the earth and the quartet became airborne, the professor yelled into the live microphone, "Ladies and gentlemen, the Wings of the Morning. . . ."

George Younce looked up toward the cockpit and the pilot was looking back over his shoulder, grinning broadly, thrilled to death to be a part of whatever he was a part of at that moment.

Over the roar of the engines, the quartet could barely hear itself singing. When Danny gave a key, the singers looked at each other quizzically. All they could hear was "Nahhyaaaaahhh!!!"—those airplane engines roaring in their ears. But they did the best they could under difficult conditions to stay on key and in stride with each other. But every key Danny gave them sounded the same.

For thirty minutes the pilot circled town and the quartet sang as hard—harder, even—than it had ever sung before, hoping that the people in the town, particularly the sponsors, appreciated their efforts.

They were perhaps expecting half the town to be standing beside the runway when the airplane landed, but as the wheels touched down and the pilot taxied the plane to its berthing place, the only person waiting to greet them was George's wife, Clara.

All hands piled off that airplane and rushed over to Clara. "What did it sound like?" "How'd we do?" "Could you hear us all right?"

Clara shook her head.

"Didn't hear a word," she said. "Not one word!"

"Not one word?" George echoed.

The quartet was flabbergasted. The professor was shaken to the marrow.

"Nothing?"

"Not a word."

At that moment, "Wings of the Morning" went flapping off into space somewhere.

The Weatherfords did a couple more broadcasts from the airplane on the ground, and the show folded up.

"It was a good idea," George said. "It just didn't work."

"Why?" someone asked.

George didn't know. But Les Beasley did. "When the engines revved up," Les said, "the sparkplugs were transmitters in themselves, and back in those days they probably didn't have any isolation and just couldn't transmit from the plane to the ground."

Every quartet in the business has had its moments like that. Well, not exactly like that—but funny enough.

The Florida Boys had a piano player named Livy Freeman in their early days. The quartet contracted to do a live radio show from an auditorium that had a revolving stage, and when the guys arrived they discovered that Livy's piano was on the rotating stage but the quartet wasn't. They moved into position, and when the engineer stabbed his finger at them, Livy hit the introduction and the quartet began to sing.

Suddenly, Livy and the piano began to move. The stage rotated, and while the Florida Boys sang, they stared as Livy and the piano moved farther and farther away, circling far across the room.

"Halfway through that first song," Les Beasley said, "we were wondering how long it would take the piano to come back to us."

It didn't bother Livy, though; he just kept hammering the piano as if the quartet was standing just behind him.

Glen Payne and George Younce remembered the time when they were singing for Rex Humbard at the Cathedral of Tomorrow in Akron, Ohio—where the Cathedral Quartet got its name—and a television promoter approached them and asked if they would like to become part of an unusual national television production.

At that time, the Cathedral Quartet would have liked to become a part of *any* television production. "We had never heard such big talk in our lives," Glen said. "The man offered us such fantastic flat rates that we bought our own airplane tickets and flew to Miami, Florida, where the first show was to be telecast."

The show was to be called "Moon Over Miami," and would feature the Statesmen and the Cathedrals.

The setting for the show was beautiful. Right on the waterfront, the show would be telecast in a large amphitheater that had a stage built out over the bay.

The show was well advertised, and the promoters anticipated a whopping success. There was just one contingency they had not properly covered. They had made no plans to control people who anchored their boats around the stage and listened to the singing from their own decks—free of charge.

On the night of the first show, no more than a hundred people sat in some of the six thousand available seats—but two thousand boats were anchored around the stage and within listening distance in the bay.

"The show was a flop from the start," Glen said, "We spent more money on our airplane tickets than we made that night. But we got some wonderful telegrams. One came from Warner Brothers Studio in Hollywood that read, 'Congratulations on your opening night in Miami,' and another came from Paramount Pictures that read, 'Congratulations on your opening success in Moon Over Miami.' Somebody had sold those studios a bill of goods, because the studios had never heard of us."

Unusual things happened during ordinary singing performances.

One evening the Kingsmen sang with a local group in an auditorium in Dalton, Georgia. The local group was on stage singing when a fight broke out in the audience between the bass singer's ex-wife and current girlfriend, and the police had to be called to pull the women apart.

Jim Hamill said that was the funniest thing he ever saw. Everybody in the house could hear the two women screaming at each other, and that poor bass singer standing up there singing. "Well, Jubilee's acoming, it's acoming in the morning. . . ."

He could tell from the sounds of the fight that Jubilee hadn't arrived yet.

John Broome was a four-hundred-pound-plus drummer for the Kingsmen in the 1960s and early 1970s. He sat on a three-legged stool among his drums and cymbals and played them with a rhythmic clatter. Once at a mobile home park in Fletcher, North Carolina, where the Kingsmen had been contracted to sing for their television sponsor, the stage was a flatbed truck, and in the midst of a song, one leg of Broome's stool slipped over the side of the truck and when he felt himself falling overboard he grabbed his drums and cymbals to hold on— and took the whole works over the side with him.

On another occasion in the Asheville City Auditorium, Broome set up his drums and cymbals on risers behind the quartet, and during one song his tremendous weight was too much for the risers. He broke through and fell to the floor in a great clash and clatter. When Jim Hamill turned around to see what happened, all he could see were Broome's big feet sticking up among the broken risers and tangled percussion pieces.

The Florida Boys worked the Iowa State Fair in Sioux City and were apprehensive to see a long line of Hell's Angels come into the auditorium. The quartet's performance was almost over when the bike riders filed in, came down to the front, and sat crosslegged on the floor in front of the first row of people. Les Beasley started to make a wise crack about leather jackets and Nazi helmets, but he changed his mind and had the quartet sing "Amazing Grace" instead. Before the song was finished, every one of the bike riders got up and quietly left the auditorium.

When Cat Freeman sang first tenor for the Statesmen, Hovie Lister always introduced him as "Sister Cat," and Cat responded sometimes during the performance by making believe he was powdering his face, putting on lipstick, or reaching inside his shirt to adjust his bra.

George Younce filled in on the bass for the Florida Boys for about three months once, and during that time the quartet booked a performance in a Pensacola theater only about three blocks from the quartet's office.

"The guy who promoted the thing," Les said, "had a film on the life of Christ that had been made about 1918, and he hired us and some other group and Martha Carson to do matinees and evening performances, three shows a day."

George picked up the narrative: "Me and Les were standing there listening to Martha wind up her part of the show. Her popularity was already gone—and we must not have had much ourselves because we lacked thirteen people having anybody there that afternoon.

"When Martha went off, this other group came on," George said, "and the tenor had seen Cat Freeman do this thing and had copied him. While the lead singer was trying to sing 'How Great Thou Art' in the most serious vein he could summon, the tenor suddenly pulled out an imaginary mirror and began to primp on stage. He put on eye shadow and I was laughing so hard at the inopportune time he had chosen to do his comedy that Les thought he would have to carry me out. When the guy brought out his little imaginary purse and started putting on lipstick, with the lead singer singing, 'Oh, Lord, my God. . . .' and glancing over at the tenor, I just broke up."

Strange things happen in the audience at gospel sings.

One night with the Florida Boys on stage, a kid in his early teens in the audience began playing with a flashlight, and after a while he became rather disconcerting. Derrell Stewart began to watch the kid more than the piano, and finally the kid's mother saw what he was doing, and jumped up and began beating him over the head with her purse. The quartet came completely apart on stage. Derrell fell off the piano bench laughing.

The Kingsmen were singing one night when a young boy began misbehaving in the audience. On stage the quartet heard the boy's mother say loudly, "If you don't quit, I'm gonna bust your rear end!" He continued to misbehave, and finally his mother picked him up and headed up the aisle for the rear door. Before they went through the door, the boy yelled, "My God, somebody pray for me!"

The Blackwood Brothers had been to the Holy Land where they visited Mount Calvary, and when they returned to the states they had a show booked in Iowa. From the stage, bass singer Ken Turner began telling about the visit to Calvary, and he said, "We were on top of that mountain . . . that mountain . . ." and he turned around and whispered, "What's the name of that mountain?" "Mount Calvary," James Blackwood whispered. "What's the other name?" Ken asked. "Golgotha," James said. "Oh, yes," Ken then said to the audience, "we were on top of Mount Golgother. . . ."

One of the funniest cracks Ken Turner ever made came unwittingly one evening as he gave his testimony.

"I was in the army stationed in the Philippines," Ken said. "Over there, there wasn't anything but dirt and grass and God-forsaken country. I was living in sin—just having a *good* time!"

And then, try as you might, things sometimes will not come out of your mouth right.

When J. G. Whitfield sang bass for the Florida Boys, they went to Thomasville, Georgia, one evening to sing on a program with the Le-Fevres, the Sunshine Boys, and a couple of other groups. The stadium was filled with people, and on the Florida Boys' first stand, J. G. decided to do a song entitled "There's a Leak In This Old Building," a song that Elvis Presley also sang. Whit made a long spiel to introduce the song, and in the process managed to forget the song's title. He fumbled and stuttered around for a minute, then said, "Ladies and gentlemen, this song is called 'I Gotta Leak In This Old Building."

"For some reason," said tenor singer Coy Cook, "we just couldn't get that song going right that night—and if we could have, nobody would have heard it. They were laughing too hard."

Fred E. Daniel sang first tenor for the Blue Ridge Quartet for several years, and at public appearances if anyone complained about the sound system being too loud, the rest of the guys sent the complainant to Bill Crowe.

One night a woman approached Kenny Gates and said, "The PA system is too loud."

Kenny pointed to Bill Crowe and said, "He's the man who takes care of the PA set. Go talk to him."

She went over to Bill and said, "The PA set is too loud."

"Sorry," Bill said, "I didn't hear you."

"The PA set is too loud."

"What?" Bill cupped his hand behind his ear.

"The PA set is too loud."

"I'm sorry," Bill said, "I can't hear you."

"THE PA SET IS TOO LOUD!!!" she shouted in his ear.

"Lady, I can't understand a word you're saying," Bill said. "The PA set has been so loud all night it's got me where I can't hear a lick!"

Quartet singers should always look before they leap. At least, they should look *where* they leap.

In Jacksonville, Florida, at a concert, Derrell Stewart, piano player for the Florida Boys, was singing the lead on a song. All the house lights were down and two powerful spots were on Derrell. The audience became so responsive, he thought he'd better get down among them; so he moved to the front of the stage, and when he gauged the distance to the floor the spots blinded him and the floor appeared to be closer than it was. He jumped anyway, and when he hit the floor the mike went one way and he went the other. He began crawling on his knees, hunting the mike and trying to regain his breath, and the spotlight operator began moving the light around, hunting Derrell, and it took a minute and a half to get all components together again and resume the song.

That wasn't as bad as a local group that went out in the audience one evening with long-cord mikes, and when they finished the song and the audience was going wild, they tried to make a dramatic remount of the stage. Racing down the aisle, they jumped to the stage together—and one guy jumped in the orchestra pit, landing with a resounding crash.

Radio was a great medium for quartets. Lee Roy Abernathy once told a disk jockey convention, "Let me tell you, what people hear on the radio in the morning sets the mood for their day. Their whole day is colored by what they hear. Don't let people tell you, 'I don't pay attention to that.' They do. And you can't live with the kind of stuff they're playing now. If you could change the music in America you could change the world. Good old gospel music would do it."

Lee Roy then added, "I'm not in the record business. I used to be. But do you know why I quit the record business? Because I was never able to make any quartet sound as good as its members thought they were."

* * *

Quartet men were very professional when it came to radio. They knew the ins and outs and the whys and wherefores.

The Sunshine Boys were based in Wheeling, West Virginia, in early 1950, doing regular daily programs on Station WWVA. At night they sang concerts in the area and sometimes didn't get home until the wee hours of the morning. Then they had to be at the studio for an early morning broadcast, and they weren't always in the best mood for that early show.

One morning J. D. Sumner and Freddie Daniel were arguing about something in the studio and the clock was coming up on six-thirty, which was air time for their show.

At five seconds before the show, Freddie threw a songbook that hit J. D. in the face.

J. D. looked at Freddie, shook his finger at him, and said, "Fat boy, as soon as this program's over I'm gonna . . ." Blooie! Eddie Wallace hit a run on the piano and rolled into the theme song. . . .

" . . . whip your . . ." J. D. said, "I'm going home. . . ." He hit the song right on cue, and after the program he and Freddie laughed about what they earlier fussed about.

Television, of course, added visuals to what the quartets had known on radio.

And with visuals they had to be extremely careful.

The Florida Boys did a guest television show once with the Homeland Harmony Quartet, and when Connor Hall and the Homeland Harmony got on camera, Derrell Stewart found a half-gallon can of orange juice back stage, which he rolled slowly across the stage in front of the quartet, out of sight of the camera. Every member of the Homeland Harmony, with eyes flared wide, followed every roll of that can, all the way across the stage—without missing a word of the song.

Perhaps the toughest call for any quartet is being asked to sing in an old-folks home. Most of those who reside in these homes have long since lost their inhibitions and usually say whatever comes to mind.

George Younce said the Cathedrals sang in an old-folks home in Uniontown, Pennsylvania, and the manager of the home cautioned the quartet, "Don't talk to the people. They're so old there's no telling what they might say back. Just go in and sing to them."

After the quartet sang four or five songs, the pianist, Lorne Matthews, leaned over on the piano bench and asked, "What special songs would you like to hear?"

A woman in a wheelchair spoke up, "Well," she said, " 'Breaking Up That Old Gang of Mine' has always been a good one."

"I don't believe we know that one, honey," the pianist said.

"Well, what'd you ask for," the woman snapped back, "you little son of a bitch."

The Florida Boys worked an old folks home once, and in the midst of the performance, a resident woman spoke up. "I thought the real Florida Boys was gonna be here," she said. She had been watching reruns on television and the quartet's personnel had changed.

"We *are* the real Florida Boys," Les Beasley answered, and he remembers thinking, "Gee, she's really old."

"Not the ones I seed on TV," she said.

Les stuck his face forward. "Don't you remember seeing me on TV?" he asked.

"Yeah, I remember you," the woman said, "but I don't know who the hell the rest of 'em is!"

The Cathedrals were invited to a home in Alabama for dinner. The mother of the host was an invalid and a sour person. She was also hard of hearing, her son said.

"Say," the son said, "how about singing Mother a song?"

That may be the toughest request of all for a quartet—to sing a song for a person in a private home. But the Cathedrals hummed up the key to "Wonderful Grace of Jesus" and broke into song. The son pushed them up close to Mama so she could hear. On the end, the Cathedrals, as always, took the song up high and loud.

"How'd you like that, Mama?" asked the son, bending over her.

"Next time," Mama snapped, "don't do it so loud!"

Sometimes—actually, most of the time—outtakes from television shows are better, and far funnier, than the shows themselves.

Once the Rangers Trio and Chuck Wagon Gang were filming their "Gospel Roundup" television show, and Rose and Anna, the female voices of the Gang, were all dressed up in beautiful new dresses. They really looked uptown that day.

Ronnie Page was master of ceremonies for the show and had engaged Rose and Anna in a bit of banter between numbers.

"Rose," he said, "what did you-all do before you started singing with the Chuck Wagon Gang?"

"We hoed cotton," Rose said.

"Really?" Ronnie said. "Did you really hoe cotton?"

"Yes," Anna said, "that's true."

"Well, I'll tell you," Ronnie blurted, "you don't look like a couple of hoers to me."

When Jimmy Jones sang with the Revelaires, they were singing in Alabama with some local quartets, and all were standing backstage talking just before the singing began. The big song at that time was "Brother, Do You Know Where God Lives?"

A woman came backstage, saw Jimmy, and walked over to him. She offered her hand and said, "Mr. Jones, I sure enjoy your singing, and by the way, do you know 'Where God Lives'?"

"Well," Jimmy, engrossed in another conversation, groped for words, "I'm not right sure, but last I heard, he was over in Wofford County somewhere."

CHAPTER TWENTY-THREE

Everybody Had a Quartet

Through the great growth years of gospel music in the South, folks in every town and community were within earshot of a good quartet.

Areas like Florida, Texas, Tennessee, Alabama, Georgia, and North Carolina were hotbeds of quartet singing. Not only did those states produce great singers, they had their share of great quartets.

Take North Carolina. Tar Heel singers were the backbone of a lot of good quartets down through the years. Particularly in low bass singing has North Carolina been productive, turning out such basses as London Parris, George Younce, Rex Nelon, Calvin Runion, Jay Simmons, Bob Thacker, Ray Dean Reese, and Jody Medford. All of those but Younce, Simmons, and Thacker are from the Asheville area.

Just after World War II, North Carolina was fertile ground for quartets. The Rangers worked on Charlotte Radio Station WBT for several years.

Raleigh Radio Station WPTF had the Lone Star Quartet at the same time. Carl Raines, who had been with the John Daniel Quartet for a lot of years, was the bass singer. He sang through the war years with the Lone Star, until 1946. Bert Carroll was the tenor, Elmer Johnson the lead, and Elmo Fagg sang baritone. Jack Taylor played for the Lone Star; he later went to the Stamps-Baxter Quartet, along with Carroll, and then became editor of Stamps-Baxter songbooks.

Clarence Turbyfill of Newton, North Carolina, replaced Elmo Fagg with the Lone Star Quartet in 1946 when he got out of the navy.

Elmo went to Burlington, got on the Tobacco State Network, and started the Blue Ridge Quartet there.

In Asheville, the Carolina Quartet and Friendly Five held forth on WWNC every Sunday, and a bit later Riley Smith had the Tonemasters in Asheville. They sang quite a bit in other areas.

There were hundreds of great singers scattered around the Southern states who never made the big-time, mostly because they were satisfied working the jobs they had and singing part-time. One was Clyde Williams, a bass singer from Asheville. Clyde sang with the Friendly Five. Once, he left the quartet and Rex Nelon, then nineteen years old, replaced him. Rex admitted to being a rather egotistical kid, and one Sunday evening when Buncombe County singers gathered at Alexander for a singing, Rex found a seat beside Clyde Williams.

"I thought I would sit beside him," Rex said, "and let him hear what a singer had replaced him. But when they started on the first song and Clyde started singing the bass, I honestly thought I'd lost my voice. I couldn't hear anything but him. I cupped my hands up to my ears just to make sure I was singing, and the longer I sat there the smaller I got. When it came our time to sing, and I walked out with the Friendly Five, all I could think of was 'What a bass singer that guy is—and what am I doing here?'"

The hills were alive with good singers in those days—and the flat lands, too. Most rural churches sang gospel and spiritual music, and shaped-note, do-re-mi singers developed everywhere. Many, like Clyde Williams, didn't care for the travel and the constant running around. He worked a job and was satisfied to sing part time, staying home with his family.

The Johnson Family sang out of Charlotte. Ma and Pa Johnson lived on a farm and came to town to sing with Arthur Smith and others on a daily variety show. They had a singer called Booger Red who became a Methodist preacher. Betty Johnson had a beautiful voice. She went to New York and sang on the Ed Sullivan Show and married a producer. The Johnson Family sang on the Sullivan Show three or four times. Because of her appearances with Sullivan, Betty Johnson landed jobs in several Broadway shows and became known nationally. She sometimes returned to Charlotte as a star with Broadway shows.

Late in 1946, Carl Raines and Clarence Turbyfill quit the Lone Star Quartet and moved to Winston-Salem to form the All-Star Quartet. Jack Pittman sang tenor in that quartet. They made a poor judgment in hiring a young man who was an alcoholic, a great singer just out of a treatment center. After three or four months he fell off the wagon and broke up the quartet.

During the war, the Rangers left WBT and the Swanee River Boys with Merle and Buford Abner sang in the Rangers' place.

Arthur Smith and the Crackerjacks had a variety show on WBTV in Charlotte after television took its foothold. They usually did a gospel song or two on every show, and their Crossroads Quartet became quite popular in North Carolina. The quartet had a different sound. Tommy Faile sang bass, Arthur's brother Ralph sang baritone, Arthur handled the lead, and whatever girl singer they employed at the moment sang soprano. Arthur Smith wrote some great songs, including "I've Been With Jesus," "I'm So Happy," and "Climbing Jacob's Ladder."

They were tied to WBTV, which limited their range for personal appearances, but they never worked strictly as a gospel quartet, anyway. When they took their road show out, it was a full variety show, with country, gospel, pop, and a lot of great instrumentation and comedy.

With all this Southern gospel on radio, once television came, management was open to gospel on TV. Pat Patterson came home from service after the Korean War, and his sister, who worked at WBTV, got him an appointment with the powers-that-were, who arranged for an audition of a new gospel quartet to go on staff over Channel 3 (WBTV). Patterson got the remnants of the Crusaders Quartet, after Bobby Strickland's death, and took three Crusaders into his quartet: Bill Hefner, Buddy Parker, and Herschel Wooten. They hired David Reece, an announcer on WNNC in Newton, to play the piano, and called themselves "The Southerners." But the station wanted a different name and renamed the group the "Harvesters Quartet."

They were one of a few quartets that started off on top, with fulltime salaries from the station, a television show twice a week, and a Columbia recording contract.

Around the first of 1948, Elmo Fagg moved his Blue Ridge Quartet to Spartanburg, South Carolina, onto WSPA Radio. Elmo hired Clarence Turbyfill to sing lead, but when he recognized Clarence's good falsetto voice, he put him on first tenor. The Blue Ridge had a recording contract with Decca.

When David Reece left the Blue Ridge and went with the Rangers as pianist, Clarence Turbyfill drove up to Lincolnton, North Carolina, and hired Kenny Gates as pianist. Kenny was playing at that time with the old Drum Funeral Home Quartet and with a dance band on Saturday nights out at Jones Airport.

Two Burke brothers, Charles and Udean, in Newton, started an act like Lee Roy and Shorty's Happy Two. They sang around the neighborhood and occasionally got to sing on programs with the LeFevre Trio and the Rangers. Once when they sang on a show with the Statesmen, Charlie said, "We thought we were in the presence of God."

Clarence Turbyfill got married and quit the Blue Ridge Quartet, and Elmo hired Ed Sprouse, a Mississippian, to replace him. Sprouse's first appearance was to be at an All-Night Singing in Catawba, North Carolina. Lee Roy and Shorty were to be there, and so were Charlie and Udean Burke.

Came the night of the singing, and Sprouse was flying into Spartanburg from Mississippi. His plane was delayed in Atlanta, and he was late. Spartanburg was an hour and a half from Catawba by fast automobile.

The Burkes went on stage. They only knew five or six songs they could sing together; so they sang two or three songs and saved the other three for later.

Shorty and Lee Roy came on and sang five or six songs and entertained with comedy for about an hour and a half.

When they were so tired they couldn't go any farther, Lee Roy announced intermission. "After intermission," he said, "the Blue Ridge Quartet's tenor will be here."

Unfortunately, the tenor didn't show up then, either, so Udean and Charlie sang their other three songs, and Lee Roy and Shorty entertained a while longer, and then the Blue Ridge Quartet came on with Shorty singing tenor for the still-missing Ed Sprouse.

They did four or five numbers and dismissed the crowd, and as the crowd went out of the building, Ed Sprouse came in.

Lee Roy still likes to tell about that night when he and Shorty, with some help from Charlie and Udean, put on an All-Night Singing all by themselves.

Through the years, many other good quartets and singing groups have sprung up in North Carolina: the Kingsmen, the Inspirations, the Pine Ridge Boys, the Hopper Brothers and Connie, the Singing Americans, the Primitive Quartet, Down East Boys, Dixie Melody Boys, the Kingsboys, HeavenBound, and the Anchormen, to name a few.

Tarheelia has never lacked for good gospel singing.

"Well, we are blessed today with a lot of good groups," Charlie

Burke said, "more than ever before. Back in those old days just after the war, you could just about count the leading professional groups on the fingers of two hands.

"There were a lot of semi-professional quartets on radio then, and some of them could outsing the pros. They rehearsed and took it more seriously. They just didn't reach out as far as the others did.

"All of these groups came out to the schoolhouses back then," Charlie continued. "A lot of churches thought the music was too jazzy and wouldn't let quartets in. Also, a lot of gospel fans today think it's awful that a gospel quartet like the Stamps Quartet would get up and sing a Western song or something besides gospel. But back in the forties, they sang gospel, which was their thing, and then they did the old Western songs, or some good folk songs, and had a comedy skit.

"When Carl Raines was with the Lone Star, he had a 'Joe Squashhead' act that left the audience in stitches, they laughed so hard. I do that act sometimes now, and that's where I got it, from Carl Raines. He'd come out all dressed up and do some comedy stuff and then have a boy do a solo while he went backstage and changed again.

"Same thing with the Swanee River Boys, and a lot of others; they had great comedy routines. They were all entertainers."

Newcomers were not molly-coddled in those days. They had to know music and be ready to sing at a moment's notice. Sight-reading was required of singers then.

"When a group hired you," Charlie Burke said, "they'd lay out a brand new Stamps-Baxter book and say, 'Let's do that song,' and you had to sight-read it or be left behind.

"Too," he added, "a lot of mornings, those quartets would get to the radio station and the quartet manager would come in unprepared, grab a songbook, and say, 'Okay, we'll do twenty-seven, sixty-eight, forty-three, seventy-six, and a hundred and ten,' and you had to sing those songs on the air without missing a note.

"The Blue Ridge Quartet were good sight-readers. Glen Payne is a great sight-reader; he started in those days when it had to be done.

"Those old men in the quartets," Charlie said, "had sung enough that they didn't want to be bothered with rehearsing, and a new kid who came into the quartet had better be able to read notes and sing them at the same time.

"Stamps-Baxter took a lot of criticism from pastors and others over the years," Charlie said, "and most of the criticism wasn't justified.

Stamps-Baxter trained a lot of sight-readers who went on into churches or revivals, and some of them were good readers but didn't know how to select songs for a service. Consequently, some of them would come up with bouncy numbers just before a very serious sermon, choosing songs right out of the convention books. They sang a lot of songs that they shouldn't have sung right before a man preached a sermon. So some preachers got turned against the Stamps-Baxter books, but it really wasn't the book's fault; it was a problem of the singing leaders who were misusing the books."

CHAPTER TWENTY-FOUR

They Wanted to Sing

Those who came forth to sing the gospel before World War II and for fifteen or twenty years following the war were something akin to Daniel Boone venturing into the wilderness: They faced the unknown with all of its deprivations and hardships. Like Boone, those singers thought their venture held the promise of eventual success, whatever they envisioned success to be, else they might have chosen something else to do.

Or was that the case? In most instances, it apparently was, but there were exceptions—like Eldridge Fox.

Eldridge's apprenticeship was not always pleasant. There were times when he and other members of his quartet had to sell blood to get money for food.

"Before the Kingsmen were born," Eldridge said, "I had a group called the Ambassadors. Part of us later became Kingsmen. We had it rough. We came in on many a Monday morning and went downtown in Atlanta and sold our blood to get money enough to eat until we could go out singing again."

If you follow that logic far enough, you'll determine that collective starving was easier to take than individual starving.

"One weekend we went out for three days of singing, and all we had to eat that whole weekend were five Pepsies and one pack of crackers," Eldridge said. In that quartet with him were Jim Kirby, Calvin Runion, Jim MacCauley, and a guy from Atlanta named Dalton.

"Once in a while," Eldridge said, "we made enough money to have seven or eight dollars each when we got back to Atlanta, and we re-joiced then because we didn't have to sell our blood. If we didn't make it, though, we got six dollars a pint for blood, and that kept us until we went out again. We kept that blood bank stocked for a long time."

Eldridge moved from Atlanta back to his home in Asheville and began playing piano for the Kingsmen Quartet. The early Kingsmen were a group of guys who really wanted to sing. Included were Jack Henderson, Frank Cutshall, Reece and Raymond McKinney, Eldridge Fox, Calvin Runion, Ray Talley, Kermit Jamerson. All of those didn't sing at once, but they were the principals of the Kingsmen during their early days. Martin Cook was the Kingsmen's first pianist.

They worked and struggled for four or five years, singing for a bus. Everything they made singing, and all they could spare from their regular jobs, they put into paying for the bus. Each member of the quartet bought his own food, his clothes, chipped in to buy fuel for the bus and pay for bus repairs, and pooled their money to make payments on the bus.

"I don't know—and I'm not kicking—," Eldridge said, "but I wonder if a lot of kids nowadays would go through what we did to sing. I hope they would.

"The first mode of travel the Kingsmen had," he said, "was an old Chrysler limousine, a three-seater. We thought it was the prettiest thing in the world. It was about twenty years old, I guess; it looked to be a block long, and we had *The Kingsmen* emblazoned on its sides. The K was made out of a musical note with a crown on top. We were in high cotton riding in that limousine.

"We took it to Cherokee one night, about fifty miles west of Asheville, and had a singing on the Indian Reservation. It was a big singing for us—maybe fifty people there—and on top of Soco Mountain coming back to Asheville the brakes gave out on that limousine. Soco is a steep mountain with a winding road down its eastern and western slopes. We held on for dear life and rode the limousine to the bottom of the mountain with no brakes. It's a wonder we hadn't all got killed in that thing!

"But we felt a calling of the Lord," Eldridge said, "and that was the main and most important thing. We felt that singing was what we should be doing, and we were young and full of whatever; and we really wanted to sing. We thought the sacrifice had to be there if we sang. We never knew that the Statesmen and the Blackwoods and people like that were making good money singing. We wanted to sing and we had to pay to do it. That's how simple our philosophy was."

At that time, in the 1950s, perhaps into the early 1960s, the guys who sang with the Kingsmen were almost afraid to dream of ever hitting the big-time.

"If I had had the ability to draw on a blackboard what I wanted to do in my lifetime," Eldridge said, "I would have drawn exactly what the Lord has let me do. That would have been a dream for me to make a vocation out of singing. Naturally, I think everybody thinks that somewhere down the road he might be able to hit the major leagues, but none of us ever allowed ourselves to think that was even possible.

"We were thinking of doing exactly what we were doing for the rest of our lives, and I guess if we'd stopped long enough to take a good look at it, our futures would have appeared to be pretty grim.

"The Statesmen and Blackwood Brothers were the groups we looked up to. We liked the Homeland Harmony and the LeFevres and all those other groups, and I'd have crawled fifteen miles to hear any of them sing—but the big boys on the block were the Statesmen and Blackwoods, and for us to think, even to dream, that we could do what the Statesmen and Blackwoods were doing . . . well, that never entered our minds."

To say that theirs was a dream world would be putting it mildly. They really looked up to the Statesmen and Blackwood Brothers.

To them, low down on the totem pole as they were, those at the top had no warts.

They just couldn't have.

Could they?

Eldridge was a youngster, fresh out of high school, when he went to Atlanta to work for the Statesmen. He had written some songs and the Statesmen picked up three or four of them for their publishing companies. The Statesmen had bought the J. M. Henson Music Company, the Lee Roy Abernathy Music Company, and the Vep Ellis Music Company, and they intended to plunge deeply into publishing gospel songs. Thus, when groups recorded the music of any of those three companies, the Statesmen received royalties, a perfectly legitimate way of doing business.

The Statesmen recorded some of Eldridge's songs, including a winner entitled "What Love." It was so successful that fifteen years after their first recording of the song, they recorded it again.

The Statesmen hired Eldridge to operate their music companies, and he moved into Jake Hess's basement in Atlanta and worked from there.

The Statesmen were scheduled to leave soon on a five- or six-weeks tour of the West Coast, and Hovie Lister told Eldridge he wanted him to do two things while the quartet was gone: to monitor Warren Roberts, an Atlanta disk jockey, to see which groups he was playing most; and to compile a songbook using only those songs written by members of the Statesmen Quartet.

Eldridge immediately began to bug Jake, Rosie Rozell, Doy Ott, the Big Chief, and even Hovie for songs they had written.

"It was like pulling teeth," Eldridge said, "trying to get songs out of most of those guys. Nobody would give me enough songs but Big Chief."

Rosie gave him a couple; Doy chipped in two or three; Jake found one or two; Hovie gave him one; and Big Chief inundated him with songs.

Every time Eldridge turned around, Chief handed him another batch of songs, usually saying, "Here's another song or two for the book."

"I loved to see the Chief coming," Eldridge said. "Nobody ever knew how good he could sing. He could sing as low as J. D., but Hovie never would let him sing like that. It wasn't the Statesmen style. When he came into Jake's basement, I'd get at the piano and Chief would sing his songs to me. Boy, was he great!"

While the Statesmen were touring the West, Eldridge put the songbook together. They returned to Atlanta on a Monday, and no one was interested in seeing the songbook. Scheduled to go on the road again on Wednesday, they quickly left for home.

The Statesmen kept their bus at the Greyhound garage and when they met there on Wednesday to go back on the road, Eldridge, with some trepidation, showed up with the manuscript for the songbook. He was nervous because the book leaned heavily to Big Chief's songs. Each man had one, two, three, or four songs in the book except Chief, and he had fifty.

The day was rainy, and as the bus rolled down the road, Eldridge began showing the book. Jake, his buddy, said, "Looks real good." Chief thought it was great. Rosie didn't really care. "It's nice," he said after thumbing through it. Hovie thought it would do just fine.

But Doy took his time perusing the manuscript. Carefully he counted how many songs each man had in the book, and finally he sat back and said, "Looks like another of them Wetherington productions to me."

The bus was old and the air conditioner was broken. Several windows were down, and Doy threw the manuscript out a window.

"Six weeks of work went out that window into a mudhole," Eldridge said.

They didn't even stop the bus to get the manuscript.

When Eldridge got back home, he thought, "Maybe those guys are human after all."

The incident didn't ruffle Big Chief's feathers. He was an even-tempered guy whom everyone loved. He could sing—Boy, *how* he could sing!—and Hovie was criticized by many in the industry for "not letting Big Chief sing lower than he does."

He was, indeed, an exceptionally low bass singer, but his moderately low tones more fitted the Statesmen style, and Hovie held him there, even in the face of criticism from his peers. Hovie did not build and guide the Statesmen without knowing exactly what he was doing.

Buddy Liles, bass singer for the Florida Boys, feels indebted to Chief. "He was one of those guys who was behind the scenes," Buddy said, "and he was a pusher, a hard worker. Once when I sang with the Orrell Quartet, we were in South Bend, Indiana, on a program with the Statesmen, and Big Chief said he wanted to talk to me the next day in Chicago where we were staying at the same hotel. He bought my breakfast and we talked for nearly two hours. I got more help from that conversation than from anything else that ever happened to me. We talked about the general do's and don't's of the gospel music business, about stagemanship, presentation, songwriting. I guess what he did was give me a pep talk—and it was great!"

Jim Hamill thought Big Chief was a prince of a fellow, except for one fact: He forgot the rudiments of arithmetic on a golf course.

"Big Chief loved to play golf," Hamill said, "but he never could keep his score straight. He'd hit a drive into the woods, and you'd hear him in there hacking at the ball; and now and then you'd hear the ball bounce off a tree limb, and you'd actually see him take about nine strokes. But when you finished the hole and asked Chief what score he had, he'd think a minute as if he were looking back and counting his strokes, and then he'd say, 'Had a five.'

"Yes, sir," Hamill concluded, "he was a super guy—if you could overlook his golf."

* * *

Even for some members of the Statesmen Quartet, the starting-out years were lean. Jake Hess faced literal starvation a few times in the early days. So did Big Chief.

Once Jake and Big Chief resorted to stealing peaches to keep the wolf away from the door.

"We were so hungry," Jake said, "that we didn't think of it as stealing. We thought we were kinda borrowing 'em, or I guess we thought whoever owned the orchard wouldn't mind keeping some singers from starving."

In the 1940s and 1950s, and even the 1960s, singing for a living did not insure one of being able to eat three times a day. It didn't even mean a fellow would eat at all every day.

Paris Mountain, just north of Greenville, South Carolina, will forever remain a favored place in Jake Hess's heart. "That," he laughed, "is where me and Big Chief kept from starving to death."

They were singing with the Melody Masters just after World War II and they had no money. "I mean not even a dime," Jake said. "Nobody in the quartet had any. We had gone one day without food and up till about two o'clock the next day. Now, you can easily go two or three days without food if you know when that next bite is coming and where it's coming from, but we didn't know when we'd get to eat again. We were literally starving."

The Melody Masters had an old Buick, and Jake and Big Chief drove it up Paris Mountain, looking at the peach orchards. The trees were bending low with peaches, and harvest time was at hand. Carefully reconnoitering, when they came to a place that was out of sight of people, they picked peaches and dumped them in the Buick.

"We loaded that car down," Jake said. "The Melody Masters had Big Chief, Alvin Toodle, Calvin Newton, and me singing, and Wally Varner playing the piano; and we all lived in one room. We ate peaches for three days without having a bite of anything else."

Someone asked Jake, "Did it ever cross your mind to do something else for a living?" and Jake looked as if he'd been struck with a whip.

"No, no!" he said. "Listen, we never thought anything about making a living in those days. We wanted to sing! When somebody goes to get a job today, he asks, 'How much will I make a week?' but back in those days we never thought about whether we would make anything. We only thought of how many new songs we could sing and how many places we could go. We just loved to sing. And being hungry didn't bother us. We didn't even think about being hungry till we were about to starve to death."

It's hard for Jake Hess to remember when he wasn't singing. Born in Limestone County, Alabama, Jake started singing when he was five. He sang with three of his seven brothers—Ollie, Butch, and Cleveland. "I was just a kid," he said, "but I was the star because they had to stand me in a chair for people to see me. The saddest day of my life came when I grew up and realized that people liked me because I was young and not because I could sing."

His first paying job came when he was fourteen when he hooked up with Louie Auten and the Tennessee Valley Boys. Then he went with the Melody Boys, and after that he began working with the John Daniel Quartet.

"I was with the John Daniel Quartet three times," Jake said. "John Daniel fired me three times. He gave me a five-dollar raise once and fired me before I drew a paycheck.

"Through World War II, I thought I was fantastic because I could get a job singing anywhere," he said. "It never dawned on me that all the good singers were either in the army or in defense plants. I'd get a job and work three or four months, go somewhere else, stay there three, four months, just move around. I was the most unreliable, unpredictable fellow in the world—and I had a wonderful time."

Jake's style of singing has always been distinctive. He has had a marvelous singing voice all his life. He developed a style that was unique, raising his eyebrows till the whites of his eyes showed, hunching his head down between his shoulders, raising his hands slowly, palms down. When you saw Jake Hess sing, you knew you were watching someone special. You didn't even have to listen to his voice; a deaf person could enjoy watching him sing.

"I don't know where I got that style," Jake said. "It's always been comfortable for me. I do know that people used to compare James Blackwood and me. When they heard James sing they'd say, 'Man, isn't he terrific? I could never do that.' And when they heard me sing, they'd say, 'Hey, I can do that.'

"If there was anyone I copied," Jake continued, "it was a guy in Birmingham by the name of Ernest Braswell. He was one of the finest singers who ever lived. I don't know why he didn't travel with quartets and sing; some good singers just don't like to travel, and maybe that was it. He sang with the original Deep South Quartet in Birmingham where I first heard him, then with the Radioaires. He looked like he lived every word he sang, and he was so clear I could understand every word. I don't know if he's still alive, but to me he was the greatest lead singer who ever lived."

Even though John Daniel fired him three times, Jake looks back and remembers Daniel with fondness. "He was like a daddy to me," Jake said. "Who else would let a brash kid get under his skin three times?"

When the war ended and the big quartets began to travel more, Jake went to Florida and sang in the Sunny South Quartet with J. D. Sumner. They were based in Tampa and Jake wanted to get away; so he swapped places with Lee Kitchens, who sang with the Melody Masters. That's where Jake and Jim Wetherington became acquainted.

The Melody Masters moved from Florida to Nebraska and went on staff with Radio Station KFAV in Omaha. KFAV had thirty-two staff musicians, all of whom worked out of Lincoln, Nebraska, and the job paid good wages. For the first time in his life, Jake made enough money to live on.

But money still didn't mean as much to Jake as singing. He took a cut in salary to join the Statesmen in 1949, a move that cinched his later inclusion in the Hall of Fame.

"I sang with the Statesmen fifteen years," Jake said, "and we all look back to that time and say, 'Those were the good old days.' If we had anything over other quartets, it was that we loved what we were doing so much that we lived it."

Evangelist John Rawlings preached in Asheville once on the same evening that the Statesmen sang in the Asheville City Auditorium. After his service, Rawlings went out to eat with friends and came back to the George Vanderbilt Hotel, where he was staying, about one o'clock in the morning. When he came into the lobby, Rawlings heard music coming from the mezzanine, and being from Arkansas and a lover of gospel music, Rawlings thought this singing sounded exceptionally good. He walked up the stairs to the mezzanine and found the Statesmen gathered round a piano working out a difficult part of a new song. They had sung the song that evening and weren't satisfied with the way it sounded; so instead of going to bed and working the bugs out of the song the next day, they went immediately to work while their errors were still fresh in their minds.

"Those guys were so concerned about precision and doing their best," Rawlings said, "that they were there in the middle of the night working things out."

The concern of the Statesmen Quartet for excellence was unsurpassed.

Jake Hess is a tough one. He has lived through two operations for cancer, two heart attacks, two open heart surgeries, and a list of other ailments as long as his arm.

He left the Statesmen December 7, 1963, and formed the Imperials with Sherrill Nielson, Gary McSpadden, Armond Morales, and himself singing, and Henry Slaughter playing piano.

"When I organized the Imperials," Jake said, I wanted a quartet that could stand flatfooted and sing all night if necessary and never repeat a song, never take an encore. That's what I had with the Imperials. If people liked what we were doing and wanted us to sing more, we sang another song. I got that idea when I overheard a lady say, 'If you like the song, applaud just to be courteous. If you applaud too much you'll just hear the same song over and over.' It took me a year and a half to get the Imperials together, and in the four years I sang with them we never repeated a song."

Jake never passed up an opportunity to sing. "I sang every chance I got," he said. "You may say, 'No one asks me to sing,' and I will answer, 'Ask them.' All my life, since I was five, I've been shaking people's pants legs and saying, 'Hey, if you don't have anyone to sing here, I'd like to sing.' I guess I might have been a little overbearing, but most people understood. You can get by with that when you're a kid, but you've either got to have an awful lot of brass or be awfully good to get by with it when you're grown up."

Talk to any of those who have been around a number of years and you'll usually hear a story of bad times.

Like Buddy Liles. He sang with a quartet called the Olson Brothers of Portland, Oregon, early in his career, around 1964 to 1966 when money was scarce.

"We blew three bus engines on one trip," Buddy said, "and there weren't many quartets in those days that could survive that. We blew the first one in Southern California, had it fixed, and then blew it again in Northern California. Somebody fixed it up again and we went on into eastern Oregon and blew it again.

"Since we couldn't get back to Portland to get a warranty," he said, "we had to have it fixed again. There were four guys in the group and every one of us was flat broke. Honestly, we didn't even have a dime between us.

"Finally, to keep from starving, we went into restaurants, studied the menu a long time while we ate all the salad crackers and water we could get, then changed our minds about eating there and left.

"We reached the point that I finally contacted my dad, who wired me some money to Boise, Idaho, and we eventually got back on our feet. But we went four days eating only crackers and water."

Because of the hardships of singing, many good singers quit the business and found something more dependable to do. Others thought about quitting, but stuck it out—like Glen Allred of the Florida Boys.

"Yes, sir," said he, "there were a lot of times I thought I ought to do something else. A lot of 'em. There were times when I thought every day was going to be the last one. It was hard to carry on, and I thought sometimes maybe I was gifted to do something else, but I never could figure out what it was; so I stayed with this."

After Wally Fowler revolutionized the gospel singing business with his first All-Night Singing in 1948, everybody and his brother tried to get into gospel music. Hard times hit the business about 1955.

"All-Night Singing was a magic phrase," Brock Speer said. "It was a money-making phrase. Wally put all-night singings everywhere and made quite a contribution to the business. Quartets began doing a more professional job, singing in less of a convention style and more of an entertainment style. It got too entertaining and that might have helped cause the slump. I think groups now are more serious spiritually about what they do."

Jack Clark agreed, and he is one who had time to study the situation that existed in the mid-1950s. It was at that time that his star began to rise.

"I don't think the emergence of rock 'n roll music had anything to do with the slump in quartet singing in the middle fifties," Jack said. "I think it was a simple problem of oversaturation.

"The quartet business was good in the late forties and early fifties, but the entire nation wasn't ready for it. The business became so good that suddenly everybody had a gospel quartet trying to book dates, and there were just not enough dates to go around. As a result, a lot of quartet people had to go back to doing something else. The business became overpopulated and had to go through a weeding-out process.

The ones who were really good, really dedicated and took care of their business, survived. The rest fell by the wayside.

"After that," he said, "and only after that, was when the real growth in the gospel quartet business began to take place, and there has been a pretty steady growth since."

It was not only singers who overpopulated. Others did too,

"When business got good in the early fifties," Jack said, "there were three promoters working in Chattanooga. They had a gospel singing in Chattanooga Memorial Auditorium every other Saturday night until people got tired of it. Then people who still loved gospel singing realized they'd had enough and began going elsewhere on Saturday night. Crowds fell off and promoters floundered."

It was during that slump that Jack Clark came out of West Virginia to make his musical mark. At the end of 1955 he went to California to play piano for a quartet called Bob Jones and the Songfellows. But very little time was required for this West Virginia hillbilly to realize that he did not like California.

He heard that Connor Hall needed a pianist for the Homeland Harmony Quartet in Atlanta, and even though he knew the Homeland Harmony had been affected by the slump in business, he got on the horn and called Connor. Neither Connor nor Jack knew the other personally, but Harold Lane, who had sung with Connor, had known Jack Clark in their native West Virginia, and he recommended Jack to Connor.

"Well, he gave you a nice recommendation," Connor said to Jack on the phone, "but we don't have a job for you because I've just lost three members of the quartet and business is bad. If I had you here I probably couldn't pay you anything."

But Jack was willing to come to Atlanta on a chance. He was sick of California. After a couple of days, he telephoned Connor again and all but begged for a job.

"I don't even know if we're going to keep singing," Connor told him. "I really don't have a job for you."

After the third or fourth phone call, Jack told Connor, "I'm willing to take a chance. All I want to do is play the piano, and I want to play it back there."

Connor continued to hedge, and Jack finally said, "Look, I'm going to be in Atlanta next Thursday morning. Do I have a job when I get there or not?"

Connor always had trouble saying no to anyone.

"Well, since you put it that way," Connor acquiesced, "come on. We'll see what we can do."

Connor put three inexperienced men—Jack Clark, Rex Nelon, and Jim Cole—on stage with himself and James McCoy and made it work. After a time, they turned into a really good quartet. But it wasn't easy.

After they had been singing together for eight or ten months, the Homeland Harmony allowed itself to be booked into Texas for a tour of several towns. They were gone nine days, traveled 3,700 miles in Connor's car, and when they got back to Atlanta and subtracted car mileage, hotel bills, and eating expenses, and split the rest of the money equally between the five men, each man took home, "as I recall," Jack Clark said, "either $8.67 or $9.37. That was for nine days of work."

But the Homeland Harmony Quartet wanted to sing.

"This is something I do not see now," Jack Clark said. "The kids are getting jobs too easily, and you see a lot of them come and go. When I got in the quartet business, we didn't come and go—we came to stay. Whatever price we had to pay, we paid.

"I kept all my date books," he said, "and I can go back and show you a lot of weeks when we made $16, or even two or three dollars, and once in a while as much as $38. Money counted a little different in those days, but not that much. We really didn't make a living for a long while, but we learned the quartet business."

Jack Clark went on to play piano for the Harvesters Quartet in Charlotte, working with Bill Hefner.

"Bill was a good tenor," Jack said, "a super salesman, and one of the funniest guys I've ever known. But he was moody. There were days when we got on the bus with Bill and laughed and had a great time for days, and then there were other times when you spoke to Bill and he looked right through you without knowing you were there. We had a tendency to get aggravated with him, but he was just that way.

"The time I spent with the Harvesters was happy time," Jack said. "We played a lot of golf, had a good time together, and worked extremely well together on stage.

"Bill Hefner is an achiever. I asked him once what he was going to do when we disbanded the Harvesters, and he said, 'I don't know. I'll do something. I think I can make as much money messing around as working for somebody!'"

And he did do something. He became a Congressman, a representative for the Charlotte district in North Carolina.

* * *

London Parris's difficulties in starting out never reached starvation, like Jake Hess and Eldridge Fox. London's hardships were with his voice. He had the depth to sing great bass, but knew nothing about how to use his voice—until he met the right man.

Born in Alexander, North Carolina, just north of Asheville, in 1931, and named Conley Parris, London grew up with quartet singing all around him. His father, Will Parris, was a great bass singer. His brother Hugh was a good bass singer, and his brother Rex may have been the best in the family. Dennis Parris, London's cousin, taught singing schools and was a fine singer. So London came from good singing stock.

He sang a bit before he went into the Air Force in 1950, signing up for a four-year hitch. Stationed in Macon, Georgia, London met Deacon Utley and the Smile-A-While Quartet, and then London began singing with a semi-professional quartet called The Travelers, out of Macon.

Once they went to Fort Payne, Alabama, to sing in a ball park on a warm summer evening in 1952. Lee Roy Abernathy and Shorty Bradford were there, singing as the "Happy Two." They pulled their four-door Cadillac into right field and opened all four doors, making themselves a makeshift dressing room.

Conley Parris, known then as "Sarge" because of his Air Force rank, moseyed over to say hello.

"Hello there, fellows," Sarge said.

"How you doing?" Lee Roy asked.

"Just fine," Sarge said, and he coughed.

Lee Roy's head snapped around. "You hear that, Shorty?"

"Hear what?"

"That boy's cough," Lee Roy said. "He's got that sub-bass register."

" 'Bout to get a little cold," Sarge said.

Lee Roy turned around. "Do you sing?" he asked.

"Oh, Lord, no," Sarge said, dodging the issue. "Never sang a song in my life."

"Listen," Lee Roy cocked his ear toward the stage near the pitcher's mound. "They're singing 'Rock of Ages' out there. Sing it with them."

"Rock of ages . . ." Sarge sang, his voice pitched too high.

Lee Roy laughed. "You can beat that, can't you?"

"No, but I wish I could," Sarge said. "I'd love to be a singer. I'd give anything in this world to be one."

He was pulling Lee Roy's leg a bit, but he was talking to the right man, though he didn't know it then.

And Lee Roy, like an elephant, never forgot.

Two years later, Lee Roy and Shorty were singing with Connor Hall and Aycel Soward in the Homeland Harmony Quartet, and Aycel quit. The quartet had a television show, and Lee Roy announced on the air that they needed a bass singer. What better way to find one?

Fifty-five men responded, and the quartet tried out all of them, but not one could do the job.

Suddenly, Lee Roy sat upright. "Say, Shorty," he asked, "do you remember that feller in the ball park with us?"

"Where at?" Shorty asked. Lee Roy knew that Shorty was an observant man; he noticed every little thing. He was anything but the fool he sometimes appeared to be on stage.

"Fort Payne," Lee Roy said. "He walked off down there. . . ."

"I remember him," Shorty said. "Tall and slender."

"That's him."

"I don't know *who* that was."

"Did you not talk to him any more?" Lee Roy asked.

"No, I didn't," Shorty said. "Only other time I saw him was after the singing when he got in the car with Deacon Utley and left."

More than two years had passed.

"Reckon you could find him?" Lee Roy asked, knowing how much Shorty loved a challenge like that.

Shorty picked up the telephone receiver and said into it, "Macon, Georgia, please. I want the residence of Deacon Utley."

Deacon's wife answered the phone. "No," she said, "they're practicing at another house tonight. I can give you the number over there."

In a moment Shorty had Deacon Utley on the line.

"Deacon," Shorty said, "there was an old boy at the singing at Fort Payne with you one time—old tall, slender boy. Do you remember who that was?"

"Yeah," Deacon said. "That was Conley Parris. He's sitting right here. Just got out of the service."

Shorty said, "Put him on," and handed the phone to Lee Roy.

"Hello," Conley said.

"Conley?"

"Yeah."

"Be at my house tomorrow night at five o'clock."

"Who is this?"

"This is Lee Roy Abernathy."

"You mean you and Shorty?"

"Me and Shorty are the ones you talked to over there at Fort Payne," Lee Roy said, "The quartet wasn't with us."

"Where do you live?" Conley asked.

"I live in Canton, Georgia," Lee Roy said, "forty-four miles north of Atlanta."

"Well, I'll be there," Conley said.

He showed up at five o'clock the next day, just in time to get in the car with the Homeland Harmony Quartet and go to Sylacauga, Alabama, for a concert.

Lee Roy almost had to grit his teeth at some of the notes Conley Parris hit that night, but he recognized a natural depth of voice and knew he could make a bass singer out of this man.

The next day, the quartet went to Atlanta to sing on television, and as they entered the parking lot, Lee Roy turned to Conley and said, "What do they call you?"

"They call me Sarge," Conley said.

"Ain't no Sarges on my television show," Lee Roy said. "Now, let's see—Parris . . . France . . . Paris . . . London . . . That's it!" he snapped his fingers. "That's your name. We'll call you London Parris."

"Shore enough?" London said. He has been known as London since.

Lee Roy claims the Homeland Harmony Quartet split up over London. "He couldn't seem to sing a lick," Lee Roy said. "The other boys finally left and got A. D. Soward to come back. I took London and built the Lee Roy Abernathy Quartet."

London moved to Canton, Georgia, and worked with Lee Roy for a year, taking a singing lesson every day. He walked four miles to take those lessons. He was a dedicated man.

But it was six months before he could properly sing a low C.

"When it came time for him to hit it," Lee Roy said, "I'd make him turn it up instead of down. So one week in practice he got where he could hit the low C. I saw that he could do it, but I bided my time."

In about a week, Lee Roy said to London, "Now, any time you want to try that low note, feel free to do it, because you can sing it now."

The next time the quartet was on television, London turned a song down to a low C and when he popped it perfectly he grinned and said, "How you like that, 'Fesser? How you like that low C?" He didn't even remember he was on the air.

London went on to great heights as a bass singer. He could sing the low G's and F's, but he loved best to sing C's, B-flats, and A-flats. "I just enjoy the good old four-part harmony," he said, "and when you get an octave apart, sometimes you don't have that good harmony that you do when the bass stays up in that other register."

London sang for years with the Rebels Quartet, then for five years with the Blackwood Brothers, then with his own quartet, the Apostles, who won a Dove Award their first year out.

He came off the road because he wanted to spend more time with his family, and gospel music was the worst for it.

London Parris had one of the great voices.

In these pages, we have met people who became gospel singers to escape the toils of the cottonpatch. We have met those who sang while starving, who didn't realize they could make a living singing—and didn't care because they only wanted to sing.

Here is a man who started singing so he wouldn't have to mop floors. His name is Jerry Goff.

He had come from the West, where he grew up in Oregon, Washington, and Arizona, to study at Lee College in Cleveland, Tennessee. His dad was a graduate of Lee, the Church of God college, and was then a leader in the Church of God.

Jerry got a job mopping floors and washing dishes in the Lee cafeteria to pay for his tuition and other fees. He had worked in the wheat and pea fields of Oregon that summer and saved every penny he made for spending money in college.

That was 1953. The head of the Lee College cafeteria was a man named Pigg. Once Mr. Pigg came through the cafeteria and encountered Jerry Goff pulling a two-foot mop across the floor, sweating and laboring. Mr. Pigg engaged Jerry in conversation, and the subject finally came around to money.

"How much money am I making mopping these floors?" Jerry asked.

"You are making thirty-five cents an hour," Mr. Pigg said.

"Thirty-five cents!" Jerry exclaimed. "Man, you mean I'm only making that much? I can make more money than that hauling bricks."

Jerry removed his apron and hung it over a chair and headed for the door, leaving soapy water on the floor.

An angry Mr. Pigg shouted after him: "I'll have you given demerits." A total of 101 demerits meant dismissal from school, but Jerry knew he wouldn't draw that many demerits for quitting his job.

The head of the college's work force telephoned Jerry and asked him why he quit in the middle of a job.

"Why does a man have to wait till the job is finished before he quits?" Jerry asked. "If he quits, he quits. And I quit!"

Jerry still had his spending money, but he needed an income to pay his college fees; so he formed a quartet from the student body, and for singing dates leaned on a lot of preachers who knew his dad.

He called his quartet the Continental Quartet. He spent his wheat-and-peas money for a 1949 Packard, promised his quartet they would split whatever they made singing, and hit the road.

The quartet was quite tuneful, and Jerry found that people loved the new songs he wrote. He kept writing songs and found that he was good at it.

The following school year, Jerry formed a new Continental Quartet from the student body because several members of the original group had been graduated. He managed to pay his men $20 to $25 a week, which wasn't bad pay for college students in those early-1950s days.

After two years at Lee, Jerry transferred to the University of Tennessee at Chattanooga and earned a bachelor's degree in radio and television production, graduating in 1957. He evangelized a year. He also earned a master's degree at Vanderbilt's Peabody College and then taught philosophy and Spanish at Fresno State College in California.

But his heart was in singing, and he came back South, sang with the LeFevres, then plunged into television production.

Somewhere along the way, he converted himself to the Southern Baptist faith.

He became involved with a good friend, Jim Thrasher, in a medical venture in which they made a good amount of money, and started his own television program called "America Sings."

He joined the Thrasher Brothers and sang with them five years, left in 1971 and formed a group called Jerry and the Singing Goffs.

Jerry also blew a mean trumpet, which he used extensively both with the Thrasher Brothers and the Singing Goffs.

Today Jerry is still in television production, and he travels the world preaching and singing.

"I have never enjoyed the ministry more," he said, "both in singing and in preaching, and I plan to continue what I'm doing now."

CHAPTER TWENTY-FIVE

Promotions

W. B. Nowlin bridges the gap between the present and the past. His walk is unsteady these days, his eye a little dim because of advancing age; but W. B. Nowlin is a giant in the industry. Because of men like him—and women, too—who were willing to risk their money on the chance of making a little more, or at least breaking even, those great gospel quartets of the 1940s, 1950s, and 1960s had places to sing where they, too, could piece together a living. Most of the time.

W. B. Nowlin promoted Texas, which, in many minds, made him big to begin with. He also promoted Arkansas and Oklahoma, and sometimes Missouri, and often in other states. At one time or another, he promoted almost all the states in the forty-eight with country, gospel, and even popular music stars.

W. B.'s patented "Battle of Songs" became an early trademark in the promotional world of gospel music, and dozens of other promoters keyed off his productions in building their own.

No one was ever better grounded in gospel music than W. B. He dated back to the early days, though not all that time as a promoter. He worked for V. O. Stamps, who looms on that distant horizon as one of the biggest figures of the early days of quartet singing.

The early days of W. B. Nowlin's life paralleled those of many another man who made his roundabout way onto the stage and away from the cotton patch.

Born in 1905 in Texas, W. B. married a schoolteacher in December of 1925 when he was twenty years old. Unfortunately, the mentality toward women being what it was at the time, the school board refused to hire Irene Nowlin for the 1926–27 school year because of the possibility of having to replace her in midterm because of pregnancy. School systems simply frowned on hiring young married women.

W. B. hadn't finished high school when that setback was thrown into his life, and he had to go out and find a job. Locating employment early in 1926 wasn't as easy as one might think, and W. B. finally had to invent a job. He talked his brother into letting him help make his crops. His brother was a farmer with rather large acreage, and W. B. knew how to make a crop. He worked hard that spring and summer, and when the crops were finished in July, W. B. moved to Cisco, Texas, and went downtown to pound the pavement looking for work.

In a department store called Eckhorn, he found a job. Eckhorn was a chain with twenty-four stores; J. C. Penney at the time had sixteen. W. B. braced the store manager, a man named Joyner, for a job. After Joyner looked him over, he asked, "How much experience have you had?"

"I've never worked in a store," W. B. said, honestly, "but if it's experience you're looking for, I've got plenty. I've got a lot of experience baling hay and milking cows. I'm right off the farm."

Joyner liked W. B.'s approach. He said, "Okay, I need three references. Bring them to me Monday and I may be able to hire you." On Monday, W. B. brought him three acceptable names and got the job. He was thrilled to death at being able to work elsewhere than on the farm.

He caught on quickly, and after six weeks Joyner thought he had W. B. trained well enough that he could leave him in charge of the store through the lunch hour. From eleven-thirty till one o'clock, only two people were in the store: W. B. downstairs, and a woman clerk on the balcony. From an alcove in a corner, W. B. could see the entire store without being seen except from close up, and when business was slow, he often stood in the alcove watching the store.

One day two women came in and walked up the stairs to the balcony. One asked the saleslady to accompany her into the dressing room to help with a dress, and while they were in there, the other woman looked around, and seeing no one—W. B. was standing in the alcove— she took a thin chiffon dress off the rack and put it in her umbrella.

"Oh, Lord!" thought W. B. "What can I do?" He wished Joyner was back. But Joyner was late, and the two women were leaving the store. As W. B. stepped out of the alcove and walked toward the front door to intercept the women, Joyner came in. Joyner bowed and spoke to the women and just as they reached the door, W. B. caught the woman with the umbrella by the arm.

The action startled Joyner.

"This woman has been shoplifting," W. B. said, and Joyner's brow clouded.

W. B. opened the umbrella and the chiffon dress fell out, the tags still on it.

"Young man, you scared me," Joyner said. "The six weeks I've trained you were about to go down the drain."

W. B. worked in that store for a year and a half, then in 1929 he had an idea that changed the course of his life. A piano company was spending millions of dollars furnishing schools all over the country with songbooks at a low price in order to advertise pianos. W. B. had the idea of selling local ads to pay for the songbooks, thus getting them for schools free. To prove his idea, he told twelve ads in Cisco and had them printed in the songbooks for Cisco's school. By doing this, he got one hundred free songbooks for the school. The printing company talked him into selling thirty-six dollars more in advertising so that both he and the printing company could make a profit, and he did. That turned into a ten-year job for W. B.

And that began his long association with the Stamps-Baxter Music Company of Dallas, Texas, which had compiled the songbooks.

In 1930 W. B. broadened his original idea. He thought of getting women in communities to sell ads for the songbooks, and the idea worked.

"It was almost like a license to steal," he said many years later. "The women never missed. Who could turn down a pretty lady selling an ad for her children's school?" The ads cost from a dollar-fifty to six dollars each.

Schools used the songbooks in their assemblies. The books contained songs like "Columbia, The Gem Of The Ocean," and "Old Black Joe," a song you'd get in trouble using today.

After W. B. sold out a territory, he felt he could go back over that territory with a new book and do as well again. So V. O. Stamps compiled a new book containing 112 songs. He put a patriotic drawing on the cover and called the book "All America Sings." Through W. B.'s efforts, millions of copies of this book were sold.

W. B. Nowlin continued to be an idea man, and through his association with V. O. Stamps he felt he could do almost anything within reason to sell songbooks. All of his ideas were legitimate and legal. He never traveled the dark corners of salesmanship; he kept everything open and above board and made sure that others profited for their labors. By 1935 he had seventy people in different states selling songbooks for him. They sold ads for the books, and Stamps-Baxter printed the books with the ads in them and shipped them out. The salespeople made good money, and the more they made the farther afield they ranged. All concerned made a fair profit, and thousands of schools were furnished free songbooks.

W. B. widened his field again in 1939. He sent letters to a thousand preachers of seven denominations, asking them to help him compile a revival songbook that would meet their specifications. He asked each preacher to select ten songs he would demand in a songbook for revival meetings. When the book was finished, it contained more than a hundred songs, each requested by more than two hundred ministers. The book was nondenominational and any church could use it. The secret of selling was to get local women to sell ads for the songbooks, working in the field with one of W. B.'s trained representatives, and for their churches the women got free songbooks for revivals. The ads sold easily because merchants knew their money would help the local churches.

"We moved more than two million of those books," W. B. said. "I was the biggest customer the Stamps-Baxter Music Company ever had. We worked together well, and I traveled all over the country."

W. B. visited the capitals of all forty-eight states in 1938 and got the State Superintendent of Public Instruction, or his counterpart, in every state to endorse the songbooks. These endorsements were valuable tools when W. B. called on local superintendents for songbook sales.

He made another discovery in promoting songbooks, a discovery that concerned the U.S. Mail. "I mailed advertisements to thousands of local superintendents and principals," he said. "For three or four years, I sent this mail third class because the rates were so much cheaper. We got back an eight- to ten-percent response. When someone suggested that my returns would be higher if I sent the advertisements air mail special delivery, I tried it. The recipients had to sign to receive their letters—and I got a ninety-four percent response! The way we sent the mail added importance to it."

V. O. Stamps was a big man. He weighed 235 or 240 pounds. He was a genial and smart businessman, just what a fledgling business like Gospel Music needed at the start. He enjoyed sharing the profits with others, especially since the Great Depression was ravaging the country and dollars—cents even—were scarce.

Once he devised a bonus plan through which people who really wanted to work, those who sold more songbooks, would make more money than those who dragged their feet. He drafted a letter describing his bonus idea and called W. B. in to read it.

Through the letter, he used the word "royalty."

"Why don't you call it a bonus?" W. B. asked.

"Because I couldn't think of 'bonus' to save my life," V. O. said. "That's why I asked you to read it."

V. O. had a radio show from 6 o'clock to 6:30 on Saturday morning, and his audience numbered in the tens of thousands—maybe even millions. He announced his bonus plan and a new songbook on the air. "Now if you're a schoolteacher," he said, "just tell me who you are and where you teach on a post card, and I'll see that you get a free copy of this book and complete instructions on how your school can secure a quantity of songbooks without charge."

On the following Thursday, V. O.'s desk was piled with bound stacks of post cards, more than 3,500 of them, answering his appeal.

W. B.'s part of the deal was to send a songbook to each teacher and ask her to pick out two good schoolchildren, take them downtown and sell so many ads for the songbooks. He directed that a certain amount of the money collected be directed to him to pay printing and delivery charges and to net himself and V. O. a fair profit—and the teacher got to keep the remainder.

V. O. turned a profit of $2,900, with which he bought furniture for his new home.

No one had to go on the road. The entire transaction took place by mail.

The Stamps brothers, V. O. and Frank, did not get along as well as brothers should. Once V. O. had to take Frank to court to make him quit calling his quartet the Stamps Quartet. V. O. had a copyright on the name. The judge told Frank that he could continue to use the name, but he would have to add something to it to make it different from V. O.'s quartet name. Thus, the Stamps All-Star Quartet was born—and all those other Stamps-Something quartets.

"V. O. was the greatest personality," W. B. said. "Frank never could make his message stick like V. O."

A Texan named Tom Hunter wanted to oppose the powerful W. Leo Daniels for the governorship of Texas, but figured he didn't have a chance unless he could find someone who could take a lot of votes away from Daniels. Hunter offered V. O. Stamps $50,000 to run against himself and Daniels.

"No way," was V. O.'s response. "I've got the biggest business of its kind in the world. I've got a million friends. I don't want to be governor—but mark my words, Mr. Hunter, I could beat W. Leo Daniels and you, too. If I ran for governor, I would be elected. You are underestimating me, sir."

He turned down the offer.

V. O. died in 1940 at the age of forty-eight. W. B. Nowlin remembers the day well.

"V. O. had a blood clot develop on Monday while his quartet was doing a program," he said. "He was rushed to the hospital and things looked bad."

W. B. and V. O. had eaten lunch together every Thursday for years. That's when they did their business, over a lengthy lunch. V. O.'s niece, Grace, was his secretary.

On Thursday morning, W. B. walked into the office and spoke to Grace. "This is the biggest, emptiest office in the world without V. O.," he said.

"You can say that again, Mr. Nowlin," Grace said.

W. B. sat down in V. O.'s chair, and the telephone rang. He answered. It was Dwight Brock calling.

"W. B.?" Dwight inquired, making sure who he was talking to.

"Yeah," W. B. said. "It's me."

"I'm glad you answered," Dwight said, "because I've got bad news. V. O. just passed away."

W. B. looked at the clock. It was nine o'clock.

"It was his heart," Dwight said. "Boom! He went just like that. You and Grace had better try to notify everybody before noon. This is sudden."

W. B. said later, "We told everybody in the office and you'd have thought an old hawk had flown down and picked up the hen and left a bunch of scared little chickens. There were two over here, and three yonder, talking quietly, and grieving. The whole place just shut down."

J. R. Baxter, Jr., V. O.'s partner, moved to Dallas and became president of the Stamps-Baxter Music Company. Frank Stamps came off the road and moved into the Dallas offices, too, and worked out of there for a while.

But the folks in the office knew that things wouldn't be the same without V. O.

* * *

W. B. Nowlin promoted his first live music concert in 1948. He had a half-gospel, half-country-pop show, with Eddy Arnold as the featured attraction. He booked the Stamps Quartet and the Stamps-Ozark Quartet to sing around Eddy.

The show was the featured attraction at a huge picnic—really an all-day singing and dinner-on-the-ground—in W. B.'s hometown, De-Leon, Texas. The date was July 18, 1948, and the Texas heat beat down upon the grassy park in which the event was held.

But 12,000 people paid a dollar each to hear the music and eat the picnic lunch, and it was the largest crowd W. B. ever had.

Nowlin was a popular figure in DeLeon. Everyone knew him. He had lived there twenty-six years and was mayor of the town for six years.

He was elected mayor without knowing he was running for the office. Out of town on election day, he telephoned his wife that evening, and she said, "Good evening, Mr. Mayor. How does it feel to be mayor?"

He asked, "Mayor of what?"

"Mayor of DeLeon," she said. "They elected you today."

"Well, I'll be dogged," W. B. said.

At that time, three qualified voters could put a person's name on the ballot without the candidate knowing it—and that's what happened to W. B. He was conscripted.

"The reason they wanted me," he said, "was because I wasn't obligated to anybody. We lived there twenty-six years and raised our family because it was a good place for the family to be when I was on the road."

To this day, W. B. Nowlin learns things at his concerts. A promoter's education never ends. His began with that first concert in 1948 in DeLeon. . . .

Eddy Arnold's manager was Colonel Tom Parker, who later managed Elvis Presley to gigantic fame and fortune. He managed Eddy Arnold for nine years before Elvis came along.

W. B. scheduled the show to open with the Stamps Quartet singing thirty minutes, to be followed by Arnold doing an hour's show, with the Stamps-Ozark Quartet closing the show. He thought that arrangement would work out fine.

But when Col. Parker learned that W. B. had scheduled a gospel quartet to follow Eddy Arnold, Parker had a hissy.

"Mr. Nowlin," he argued, "this isn't right. Nobody can follow Eddy Arnold. He's going to sing seven songs that have already won gold records. How is that quartet going to follow that?"

"Mr. Parker," W. B. said, "I didn't know that. And I don't know how they're going to follow Mr. Arnold—but they're going to have to because that's the way the show's set up and it's too late to change it. This is my first promotion and I didn't know any better. We'll just have to see what happens."

"Well, I'm sorry," Col. Parker said. "I wish I had known it in time."

"If you don't think it's good this afternoon," W. B. said, "we're going to do two more shows tonight and we'll change it then."

"All right," Parker said.

The Stamps Quartet warmed up the crowd, and when Eddy Arnold came on the 12,000 people began to scream and holler and have a good time and Arnold took DeLeon apart piece by piece and put it back together again. He sang the seven gold songs and a lot more, and when he left the stage the people stomped and yelled for more.

When the Stamps-Ozark Quartet came on behind Arnold, it had to wait till the crowd quieted before starting its stand.

When the quartet's emcee got the crowd's attention, he said quietly into the microphone: "Ladies and gentlemen, we don't know you, and you sure don't know who we are. We're the Stamps-Ozark Quartet, and the man who is responsible for this concert is supposed to pay us for coming on here.

"Let me tell you," he continued, "that we sing a different type of song, and today we're going to sing a song that not a person here has ever heard because it's brand new. We want you to listen to the words because they'll give you a blessing."

He stepped back on line, and the Stamps-Ozark Quartet sang "Oh, What A Savior." The crowd was quiet as a mouse. W. B. looked around and Col. Parker stood in the wings with tears rolling down his cheeks, watching that quartet. He made no effort to hide his tears nor to wipe them away. He simply enjoyed the song and he cried.

The crowd exploded with joyous applause and the Stamps-Ozark Quartet made a big hit that day. W. B. finally had to pull the singers off stage.

That was the day Col. Tom Parker fell in love with gospel quartets. In later years, any time Elvis wanted a gospel quartet to back him on stage or on records, Col. Parker got the best quartet available—first the Jordanaires, then the Imperials, and for the last six years of Elvis's life, J. D. Sumner and the Stamps Quartet.

In 1949 Col. Parker had W. B. put the Imperial Quartet on five shows with Eddy Arnold. They played Houston, Galveston, San Antonio, Laredo, and Austin. Marion Snyder was emcee for the Imperial Quartet; and he had what he thought was a lot of fun on stage, especially introducing his singers. He introduced one member as being from Birmingham "where his parents are in the iron and steel business. His mother irons, and his daddy steals."

Snyder thought that was terrifically funny, but Col. Parker called his hand. "You're the biggest ham I've ever seen," Parker told Snyder. "This is a professional show and you're trying to make a high school performance out of it. It is not necessary to tell these people where each of you is from and what your mother and daddy do for a living."

Then Parker cut Snyder down. "On the next show," he said, "instead of doing fifteen minutes, you sing for eight minutes and come off."

Snyder was livid, having his quartet's segment cut in half, but he learned a valuable lesson from a great promoter.

That night, six thousand people jammed the hall, and the Imperial Quartet did three songs. The last one was a novelty number in which the bass singer mocked a trombone with his hands and lips— and his performance stopped the show.

The six thousand came to their feet, yelling and screaming and clapping their hands, asking for more.

The show's emcee turned to Col. Parker and asked, "Colonel Tom, what you gonna do?"

"Tell 'em to sing three more songs," Parker said.

The emcee relayed the message to Marion Snyder, who hissed, "Tell him to kiss where I can't," and he brought his quartet off stage with the crowd going wild.

Parker pulled Snyder to one side and apologized profusely, W. B. remembers, and the Imperial Quartet went back on stage and did five more songs, to the delight of the crowd.

There was still animosity between Snyder and Parker when the show moved into Austin for its last date. About 5 o'clock that afternoon, W. B. and Snyder were eating at the Driscoll Hotel when Col. Parker walked up to their table.

He introduced himself formally. "I'm Tom Parker," he said, extending his hand, "manager of Eddy Arnold."

W. B. caught on quickly. He rose and took the colonel's hand. "I'm W. B. Nowlin," he said, "and this is my friend, Marion Snyder, with the Imperial Quartet."

Col. Parker took a seat. "Gentlemen," he said, "let's play tonight like we've just met right here, that we've never seen each other before and forget that anything on earth ever happened that could be in any way detrimental to this show tonight."

That was like the Colonel—always thinking what was best for the show.

"I want this last show," he said, "to be the best ever."

And what a show it was! W. B. said the Austin crowd was entertained as well that evening as any crowd anywhere, anytime.

The Imperial Quartet started with Marion Snyder at the piano sometime in the 1940s and sang until it disbanded in the 1950s. When Jake Hess started the Imperials in 1964, he telephoned Marion Snyder and asked if it would be all right to use the name Imperials, not Imperial Quartet, and Marion said, "Jake, it's a compliment that you would call me and even consider using the name."

Snyder had played piano for the Stamps Quartet in the late 1930s. He was playing for the Stamps when V. O. died. He was V. O.'s brother-in-law, having married his sister.

Promoting gospel concerts was not easy, even in the glory days of quartet singing. Beginning with his first promotion, W. B. Nowlin had many unusual experiences.

His first all-gospel concert was in Tulsa, Oklahoma, in 1949. He booked Wally Fowler and the Oak Ridge Quartet, the Stamps-Ozark Quartet, and the Imperial Quartet for eleven dates. The well-known Oak Ridge Quartet was a regular on the Grand Ole Opry, and it was featured on the eleven gospel dates. W. B. paid Wally Fowler $400 a day on that tour, which was outstanding money at that time.

W. B. booked the first concert into the Convention Center in Tulsa and handled all the preliminary details by telephone and mail. He went to Tulsa for the first time the day of the show, and the first person he visited was the manager of the auditorium.

"I've been looking for you," the manager said. "I didn't know whether you were going to show up or not."

"Well, I'm here," W. B. said, "and I want to talk to you because this is my first gospel concert, and I've got eleven in a row."

W. B. withdrew his checkbook from his pocket. "I've got my

checkbook here," he said, "and I'm going to write a check for every expense that concerns this building and you. I want you to itemize the expense here."

"Okay," the manager said, "but there's one expense you're going to fuss about, and I've got to mention it to you. The musicians union has a contract with the city. Any time anybody uses this building for a musical event, he has to pay ten union musicians forty dollars a man. You can make them come down and play in the orchestra pit before the concert and at intermission, or you can let them stay home and give me your check for them."

W. B. was puzzled. "I don't have any choice?" he asked.

"No, sir," the manager was emphatic.

Anger flooded W. B.'s body. "Sir," he said, clenching his teeth and letting his anger boil over, "I didn't know Hitler won the war!"

The manager leaped to his feet. "Get out!" he screamed. "Get out and don't come back! Find another place to hold your concert."

He threw W. B. out of his office.

That was at 3 o'clock on the afternoon of the concert. W. B. went to the bookstore which had handled the advance sale of tickets and found that 2,000 adult tickets and 300 children's tickets had been sold. The building only seated 2,800.

He went to see a friend at a record shop. "Bill," he said, "I've made a big mistake," and he told him what had happened.

"I think I can straighten it out for you," Bill said. He telephoned the city attorney, told him what happened, and the city attorney called the mayor. The mayor and city attorney came to the record shop, and everybody went to the auditorium. When they walked in the office, the sixty-seven-year-old manager wanted to throw W. B. out the window.

But the mayor was firm. He told the manager, looking him straight in the eye, "You're too old for this job. I voted for you and helped put you in as manager of this auditorium because we needed you, but we don't need you for this kind of conduct.

"Just because someone disagrees with you," he continued with the tongue-lashing, "doesn't give you the right to do something like this. You go home right now and get your wife and get out of town. Take a vacation. I don't want to see you for two weeks, and then we'll talk about your job. Meanwhile, your assistant can run the building."

Dealing with the assistant manager, W. B. had to write the check for the union musicians, but he stopped payment on it the next day and never had to pay it. Because of that incident, the city of Tulsa reviewed its auditorium policies, W. B. said, and did away with the contract with union musicians.

Two years later, W. B. took the Red Foley Show into Tulsa and had to deal with the original auditorium manager, and this time he turned out to be an agreeable man.

"Mr. Nowlin," the manager said, "you're the only man who ever raised hell about that deal and did something about it. The city cancelled its contract with the union and straightened out the mess. You come on in and we'll work together." And they did.

By the mid-1950s, W. B. Nowlin's reputation as a promoter was established, not only in Texas but in surrounding states. His business thrived, and all the quartets knew that singing for W. B. was the same as money in the bank.

The city of Lubbock, Texas, built a new municipal auditorium in 1956, and W. B. decided to open it with a gospel sing on a Saturday night. The Saturday date was the same as that of his scheduled singing in Fort Worth, so he switched the Fort Worth date to the previous night, Friday, to avoid conflict and confusion.

Since a lot of people had been attending his Saturday night singings in Fort Worth for six years, W. B. phoned a columnist on one of the Fort Worth newspapers, and asked if he would give a plug to the change in the paper.

"Sure, I'll take care of it," the writer said, "but do you know what you're bucking in Lubbock that night?"

"No, I don't," W. B. said.

"Liberace," the newsman said. "He's going to be in another hall out there on Saturday night."

"Well, that won't bother us," W. B. chuckled. "I've got the Blackwood Brothers on the program, and they've got a piano player named Jackie Marshall who plays notes Liberace has never heard."

He was being facetious, of course, but the writer, being the newspaperman he was, knew a good story when he saw one. He quoted W. B. in his column on the day of the singing.

W. B. rode to Lubbock with the Blackwood Brothers and went into the Plainsmen Hotel, where the Blackwood Brothers would stay that night. The first people he saw in the lobby were the two men who were promoting Liberace.

As W. B. walked over to speak to them, Liberace himself got off the elevator and made his way to them.

The men introduced W. B. to Liberace. W. B. knew the promoters had seen the article in the Fort Worth paper, but he didn't know if Liberace had. He also knew that Jackie Marshall was getting off the bus and would be in the lobby shortly.

He showed the article to Liberace and when the great entertainer finished reading it and a huge smile spread over his face, W. B. said, "I didn't intend for it to be printed, but there it is."

"I'd like to meet that guy," Liberace said. "I think it's a swell story."

"Here he comes," W. B. said, seeing Jackie walk into the lobby with his traveling bag in one hand and his suit over his shoulder.

"Jackie, come over here," W. B. beckoned, and when Jackie walked up, W. B. said, "I want you to meet a friend of mine. This is Liberace."

Jackie was struck dumb. W. B. had already told Liberace about Jackie's quick-play music course, *The Marshall Plan*, and Liberace said, "I'd like to subscribe to that Marshall Plan. Would you take my subscription? Maybe I could learn some new notes."

Everyone in the group laughed heartily, and Liberace laughed louder than all. His sense of humor was huge, and he enjoyed a good joke on himself.

That evening, Liberace filled the other hall, and the Blackwood Brothers and the Statesmen overflowed the new auditorium.

Whether intentionally or not, Liberace finished his show an hour before the gospel sing was over, and he hurried over to the auditorium, arriving backstage with the Blackwood Brothers on stage, just in time to see Jackie Marshall and J. D. Sumner do their Liberace routine.

Jackie imitated Liberace at the piano, and J. D. mimicked Liberace's brother, George, bringing out a huge candelabra and placing it just right on the piano, staggering around under the weight of the thing. Their routine drew swells of laughter from the capacity crowd— and the laughter turned to oohs and aahs when Liberace walked on stage in his spangled suit. He was grinning ear to ear as he walked up behind the unsuspecting Jackie. J. D. had seen him coming and had discreetly melted into the background.

Jackie almost fell off the bench when Liberace took the microphone James Blackwood handed him and said, "Jackie, that's swell— but let me show these people how I do it."

Jackie slipped off the bench and Liberace took over, and for twenty minutes he entertained that crowd royally.

He brought the 3,100 people to their feet, shouting and yelling for more, and the Blackwood Brothers, the Statesmen, Gov. Jimmie Davis, and the Florida Boys, who made up the show, all came on stage to applaud him.

Don't ever tell W. B. Nowlin that Liberace wasn't one of the world's greatest entertainers.

"Not only that," W. B. said, "but he was the most wonderful human being you'd ever want to meet. He would visit with anybody, and he was very easy to talk to."

After the show that evening, Liberace wallowed around on the ticket counter, introducing himself and talking with dozens of people. He signed autographs for most of an hour and proved extremely generous with himself and his time.

Fort Worth was W. B.'s big town. By 1956, he had had six years of concerts there, twelve to sixteen a year; and by that time, with the popularity of the Blackwood Brothers and the Statesmen soaring to an all-time high, if he didn't have them on at least every other program, he didn't have a success.

He booked the Blackwoods and Statesmen into the auditorium every two months, filling out the card with two more groups, selected from the Speer Family, the Oak Ridge Boys, the Florida Boys, and a few others.

On the other months, he booked other groups, trying to bring all the top groups to town every year—and his system worked well.

There were fourteen years during which the Blackwood Brothers and Statesmen drew larger crowds every time they came to Fort Worth to sing, a record perhaps unparalleled in all of music.

W. B. called his singings "The Battle of Songs," and the name seemed to fit. Groups battled it out on stage before capacity crowds. In 1964, Fort Worth hit its peak. W. B. promoted sixteen singings in the city that year. On four occasions he filled two buildings with people and shuttled the quartets back and forth. On two other evenings, he filled three buildings with people. In 1965 he went back to monthly promotions, afraid he would wear the town out by overpromoting.

"Too," W. B. said, "the business began to change about that time. Different things came along. Some of the groups got too commercial, for one thing." Then the charismatic movement came in—groups like the Happy Goodman Family and the Singing Rambos—and W. B. realized that his crowds were divided among themselves.

"It reached the point," he said, "that I had to segregate the crowds, and the singers, too. And that's true today. Groups like the Hinson Family and the McKameys and the Inspirations I put on one program. They have tremendous followings, but their people are different than those who like the Stamps Quartet, the Cathedrals, and groups like that.

"We know who among our people will come to each program, and we handle the telephone and mail order tickets with that in mind.

"Some," he said, "will come to both singings, but not enough to fill a house. Those things are very noticeable at the box office. We learn those things, and there's nothing we can do to change them."

Gospel music's great promoters—among them W. B. Nowlin, Lloyd Orrell, J. G. Whitfield, Polly Grimes—had always to be wary of partnerships. Usually civic clubs were fine to promote with, because their members worked for a common cause and the good of the entire community. But promoters had to be careful how they chose individual commercial partners.

In 1956, Nowlin began to promote Springfield, Missouri, with a partner who, for obvious reasons, we will call Smith, a man who owned a business and a quartet. Smith's quartet had sung for W. B. on occasion, and W. B. thought he might be all right as an on-the-spot promotional partner. Smith could do the legwork without W. B. having to visit Springfield before each promotion.

That first promotion, however, went awry from the start. Smith had his quartet members take up tickets, and in doing so managed to bilk W. B. out of $1,200.

W. B. called Smith up to his hotel room for an explanation, and Smith openly admitted what he had done. Then he added, "Mr. Nowlin, you don't think I'm dumb enough to let you come up here after I've done all this work and leave town without me having enough money to buy a sandwich. I tried to get it all."

"Well, I'll try to stop that," W. B. replied.

The following month, Smith booked another concert without W. B.'s participation, booking the Blue Ridge Quartet, the Wills Family, and the Plainsmen. W. B. telephoned those groups and told them Smith was a crook, and all three cancelled the date.

Smith filed a suit against W. B. for $135,000.

W. B. booked his next concert in Springfield without Smith and his quartet. He worked with another local quartet, whose manager was a United States Marshal, and got the fire department to take up tickets.

During the concert, two officers came backstage and tried to serve a damage citation on W. B., but the citation was made out in the name of W. B. Nolin.

"Sorry, boys," W. B. said. "I can't sign that. It's not my name."

"What is your name?" one asked.

"My name is W. B. Nowlin," he said. "It's spelled N-O-W-L-I-N."

"Okay," said the officer. "We'll take care of you. We'll get this fixed and be right back."

W. B. looked up the U.S. Marshal, told him what the score was, and they settled up quickly. W. B. returned to the hotel and checked out and went to the depot and got on the train.

When the officers returned with a properly worded citation, W. B. was a long way down the tracks.

The citation was finally served by registered mail, and W. B. went to Springfield to answer the charges. The U.S. Marshal got him a lawyer who got the suit dismissed on the grounds that W. B. had been improperly served by mail rather than in person by an officer of the law. The lawyer only charged W. B. a hundred dollars.

Six months later, W. B. booked the Blackwood Brothers into Oklahoma City and was talking to James Blackwood when a man came up and said, "Mr. Nowlin, I think you're the dirtiest man I know."

Nowlin looked the man over and replied, "I don't know who you are or I might be able to return the compliment. Who are you?"

"My name is Jones," the man said. "I'm a used car dealer. You mistreated a lifelong friend of mine and put him out of business. You ruined him."

"I don't believe I know what you're talking about," W. B. said.

"His name is Smith," the man said. "He's at my house, he and his wife and two small children because they have nowhere else to go. It's all because of you, and I wanted you to know it."

"I'd love to sit down and tell you my side of it," W. B. said, "but I don't think you deserve it. It's not like you think it is, and you haven't hurt me a bit."

Two months later, Jones showed up at W. B.'s Oklahoma City promotion again and asked for W. B. by name at the box office. W. B. recognized him but went up to him and extended his hand. Jones shook hands and said, "Mr. Nowlin, I drove up here seventy-five miles to apologize to you. My friend Smith stole the best car I had and went to

Florida, and I can't do anything about it because of our family relations. But I told my wife I had to come up here tonight and tell you I'm sorry for the way I talked to you before."

W. B. Nowlin wouldn't take anything for the life he has lived. "I sometimes think that I've had so much fun," he said, "and so much pleasure that my life has slipped away so much quicker than it would have if it hadn't been so wonderful.

"Gospel music is so clean and wholesome," he said, "that the city of Fort Worth doesn't even require a security man at the auditorium when I have a singing—and it's been that way for thirty-six years."

CHAPTER TWENTY-SIX

Small Town Doings

All promoters of gospel music during the postwar heyday of quartet singing were not giants like W. B. Nowlin, J. G. Whitfield, Lloyd Orrell, and Wally Fowler, who promoted multiple cities. Some were local men who were satisfied to bring great singing to their hometowns every month or two—with the additional hope of turning a dollar or two.

Typical of these was an automobile salesman named Riley Smith, who promoted City Auditorium in Asheville, North Carolina.

Asheville was a town of about 50,000 people located in the heart of the beautiful Blue Ridge Mountains. It was a tourist mecca where folks came to soak up the beauty and quietness of the hills.

In the early 1930s when he was a young man, Riley Smith had a gasoline station in Leicester, outside Asheville. Through the late 1930s and the 1940s, Riley, a baritone, sang in local quartets, including the Sebren Quartet, organized and operated by George W. Sebren, who owned a local bookstore which handled the latest songbooks of Stamps-Baxter, Vaughan, Tennessee, and other publishers. Sebren's largest claim to fame, however, was that he had trained and sung in the very first professional male quartet ever formed in 1910.

Riley headed the rationing board in Asheville during World War II, a thankless job, of course, but Riley Smith was a popular man because he was so thoroughly honest.

And that trait of character was in his favor when, in 1951, he decided to promote monthly gospel music shows in the Asheville City Auditorium.

He tried his hand at promotion once in 1949, paying Hovie Lister and the Statesmen Quartet $75 to sing at Vance School in West Asheville. He had known Hovie Lister since Hovie was a pup. Riley remembered Hovie's dad, W. Hermon Lister, picking Hovie up and putting him on the piano bench to play for the Lister Brothers Quartet in Greenville, South Carolina. Greenville was just down the mountain, sixty miles from Asheville.

Riley attended all the local singings: the big ones at Alexander Baptist Church outside Asheville where London Parris, Rex Nelon, Kermit Jamerson, Eldridge Fox, and other good singers learned to perform. He had attended singings in a large room above Liggett's Drug Store in downtown Asheville, and had sung in the Superior Courtroom of the Buncombe County Courthouse.

No one had ever tried to promote in the 2,500-seat Asheville City Auditorium, but Riley had a notion he could make it if he followed Wally Fowler's All-Night Singing format.

Riley had his own quartet by this time, called the Tonemasters, and his piano player was Bob Robinson, who went on to a measure of fame with the LeFevres and the Sons of Song.

The first two times Riley promoted City Auditorium in 1951, he didn't have enough people to sing to; so he gathered everyone in front of the auditorium and told them his problem. "I can save the price of the auditorium," he said, "by not opening the doors." The people understood, got their money back and seemed to be satisfied. Riley paid the talent out of his own pocket.

On the third program, he drew enough people to break even, and told his friends, "Thank the Good Lord, this things's going to go."

In 1951 he contracted top talent for $125 to $175 per quartet. He charged $1.20 for adult admission, and while he promoted for eight years, through 1958, and the price of talent increased several times, he never increased the price of his tickets.

Riley always used his own quartet, the Tonemasters, on the program, and usually split $75 among the members, excluding himself. Then he tried to have two or three top drawing cards. The Statesmen, the Speer Family, and the Harmoneers were top draws in Asheville, and if he could get the three for one program, he knew he could fill the house—almost, anyway.

The Sunshine Boys were dynamite, and they combined well with the Foggy River Boys, the LeFevres, and the Tonemasters. The Swanee River Boys, Bobby Strickland and the Crusaders, the Goodman Family, and the Homeland Harmony were good draws in Asheville.

The Swanee River Boys were different. They sang a soft and perfect harmony. There were other different groups, too, that Riley used
occasionally, like the Jordanaires, the Crossroads Quartet of Arthur
Smith, and the Chuck Wagon Gang.

"The Statesmen were the biggest drawing group I had," Riley said,
"but I liked the Sunshine Boys and the Rangers Quartet. The Rangers
were wonderful. Vernon and Arnold Hyles were terrific. They were
singers, just like the Sunshine Boys. They knew what singing was all
about. They'd come on stage singing and go off singing.

"The Swanee River Boys were solid singers, no question. You could
hear a pin drop when they sang. They didn't waste their time talking;
they sang. If they tried to talk, they fell flat; they had to sing—and
everybody listened. They sang that soft harmony that lulled a crowd—
and then the Statesmen would come out and knock the people right out
of their seats. The Statesmen could do anything they pleased on stage
and pull it off. They were great showmen; they knew exactly what a
crowd wanted—and they gave it.

"And I'll tell you something else," Riley said, "Ace Richman and
Eddie Wallace of the Sunshine Boys were great talent. They knew how
to entertain a crowd."

Asheville's All-Night Singings drew people from all over the region. Coal miners came from West Virginia and Kentucky. People
came from all over the Carolinas, from Virginia, Tennessee, Georgia,
and Alabama. They came for the singing and for sightseeing. During
the day they drove around the mountains and looked at the scenery and
enjoyed the coolness, and at night they thrilled to the singing.

By 1953, City Auditorium filled almost every month for Riley
Smith's All-Night Singings. He paid quartets top dollar. He has cancelled checks that show that he paid these amounts for some of his singings in 1953:

February 28—Revelaires (with Big Jim Waits and Dan Huskey)
$350; Blue Ridge Quartet, $350; Speer Family, $300; Foggy River
Boys, $325.

March 29—Blackwood Brothers, $450; Sunshine Boys, $350;
Blue Ridge, $300. The Blue Ridge Quartet, of Spartanburg, South
Carolina, didn't have as far to come as the Sunshine Boys (from At-
lanta) and the Blackwood Brothers (from Memphis).

April 25—Crusaders, $325; Homeland Harmony, $350; Sunshine
Boys, $375.

His biggest night came on May 29, 1954, when he finally brought
in the team, the Blackwood Brothers and the Statesmen together. He

paid them $1,100 to sing, and he still has the cancelled check, endorsed by R. W. Blackwood two months before his death in the airplane crash in Clanton, Alabama.

The weather was as bad that night as it ever had been for one of Riley's singings. It rained tremendously hard, and a cold wind blew, turning some of the rain to icy slush, even though it was late May. But late in the afternoon people began arriving in droves for the singing. The front seats went quickly, and then the rest of the auditorium filled up until the Asheville Fire Department said "No more." There were still hundreds of people lined up at the ticket windows, a line stretching more than a block from the auditorium.

The Statesmen and Blackwood Brothers were at their best that night. They entertained royally, and it was after midnight that people began to leave. Amazingly, there were still people waiting outside, and as six people left, the fire department let six come in.

Riley always ended his All-Night Singings by 3 o'clock in the morning, but this night they sang longer, and the crowd stayed. It was the last time Asheville ever saw R. W. Blackwood and Bill Lyles, except on television a month later when the Blackwood Brothers won Arthur Godfrey's Talent Scouts.

Acoustics were great in the Asheville City Auditorium. J. D. Sumner and Big Chief Wetherington could actually shake the house with their low bass notes, magnified by an exceptional amplifying system.

"I loved working with those groups," Riley said. "I didn't go into promotions to make money, and to tell the honest truth, I didn't know I was going to make a nickel, because I had made very little money singing. But I could see this thing was something people wanted, and in order to do what they wanted, I had to have money. I had to charge admission, but I kept it as low as possible."

After less than a year, Riley realized the promotions were getting too large for him to handle alone; so he asked a lifelong friend, Dan Foster, to help him. From then on, Foster ran the front of the building—the ticket sellers and door men—and Riley ran the back end—the singing itself, the talent, the problems with the singers. The two split any profits, and on the average they made $250 to $300 per singing.

Riley continued to sell automobiles the whole time he was promoting.

"I had no real problems with any of the singers until the very last," he said. "The easiest people to work with were the Goodman Family, Bobby Strickland and the Crusaders, the Harmoneers, people like that.

James Blackwood was good to work with. Urias LeFevre was a bit fiery at times, but I didn't have deep-down problems with him. I'd tell him what I felt and he'd say, 'Well, you talk pretty straight, don't you?' and I'd say, 'That's the only way I know to do it.' Hovie and I would laugh at each other and still argue. All of this was a wonderful experience for me."

Riley ran his singings on a sound business basis. "When I made a deal with any of the quartets," he said, "I promised them so much money, and they knew they would get that money. The whole secret of the thing was that I kept it on a straight basis. Then it worked out fine with all groups. I didn't deal under the table with anybody.

"Some," he said, "were harder to work with, due to the fact that they got to the point that they wanted to put on a show instead of singing. Hovie and the Statesmen started it.

"They also started another problem," Riley said. "My people came to hear the singing, but some of the groups wanted to preach instead of sing. Hovie started that, too, and I couldn't stand it because I knew my people came to hear the singing. They could go to church the next morning—Sunday—and hear the finest preaching in the land for free. They didn't pay $1.20 to come to a singing and be preached to."

Riley finally reached the end of his rope, and it was the team that brought about the end.

"They framed up on me," Riley said. "The Statesmen and the Blackwood Brothers reached the point that they didn't want to come to Asheville unless they came together, and I couldn't afford that. Their prices were too high for our town, and I didn't want to go up on my ticket prices.

"I told Hovie and James that I would not continue to promote them," Riley said, "if that was the way they were going to do."

The three, along with Urias LeFevre, sat in City Auditorium until 4:30 one Sunday morning trying to hash out this problem.

"We couldn't get straightened out," Riley said. "They were bent on doing it the way they wanted to, and I couldn't do it that way. Finally, Hovie said, 'Well, we'll just come in here with another promoter.' And that's what happened."

The next time the Statesmen and Blackwood Brothers came to Asheville, Wally Fowler promoted the singing. He rented the City Auditorium and went head-to-head with Riley Smith.

Asheville had been a good town for gospel music, but it was not large enough to support two promoters. Something had to give.

Riley went to Ralph James, manager of the auditorium. "I don't think what's happening is fair to me," Riley said. "I've been promoting this building every month for eight years, and suddenly you let another promoter come in against me. It isn't fair. No two programs—the same program—can operate successfully here in the same month every month."

"I realize that," Ralph said, "but I don't know what we can do about it. Under the law, I can't deny the auditorium to the other people. If I were you, I'd talk to Weldon Weir."

Weir was the Asheville city manager, a man who could get things done, but in this case his hands were tied.

"I live here," Riley told Weldon. "I'm a taxpayer. I've promoted this building every month for eight years, and I've never been late with a payment to the city. I can't see why you can't give me some protection, and I certainly can't see why you can't prevent putting him on in front of me."

"Well, you know what the story is," Weldon said.

"No, I don't," Riley said. "Tell me what it is."

"By law," Weldon said, "there's only one thing you can do: put on better programs."

The double promotions damaged Asheville greatly as a gospel music town. Neither promotion drew well. After a few promotions, the Statesmen and Blackwood Brothers were singing to half houses, and soon they were not coming to Asheville anymore. Riley's crowds went down, too, and he had to give up his promotions.

J. Bazzel Mull, the blind Knoxville preacher-promoter, took Asheville over and promoted for a while. Then the Kingsmen Quartet promoted for a few years.

But no one matched the promotional success of Riley Smith in the heyday of his promotions.

In retrospect, Riley said, recently, "I don't know why my singings were so successful. Nobody could understand how I could fill the auditorium when nothing else would. I don't know, either, unless it was the way I handled it, the way I felt in my heart about it. I was sincere, and the Good Lord was just good enough to me to let me do it. When I advertised groups, they came, and they were the best in the business."

For a while, Asheville was a great singing town. Then, like so many others, it died. And today it's hard to gather a crowd there for a gospel show.

CHAPTER TWENTY-SEVEN

The Whitfield Contributions

In those old convention days immediately following World War II, when thousands of men were at loose ends after fighting the toughest war in United States history, J. G. Whitfield knew exactly what he wanted to do: He wanted to sing.

He had already had a taste of it. Before he went to the Air Force, he sang with a bunch of boys who called themselves the "Happy Hitters."

It was quite natural that in 1947 when Whitfield bumped into a longtime singing friend, Roy Howard, the two decided to put a group together. They got Guy Dodd to sing tenor, Edward (Blocksome) Singletary to sing baritone, and Tiny Merrell to play piano. Howard sang the lead and J. G., the bass.

They based themselves in Pensacola, Florida, where they lived, and called themselves the Gospel Melody Quartet. Mostly they sang at conventions, churches, schools, and in some concerts in and around Pensacola.

The Gospel Melody Quartet was the forerunner of The Florida Boys, one of the most successful and lasting quartets in the business.

That era in J. G. Whitfield's life prompted him to great heights as a singer, quartet manager, one of gospel music's most successful and busiest promoters, and the industry's first successful post-war publisher as founder and owner of *The Singing News*.

Whit learned early-on that adversity is a part of the business. In 1951, with the Gospel Melody Quartet earning more success every day, Roy Howard, who seemed to be in perfectly good health, died of a heart attack soon after singing with the quartet on a Pensacola radio station.

That blow hit the quartet hard, but the boys kept on singing. They changed some members, and Whit began to put more emphasis on singing at concerts, seeming to sense that that was the direction in which the industry was heading.

In September of 1952, an eighteen-year-old, guitar-picking baritone named Glen Allred joined the Gospel Melody Quartet, and the following spring of 1953 Les Beasley was hired to sing the lead.

Feeling more professional than ever before, the Gospel Melody Quartet began to expand its horizons. The group hooked up with Wally Fowler, who promoted many of the larger cities in the South, and Fowler prompted the change of the quartet's name to The Florida Boys.

Wally was of the opinion that Gospel Melody was not a distinctive enough name, and on stage he began to refer to the quartet as the "Boys from Florida." He even used that designation on posters advertising his singings. Finally, the quartet itself began to think that Wally was right. There were a lot of Gospel Melody and Melodyaires and Melody this and Gospel that around.

One morning in 1954, J. G. Whitfield walked into a rehearsal and said, "Fellows, as of today, we're the Florida Boys."

"Just like that?" Les Beasley asked.

"Just like that," Whit confirmed. "That's the only way we can do it."

Nobody argued, and the succeeding years proved Wally to be right. "It was just like we'd jumped off a springboard," Whit said. "Everything was up from there."

While still singing with the Florida Boys, Whit went into promotions. He did it as a measure of helping his own quartet, promoting dates for the Florida Boys to sing when they weren't working for Wally. Keeping the quartet busy was the key to remaining a professional quartet in which the men involved made their living without holding down other jobs.

Whit began to promote Panama City, Mobile, Dothan, and all along the Gulf Coast of Florida and Alabama. The quartet grew in popularity because of this. Its first television job was on a show in Dothan, and suddenly the quartet's popularity zoomed to the point that it had the number three show on Dothan television. *Gunsmoke* was number one and *What's My Line* was second.

Whit enjoyed promoting. Not only did it keep the Florida Boys busy, Whit also made some extra money at it. In those early days of gospel concerts, Whit booked the Statesmen Quartet for $600 on a Saturday night and usually made money.

When Whit and Hazel were married in 1957, life took a different course, and in 1958 Whit quit the road. He left the Florida Boys, stopped his gospel promotions, and settled down at home. He had a small business in Pensacola, and Hazel had one, too; so they combined their businesses, and Whit began to live a tamer life.

It was a real shock to the Florida Boys when Whit announced he was stepping down.

"Who in the world will we get to manage and do the talking and all that?" Les asked.

"Why, I'm going to appoint you," Whit said.

"Lord have mercy!" Les exclaimed. "I've never done anything like that. I don't think I can."

"Yeah," Whit said. "You can do it."

And he did. Under Les Beasley's managership, the Florida Boys over the years have been one of the most solvent quartets in the business, and certainly one of the most active.

A lot of the Florida Boys success is attributable to the leadership of Les Beasley. Anyone in gospel music will tell you that he is one of the best, if not *the* best quartet manager in the business. He had the good sense to hire a fellow named Billy Todd to replace Whitfield. Todd had such a powerful voice that he sometimes made other bass singers sick, the way he could stand a foot from the microphone and project a fine bass foundation with admirable leads, while other basses practically had to swallow the mike to get their best tones out.

Les Beasley's sense of humor runs to the dry side. One would not look at him and say, "There goes a funny man." But there are times when Les's humor overflows.

Billy Todd always beat it back to the bus and changed from his singing suit into more leisurely clothes before the quartet went out to eat after a performance. He kidded those who stayed nattily dressed when they went to eat, often in a truck stop.

Once when the Florida Boys went to Los Angeles to do a television commercial for Cal Worthington Dodge, Cal had a 400-pound pet tiger that he called "Spot." The tiger was a friendly sort, and throughout the making of the commercial, Les eyed that tiger like he had something on his mind.

As soon as the cameras stopped rolling, Les, dressed in his stage suit with starched shirt and tie, challenged that tiger to a wrestling match there in the parking lot.

Les made the first and last moves. As soon as he made the first move, the tiger took him to the pavement flat on his back, and that was Les's last move.

Apparently the tiger liked him because he began to lick Les on the cheek. A cat's tongue is rough, like sandpaper, and the bigger the cat the rougher the tongue, because for days Les's cheek was as red as if it had, indeed, been sanded.

Billy Todd thought Les Beasley challenging a 400-pound tiger was the funniest thing he had ever seen.

J. G. Whitfield wasn't cut out for idleness. He began to sing with his brother Joe and Joe's wife Sue, with whom he went to church. Next thing he knew, they had a good group going. George Forbus sang tenor, Jack Toney sang the lead, Joe sang baritone, Whit sang bass, and Sue played the piano. They called themselves the Dixie Echoes.

Jack Toney was a gem of a discovery. He has been considered by many of his peers down through the years as perhaps the finest lead voice ever in gospel quartet singing. He sang with the Statesmen for six years, and later sang with the Stamps Quartet.

Singing with an enviable easiness, Toney makes people marvel at the quality of his voice. He would be the lead singer in a lot of all-time, all-star quartets.

When the Dixie Echoes lost Toney to the Statesmen, they replaced him with an Alabama fellow named Dale Shelnut, who also reached great heights both in popularity and in the quality of his singing. Few men ever sang better than Dale Shelnut, and Dale could handle the old Negro spirituals better than anyone who ever came down the pike.

After awhile, the Dixie Echoes picked up a Pensacola man named Hal Kennedy, a good singer and great guitar player, and they were soon in such demand that they began to sing concerts. Wally Fowler booked the Dixie Echoes for a few dates, and to keep this new quartet busy, Whit went back to promoting.

Hazel knew J. G. was cut out to be in gospel music, and she didn't object.

Soon, with quartet concerts growing in number and appeal, Whit found himself promoting all over the South, including Atlanta. The Georgia capital was so large that Whit held monthly singings there—

and Atlanta supported them in large numbers. It was one of the South's great gospel music centers, and many quartets based themselves there—the Statesmen, the LeFevre Trio, the Homeland Harmony Quartet, the Harmoneers, and various others.

At his Atlanta singings in 1964, Whit began hearing about a young quartet from the mountains of North Carolina, and thus began to unfold one of gospel music's great success stories, and a story that showed the necessity for good relations between quartet and promoter.

"At the Atlanta singings," Whit recalled, "people came to me every month and told me there was a group that I needed to check on. They called themselves the Inspirations, and they sang out of Bryson City, North Carolina. They were singing around Atlanta in churches and people who heard them sing were regular customers at my concerts."

On one particular Saturday night, Whit was bombarded with dozens of requests for him to book the Inspirations. Apparently the quartet had several church engagements in Atlanta that weekend.

"I didn't know how to get in touch with them," Whit said, "but when I got back to Pensacola the first of that week I thought I'd better look into the matter because there seemed to be special interest in the Inspirations.

He didn't have long to wait. Les Beasley called him on Monday and said, "Whit, I want to tell you about a little group up in the mountains that does a super good job. They've got a tenor that nobody likes but the people—and they're pleasing the people. They're young and you might want to look at them. They call themselves the Inspirations."

"Well, I've heard of them before," Whit said.

Les said, "I was with them this weekend, and they're doing what the people want to hear."

"What do you mean about their tenor not being liked but by the people?" Whit asked.

"Most of the singers think he can't sing," Les said, "but the people go crazy over him. His name is Archie Watkins."

"You got a telephone number?" Whit asked, "or someway I can get in touch with them?"

"Yeah," Les answered. "I brought you a phone number. These are high school boys, and the fellow playing the piano for them is their school teacher and their quartet manager. His name is Martin Cook."

Whitfield telephoned Martin Cook and booked the Inspirations for the next singing in Atlanta, which was the following month.

Martin Cook showed up with his little tenor, Archie Watkins; and with the rest of the quartet, Jack Laws on baritone, Ronnie Hutchins singing lead, and fourteen-year-old Troy Burns singing bass.

They took Atlanta by storm.

"That was the start of a success story," Whit said. "I paid the Inspirations $125 to sing for me in Atlanta that first time, and to show you how they progressed, the last time they worked for me in Atlanta I paid 'em $2,500."

As a promoter, J. G. Whitfield picked up other groups and sent them down the trail to stardom.

When Rusty Goodman left the Plainsmen and decided to go back with his family singers, he telephoned Whit. They had talked together a lot, usually about the life Rusty was leading—"the life," as Whit put it, "that most young men lead"—and when Rusty called Whit, he told him, "Whit, I want to tell you something and I'm sincere. I've got my life straightened out. The Lord saved me. Now we're putting the Family back together—me and Howard and Vestal and Sam—and we want to sing."

Whit had just started promoting Nashville, and when the Happy Goodman Family came to Nashville to cut their first album, Whit had a singing that coincided with their visit. He invited them to come over and sing a song or two.

They sang "I'm Too Near Home To Turn Back Now," and brought the house down. He booked them immediately for the following month's Nashville concert.

At that time, Whit and the Florida Boys were putting the *Gospel Singing Jubilee* together for syndicated television. Whit thought the Happy Goodman Family would be perfect for the Jubilee. He had known the Goodmans when the sisters sang and they were an exciting group then, but Vestal, Howard, Sam, and Rusty really clicked. Their singing made the people happy. Whit told Howard that they not only had the talent to sing, but the Good Lord had also given them the ability to make connection with the people.

Whit put them on the *Jubilee*, and they became the strongest group on television.

Looking back, Whit feels the year 1974 was the greatest he had in gospel music. He sold more tickets, promoted more dates, filled more houses, and made more money than in any other year he promoted.

Why? Because he had the sense to recognize the talent the people wanted—and he sewed it up. He put the Happy Goodman Family and the Inspirations together as a team and worked them every weekend that year—every Friday and Saturday night. On those two nights, they worked for no one else in 1974, only Whit. At times, he booked other groups with them to fill out a big program for a big auditorium, but ninety percent of the time he booked only the Happy Goodmans and the Inspirations.

"That was a great year for them," Whit said. "And for me."

The marriage lasted only a year, however. "They had some problems," Whit said, "and weren't able to work together more than a year. But it was super and wonderful while it lasted."

Whit probably put in more time with the Goodman Family and the Inspirations, trying to build them, than with other groups—but he did find time for others. He worked the Kingsmen a lot and helped them greatly when they became full-time singers in 1971. He continued to promote the Florida Boys and Dixie Echoes. And when the Goodmans brought the Hinsons out of the wilderness, Whit and Les Beasley put them on the *Jubilee* to help build their name.

Perhaps remembering the favor Wally Fowler did for the Gospel Melody Quartet when he forced their name change to the Florida Boys, Whit did the same for the Gospel Echoes.

Buck and Dottie Rambo were the Gospel Echoes, and Buck and Hal Kennedy were friends. This was in the days when Whit sang with the Dixie Echoes and promoted various towns around the South. Hal hammered at Whit to book the Gospel Echoes more, and Whit finally took Buck Rambo aside and had a heart-to-heart talk.

"Buck, I'd use you more," he said, "but I can't. Your group name clashes with the Dixie Echoes and you need to change it. Too, if you changed your name to *The Rambos,* you'd be promoting yourself and your family."

Buck thought about it for a minute and said, "You've got a point, Whit."

He changed the name and Buck and Dottie and their daughter Reba began appearing as *The Singing Rambos.*

"I don't reckon their singing was any better," Whit said, "because it was awfully good to start with, but changing their name got them more recognition, and at one point the Rambos were as strong as any group in the business. They had all of Dottie's great songs, and they were different. They were something a promoter put on the program that wasn't a quartet, but was very, very enjoyable as a change-of-pace."

*   *   *

With Hal Kennedy, Whit introduced the electric guitar to gospel music.

"I got credit for bringing instruments to the stage," Whit said, an act for which many dyed-in-the-wool quartet fans could kill him, because instruments have become so prevalent that many groups use them to the detriment of harmony singing.

Whit had known Hal Kennedy for many years but did not know he could sing. One day Hal brought Whit a 45 rpm record and asked him to play it. Whit listened carefully, and when the song ended, he said, "Great day in the morning! Is that you?"

"Yeah, that's me," Hal said.

"How about coming up to Joe's music store," Whit suggested, "and rehearsing with the Dixie Echoes. Let's pick a little and sing."

Hal came, and soon he was coming regularly to jam with the Echoes—and next thing he knew they had him on the bus, traveling and singing at their concerts. Picking his guitar, too.

"Hal became a star," Whit said. "He was good, and he was an extraordinarily good fellow. My hat's off to him to this day. After he left the singing field he went on to pastor a church. He preaches the good gospel."

In 1968 J. G. Whitfield had a brainstorm that added another dimension to gospel music. People all over the country, particularly the South, were starved for the news of their favorite singing groups. The only time gospel music made the newspapers was when a tragedy struck the industry, like the airplane deaths of R. W. Blackwood and Bill Lyles, or the automobile crashes that took the lives of Erman Slater and Bobby Strickland. People all over were begging for news of their singers.

J. D. Sumner was president of the Gospel Music Association and in that capacity he had engineered the publication of a monthly newsletter called *Good News*. The newsletter was printed in tabloid newspaper form, and gave Whit the idea of a newspaper devoted entirely to gospel music. As a means of reaching the public, he thought of his own rather extensive mailing list, compiled through his promotions, and those of W. B. Nowlin in Texas and Lloyd Orrell up north.

He approached J. D. one day. "I like that newsletter you put out, J. D.," Whit said, "but it ought to be a newspaper to keep our people informed as to what's going on."

"Hey, that ain't no paper," J. D. said. "It's just a newsletter I put out."

"But it ought to be a paper," Whit argued.

"Maybe so," J. D. answered, "but I got no intention of putting out a paper."

"It could be done," J. G. said.

"It could," J. D. agreed, "but I ain't gonna do it."

So J. G. did. He got together with a friend, Jerry Kirksey, in Pensacola, and they planned the paper.

In March of 1969, J. G. walked into Kirksey's office one morning and said, "Jerry, let's get the first issue out right away."

Jerry went to work. He hired Janice Cain, who attended all the singings, to write for the paper, borrowed W. B. Nowlin's mailing list and combined it with Whit's list to come up with a hundred thousand possible subscribers, hired a young fellow on the Pensacola paper to give them the expertise they needed—and in May of 1969 brought out the first issue of *The Singing News*.

Today, *The Singing News* is a monthly slick magazine, still edited by Jerry Kirksey, but Whit is no longer connected, except as publisher emeritus.

The magazine is owned by Maurice Templeton of Boone, North Carolina, and has made great strides in the industry.

CHAPTER TWENTY-EIGHT

High Jinks

"There aren't many of us left," said George Younce, "who started out in cars. Most of the people in this business today crawled on a bus and started out, but we rode for years in the cramped seats of automobiles. It's a wonder we're still here."

"Interstates and buses are the best things that ever happened to quartets," said Glen Payne.

"Yeah, thank God for J. D. Sumner," Younce said. "He built the first custom bus—but I don't know who to thank for building the interstates. Uncle Sam, I guess."

Eldridge Fox chuckled, then said, "It's hard to understand, too, when some of the younger guys start complaining that the air-conditioning is not just right, or the VCR is broken."

Les Beasley also laughed. "My new tenor singer said the other day, 'I've been working like a dog,' and I thought, 'Lord have mercy! He doesn't know what work is.'"

"It's nice to be able to ride the bus in your riding clothes," George Younce said, "and when you stop go back to the closet and pull out your nice pressed suit and stand there and get dressed in comfort. Used to be, to save a hassle, you'd put your suit on and fold your coat in your lap and then sit down in the automobile and try to get your creases straight, and then sit that way for hours so you wouldn't get your suit wrinkled and you'd look halfway decent when you crawled out that night to go on stage."

"Jake Hess could ride all day," Les said, "and get out and look like he'd just stepped out of a bandbox. And I looked like I'd been pulled through a trash pile backwards."

"We'd sit there and sweat," George said. "We were bound to have smelled like goats."

"Goats smelled good," Glen said.

"I remember taking the air conditioner out of our limousine," Les said, "because we had to have that space to carry our clothes and the PA set, and the records and all."

"There were more important things than air-conditioning," George agreed.

Buses made travel easier—that is, the effort required to get from one point on the map to another—but no one ever found a way to beat the boredom of being separated from family for long periods. So quartets resorted to humor—especially those that happened to have a real clown in their midst.

Basically, these were funny men to begin with. The road only made them more hilarious.

The Blue Ridge and the Harvesters quartets once worked a string of thirteen consecutive unprofitable dates together, and as they walked into the auditorium for the last singing, Bill Hefner of the Harvesters said, "Boys, I sure hope we break even tonight; I could use the money."

The Blue Ridge, the Florida Boys, and the Harvesters did a ten-night tour together, singing up and down the Atlantic coast, and at the end when they divided up the profits, each quartet received $33.

"But we had fun," George Younce said. He was singing bass for the Blue Ridge, and J. G. Whitfield was the bass for the Florida Boys.

"That was the trip on which Whit asked me to give him some singing lessons," George said.

George saw a good chance to pull Whit's leg. "Whit," he said, "just sing as long as you can on the same breath and that way you can keep the same tone placement."

"Oh," Whit said in his lowest bass voice, "is that the way you do it?"

"That's it," George answered. "The more you breathe the more chance you've got of losing your placement."

Whit went on stage that night and sang a while and coughed a while, then caught his breath and kept on going, singing and coughing. The others in the Florida Boys were ready to kill him when they came off stage.

"Don't kill *me*," Whit said. "Kill George."

* * *

Lee Roy Abernathy traveled with a number of quartets, most of them for only a short while, playing piano and helping the quartets with their music. One of Lee Roy's favorite characters was Aycel Soward, the great bass singer of the early days of quartet singing.

They were both with the Homeland Harmony Quartet and one day were traveling through South Georgia, bound for Florida. Lee Roy was driving, and Aycel suddenly said, "Oh, if I could have a dad-blamed cup of coffee."

Lee Roy cringed. He thought "dad-blamed" was cursing.

They came to a small town and Aycel said, "Turn left, Abernackle; I've got to have a dad-blamed cup of coffee."

They came to a small cafe and Soward grinned, "You always turn left, Abernackle, to find coffee."

Lee Roy was thought, at least by some, to be a sort of wizard. Arnold Hyles, the Rangers' great bass singer, was a superstitious man who thought Abernathy was from another planet.

One day the two found themselves in Charlotte, where the Rangers had been based for years and where everybody knew Arnold Hyles.

When they met an acquaintance of Arnold's, Arnold would say, "Lee Roy, do that penny thing." Lee Roy would press a penny onto a person's forehead, then pull it off when he took his hand away, and the person felt as if the penny were still there.

Arnold thought that was the greatest of jokes.

They met a policeman whom Arnold knew and Arnold said, "Lee Roy, do that penny thing." Lee Roy tried the penny and it wouldn't stick."

"Let's try a dime," he said.

He pressed the dime into the officer's forehead and pulled it off when he dropped his hands, but the policeman thought the dime was still there.

The policeman turned and saw a woman he knew. "Hey, Sue," he yelled, "come over here." She came and he said, "Look at my dime. Look here." He pointed to his forehead and Sue frowned. Nothing was there.

The officer looked away and saw a man he knew. "Hey, Billy, look at my dime."

Billy didn't see it, either, but he did see Arnold Hyles bent double with laughter, tears streaming from his eyes.

A moment later the officer saw his reflection in a store window, and there was no dime on his forehead. He stopped laughing.

Arnold was gone.

"Where is that old son of a gun, Hyles?" he demanded. "I'll lock him up."

The Blackwood Brothers once decided to break J. D. Sumner of smoking. James began to load J. D.'s cigarettes with explosive charges and when J. D. fogged up—BLAM! The charge would scare him out of his wits, and James and the Blackwood Brothers would laugh till they cried.

Quartets still traveled in cars and limousines at that time—late 1954, early 1955. J. D. was driving the quartet home to Memphis late one night and stopped at a truck stop for coffee. He went in alone; everyone else slept in the car.

Seated at the counter, J. D. ordered coffee, withdrew a cigarette, and lighted it.

He took two draws.

BLAM! The end of the cigarette blew off.

Scared J. D. and a dozen other people out of their wits.

J. D. looked at the little guy beside him just as he made reference to James Blackwood. "You sawed-off little runt!" he muttered.

The little fellow was off his stool in a flash, putting up his fists. "You talking to me, Buddy? Talking to me?"

J. D. laughed and talked his way out of that one.

Not only was Coy Cook one of the great tenors, he was also the goosiest man in gospel music. Jab him in the ribs and he'd jump a foot and let out a screech like a wounded mountain lion.

The Florida Boys sang in a small Alabama town and afterward stopped at a real joint for a bite to eat. The place had a dirt floor. And the roughest-looking customers Les Beasley had seen in many a day.

Hurriedly the Florida Boys ate and lined up to pay their checks. Les stood in line behind Coy, and behind Les was one of the roughnecks.

"I didn't know Coy had a glass of ice water in his hand," Les said, "and when I reached up and goosed him and ducked, he threw that glass of water over his shoulder—and into the face of that big redneck."

Les thought, "Oh, Lord, here we go." He could see a barroom brawl breaking out.

The big guy's expression began to change over and over, and Les could tell he was mulling over what had happened and what to do about it, and suddenly his face broke into a wide grin—and he didn't have a front upper tooth in his head. Knocked out in a fight, no doubt.

In a moment, the man laughed, "Haw, haw!" he said. "Little bit goosey, ain't you, pal?"

The reactions of a goosey guy can never be predicted. The Florida Boys sang for a mobile home sponsor who was responsible for putting a lot of money in their pockets. He sponsored the Florida Boys on television and was forever goosing Coy. Les Beasley cautioned him not to goose Coy so much, and it only made him worse.

On a Sunday afternoon the Florida Boys had a big singing in Dothan, Alabama, and the Farm Center was filled with people. This fellow came in late, and the first thing he did was goose Coy; and Coy's reflex action was to turn and swing at whoever had goosed him. He happened to hit the fellow flush on the chin and knocked him cold. He had to be taken to the hospital and revived, but he was a good sport. He didn't cancel his contract with the Florida Boys.

He just made sure he was on safe ground the next time he goosed Coy Cook.

The Florida Boys were traveling down the road one day with Les driving when they came upon the rear of a car bearing a bumper sticker that read, "Honk If You Love Jesus." Normally, Les Beasley does not react to things like that, but he honked a couple of times, and when he finally came to an empty straightaway and passed the car, the driver threw him a birdie.

Jimmy Taylor, piano player for the Rebels, was a feisty little guy. "He stood about five-feet-five and thought he was seven feet tall," Jim Hamill once said of Taylor.

The Rebels had a singing engagement in a small town near Syracuse, New York. They found the town, but had no idea where the auditorium was. Jimmy, driving the company limousine with "Rebels" painted on its side, pulled into a service station and asked an attendant, "Friend, where are we singing tonight?"

The attendant, a big, rough, muscular guy, looked at the car, then at Jimmy, and asked in return, "Who the hell *are* you?"

The Florida Boys and Oak Ridge Quartet once traded practical jokes. The Oaks were going to California in January in their old bus, and the Florida Boys had a bottle of something that smelled terribly like rotten eggs and then some. Some of the Florida Boys went out while the Oaks were on stage and taped a bottle of the vile-smelling stuff under a lower bunk in the Oak Ridge bus. The Oaks couldn't locate the source of the ill scent until they got to California, all with colds from riding with the windows open. They finally figured out who pulled the stunt, and the next time they saw the Florida Boys they filled the bin of the Florida Boys' bus full of crickets. For six months, the Florida Boys had crickets chirping on their bus.

It is only natural that quartet personnel, being hoot owl people who sing late and then eat in the wee hours of the morning, become associated with truck stops all over the country. It has been that way for a long time.

Jay Simmons, who sang a deep, excellent bass for the Plainsmen, the Prophets, and others, went into a truck stop with his quartet one day and thought he'd have a little fun with the waitress. Jay often asked waitresses to pray over his quartet's meals, usually embarrassing them sorely and sending them away with suspicious backward glances.

The waitress in this truck stop was an older woman. Three or four quartets were sitting around the place within listening distance.

When the waitress served the Plainsmen, Simmons looked up with baleful eyes and asked, "Ma'am, would you say the blessing for us?"

"Why, certainly," the woman said, and proceeded to pray a long and beautiful prayer, leaving Jay Simmons with egg on his face and all the other quartet people laughing at him and cheering for her.

The Florida Boys sang in concert not long ago and afterward went to a nice restaurant to eat. Standing in line to be seated, the quartet didn't miss Rick Busby when he went to wash his hands. Not paying attention, Rick went in the wrong door, into the ladies' lounge. A woman dashed out in a few moments and reported to the hostess, "There's a man in there!" The Florida Boys grinned, not knowing it was their tenor singer.

The hostess went into the ladies lounge and in a few minutes came out, pulling Rick Busby with her. He was red-faced and so embarrassed—and there stood all his singing mates, looking at his discomfiture.

Word circulated through the restaurant, and even some of the waitresses kidded Rick about his mistake, deepening his embarrassment. The Florida Boys egged it on, too. Finally, the waitresses all came over together and served Rick a large free dessert for being a good sport.

Wally Fowler hitched a ride on the LeFevres bus one night. He piled into the bunk and was snoring away when the driver went into a sharp curve and crammed on the brakes. Wally rolled out of the bunk and all over the bus, clad only in brief underpants. It made him so mad he couldn't see straight. He thought the driver had whipped the bus around on purpose.

Once the Oak Ridge, Blue Ridge, and Palmetto State quartets sang in Thomasville, Georgia. They stopped a hundred miles up the road late that night and ate, then hurried out, each trying to beat the other onto the road. Going up the interstate, they raced for position, each bus trying to outrun the others.

Fifteen miles up the road, the Palmetto State was running last, and a car whizzed around them with someone hanging out the window, frantically waving his arms.

"That's George Younce," Jack Bagwell said.

"No, it's not," said Jack Pittman. "That's a carload of drunks."

Up ahead, the Oaks and Blue Ridge were really airing out their buses. The Palmetto State couldn't keep up with them, but did manage to pass the carload of drunks.

Soon, here came the drunks again, with George Younce hanging out the window, waving and screaming. The Palmetto State went right on.

"Couldn't be George," Jack Pittman said. "He's up yonder in the bus asleep."

Finally, the drunks caught up with the Blue Ridge, and the quartet guys quickly realized they'd left George in the rest room of the restaurant, so eager were they to lead the race. And the only people George could persuade to take him to catch up with the buses were the drunks.

Coy Cook was a good bus driver. When he was with the Dixie Echoes, he was driving through Georgia, near Calhoun, when an old pickup truck stacked higher than you would believe with chicken coops was rolling along and Coy pulled in behind it. He followed the pickup a couple of miles, marveling at how many chickens were on it, and suddenly the truck pulled to the right as if to take an exit ramp.

The driver apparently changed his mind, for just when Coy

gunned the bus to pass, the truck swerved back on the road in front of the bus.

Coy hit the truck—hard. The pickup hit an exit sign at the ramp, tumbled over the railing—and scattered squawking chickens everywhere.

Coy quickly stopped and ran back to help the driver of the truck.

"Are you hurt?" Coy asked, and the driver just stared. He didn't say a word.

"Are you hurt?" Coy asked again, and still the driver said nothing.

"Should we get an ambulance for you?" Coy shouted, trying to penetrate the driver's fog.

Finally, the driver turned unfocused eyes toward Coy and said, very slowly, "I saw Death back there!"

"We better get these chickens rounded up," Coy repeated.

"But I squshed forty of 'em," the driver said.

"Well, let's catch the rest."

"I saw Death back there!"

Tiny Candy Hemphill got off the Hemphill's bus in front of the Asheville City Auditorium to walk her pet goat down the street. Her daddy, Joel, had found a small kid goat that Candy fell in love with. He bought a leash at the five-and-ten and Candy led the goat around like a puppy.

The little goat clicked along on the concrete sidewalk, pausing now and then to emit a small "baa" that was more of a croak than a bleat.

Down the street from the auditorium, leaning against a car, whittling on a stick, stood an old mountaineer fresh from the backwoods.

The little goat clicked to a stop, looked at the man, and bleated, "Ba!"

Candy walked on with the goat and the man looked the animal over, noting its extra-long legs, its funny shape.

"Hey," he yelled to Joel, who accompanied Candy. "Hey!"

Joel paused.

"What kind of a dawg is that?" the mountaineer asked.

"Dog? That's no dog," Joel said. "That's a goat."

"Goat?" returned the mystified mountaineer. "Talks like a dawg."

Never has a quartet's road stamina been tested, though, like the Kingsmen Quartet's was tested one day in the late 1960s when Bud

Roberts drove the Kingsmen bus up to the Shellanes Motel in Sheffield, Alabama.

Daylight had just broken and a soft rain was falling when Bud parked the bus on an incline and he and Jerry Redd, the insomniac tenor, went inside for breakfast, knowing the others in the bus would awaken eventually.

McKinley Quakenbush, who writes for *The Singing News*, was traveling with the Kingsmen that weekend. He was sleeping soundly in the rearmost bunk when Eldridge Fox turned over in his sleep, and on that southern incline with Eldridge turning from north to south, he just kept on going out into the aisle.

He landed with a thump that shook the bus and woke McKinley, who wondered if an earthquake had hit Sheffield. Shortly, Fox and Quakenbush dressed and went inside for breakfast. It was raining quite hard. After breakfast, the four—Quakenbush, Fox, Roberts, and Redd—decided to check into three rooms, Bud and Jerry to share one, and Eldridge and McKinley to get singles, the idea being that later in the day when the rest of the fellows woke they could shower and shave in those rooms.

Bud and Jerry awakened the motel clerk, a blonde, fiftyish woman who tried to smile pleasantly while checking the men in and couldn't quite pull it off.

She gave them a room key and they headed out into the rain as Eldridge and McKinley moved up to the counter. Before they got checked in, Bud and Jerry were back.

"There's somebody in that room," they said in unison.

"Oh," said the sleepy lady. "Let me give you another."

Then she gave Eldridge Room 47 and McKinley Room 46, charging them in advance.

They laughed about Bud and Jerry all the way to their rooms. Then they noticed that she had given both of them keys to 47. Eldridge tried his and it wouldn't work. McKinley tried his and jiggled the key in the lock and a gruff voice boomed from the inside of the room: "Who's out there?"

"Excuse us," Eldridge said. "We've been given the wrong room."

They weren't laughing so hard then.

Back to the lobby they went, and the clerk switched Eldridge to Room 33. She gave McKinley the key to 46, and he asked her to telephone the room to make sure it was empty. No one answered the phone.

Down to the rooms they went again. Eldridge was lucky. He got an empty room, but McKinley unlocked 46 and walked in and clothing and suitcases were scattered about the room. Fortunately, no one was there.

This time he met a maid and explained his problem to her.

"Here," she said, "I'll find you a room." She went down the line unlocking doors, saying "Excuse me," and "Pardon me," and once she said, "Oops, sorry!" until she came to Room 30. It was empty.

"Stand right there," McKinley said to her. "Don't let anyone else in the room. I'll go get the key."

The clerk was back in bed, but she turned out again and traded the key to 30 for the one to 46.

"Would you please make sure you've got our cards straight?" McKinley asked. "I'm in 30 and Mr. Fox is in 33."

"Already changed 'em," she said, but somehow McKinley knew she hadn't. He was tired, though, and went on down to 30. He fell in bed and immediately went to sleep.

While he slept, things transpired.

James Sego telephoned Eldridge Fox three times at the Shellanes Motel, and three times the sleepy clerk rang Room 47.

Three times the traveling salesman in Room 47, who had apparently been out on the town all night and was then trying to sleep it off, roundly cursed both the motel clerk and the surprised James Sego.

"Didn't sound a bit like Eldridge Fox," said James Sego after the third cussing. He decided, though, that whatever he had to tell Eldridge could wait until he saw him that night.

At noon, when Sego called the third time, the salesman, wide awake by this time, dressed and went up to the restaurant for lunch, or breakfast, or whatever. Afterward, the rain let up and the man took a walk. He returned to the motel at two p.m.

His biggest mistake was taking the walk and not returning immediately to his room. At about 12:15, as well as Quakenbush could determine while reconstructing the story later, the maid cleaned up Room 47.

At 12:30, Calvin Runion and Ray Talley awoke in the bus, went to the desk and asked what room Mr. Fox was in, please. The clerk—the same sleepy one—looked at the register list and said, "Forty-seven."

"May we have the extra key?" Calvin asked, and the clerk gave it to him.

So Calvin and Ray unlocked Room 47, saw no one was there, figured Eldridge had gone to eat, and made themselves at home. They showered and shaved, used all the towels, turned on the TV and stretched out on the bed to watch it.

At 1:45 they headed for the restaurant for lunch, and as they stepped out of the room they met Eldridge coming up the walk.

"Where you been, Foxy?" Ray asked.

"I just got up," Eldridge said. "I been in my room asleep."

"Yes, sir," Calvin laughed. "He's been in his room asleep." He nudged Talley in the ribs with an elbow and they hee-hawed. "He's been in his room asleep." It was a leg-slapper.

"I dunno what's so funny," Eldridge said, "but I've been right in there since 7:30." He pointed to Room 33.

"In there?" Calvin asked.

"If you've been in there," Ray asked, "then who's in there?" He pointed to Room 47.

"I don't know who he is," Eldridge said, "but he's the crabbiest man in Sheffield. Me and Quakenbush tried to unlock his room by mistake this morning, and he told us where to go in no uncertain terms."

"You're not ribbing us?" Ray asked.

"Let's go eat," said Calvin.

"Yeah, quick," Ray said.

It was around two o'clock when Frank Cutshall, the last of the Kingsmen to wake up in the bus, got up and dressed. About the time he walked into the motel lobby and asked the lady which was Mr. Fox's room, the traveling salesman returned to his room.

"Forty-seven," the lady told Frank and gave him the last key she had to the room.

Unsuspecting, Frank went swinging down the stairs, his own towel draped over his arm, humming to himself. He sauntered up to Room 47, unlocked the door, and stepped into a hornet's nest.

There stood a strange man. Halfway between the water-splashed bathroom and the rumpled bed, he stood staring at his room. To say that he was mad would be putting it mildly.

He looked at Frank. Frank looked at him.

Frank broke the silence. "Where's Foxy?" he asked.

The man flew into a rage. "Get the hell out of here," he screamed.

And as Frank began to put some distance between himself and Room 47, he heard the man yell, "If I ever hear of Foxy again, I'll. . . ." His voice trailed off to nothing as Frank went into overdrive at the top of the steps and approached the bus in a blur of speed.

The Kingsmen gathered in the restaurant, reconnoitered the situation, concluded that someway (they didn't know how) they had been outflanked (they didn't even know by whom), boarded the bus and headed out of town.

CHAPTER TWENTY-NINE

It Ain't Peanuts

Quartets are recognized by those in their hometowns as boosters of the local economy. Some of them become closely identified with their hometowns, or at least with their home areas. No other quartet in the business has become so recognized and identified with an area as the Inspirations with Bryson City, North Carolina, and the Great Smoky Mountains.

People from Bryson City vacation in other areas, and as soon as they tell someone where they're from, the other person will immediately say, "Oh, that's where the Inspirations live." Or, at the least, they say, "Oh, Bryson City. What's that singing group that lives there?"

The Inspirations put Bryson City on the map.

Not many people stop to consider it, but the Inspirations have become one of the largest industries in the Bryson City area, and the same holds true for other quartets in other towns. Depending on who you talk to around Bryson City, you'll find that the people of the area consider the quartet to be worth anywhere from five million to ten million dollars a year to the region.

Don't jump to conclusions: Those figures do not represent income for the Inspirations; they represent income for the people of the Bryson City area as a direct benefit of the presence of the Inspirations in that town. The quartet is a tremendous boon to the local economy.

Because of the Inspirations, untold thousands of tourists visit the area. Many come to attend the singings the Inspirations hold in Inspirations' Park in the Smokies. Others come through the area and stop off in Bryson City just to be able to say they've been there where the Inspirations live.

"All day long, every summer day," said Martin Cook, manager of the Inspirations, "people stream in and out of our office to have a cup of coffee and say hello, and then they go home and can truthfully say, 'I've been to Bryson City.'"

Each summer, the Inspirations promote eighteen to twenty days of singing "on the mountain." That phrase, "on the mountain," is the way everyone in Bryson City refers to Inspirations' Park. During those days, every motel for miles around is filled, thanks in part to the singings. Restaurants are overrun, and tourist souvenir shops are constantly busy.

"We generate a lot of business in our area," Martin said. "People from all over the country come to our singings. We've counted license plates in our parking lot from every state, every province in Canada, and from some foreign countries. All those people spend money here in the mountain area and boost the local economy."

The Inspirations pay thousands of dollars in North Carolina taxes every year, individual income tax, franchise tax on their singings, personal property taxes on property, including the restaurant and motel they own in Swain County.

"You'd be surprised how many families have moved into this area," Martin said, "built homes and settled down here just because of the presence of the Inspirations. And they buy cars, clothes, building materials, groceries, everything locally. They help build the economy."

The Inspirations spend around $60,000 each year to advertise and promote their singings. They spend this money with local printers and the post office and for help in promoting and conducting the singings.

"We advertise our singings all over," Martin said. "We advertise heavily in places like Atlanta and Charlotte, and to show the extent of our advertising, we advertise in twenty-two newspapers in South Carolina alone."

The Inspirations mail more than a quarter of a million pieces of mail every year. Their mail order business is tremendous, and their dealings with the Post Office in Bryson City forced that firm to hire two additional people for its staff.

Perhaps the Inspirations' biggest contribution to the area is in promotion. Wherever they go, they promote their home area, always identifying themselves with Bryson City and the Great Smoky Mountains. For many years, before millions of viewers, they sang and plugged Bryson City on the *Gospel Singing Jubilee*. It would be impossible to estimate how many people visit that area because of the Inspirations' promotion of the region.

When people think of Bryson City and the Great Smoky Mountains, they think of rhododendron blooming on Mount Le Compte, of the black bears in the Smokies, of Indians in nearby Cherokee, and of the Inspirations.

The quartet has become a tremendous plus for the people of Western North Carolina and East Tennessee.

In location and personnel, the Inspirations are more established and recognized with a geographic area than any other gospel singing group has ever been.

They are an example of what quartets mean to the towns and areas where they live. The Inspirations are probably into promotion of gospel singings more than most or all other quartets, but many others make a good portion of their year's income from promoting gospel shows, which boosts the economy in their places. Almost all groups have their own homecoming sings; and others, like the Palmetto State Quartet in Greenville, South Carolina, promote singings in their home towns several times each year.

Quartets certainly pay their way—and always have—and sometimes they pay the ways of many others, too, when you figure what they mean to the economy.

CHAPTER THIRTY

Television!

Whatever dominance the Blackwood Brothers-Statesmen team held over gospel music was finally broken. Not by chance; not by any other alliance of quartets; not by competitiveness in the field; not by drawn swords—but by that phenomenal entertainment medium that took over America: television!

The Statesmen and Blackwoods were predominant in putting quartet singing into television; and TV eventually forced a loosening of whatever hold those two superior quartets had over the rest of the field.

The team had put gospel music in the big-time. Most in the entertainment world still liked to snicker behind their hands at the fellows who ran around the South singing about a better world, better times, joyous tidings, and the good things to come by living a Christian life.

Both the Statesmen and Blackwood Brothers had sung frequently on national television. When they each won Arthur Godfrey's Talent Scouts by obliterating all competition on the nights they appeared, they had put quartet singing in the public's eye coast to coast, and had, indeed, pioneered the music all over the country, particularly on the West Coast.

But all things run their course, and the tides of time finally caught up. Television gave the other groups the assist they had been looking for. While the team had maintained a sort of control over other groups, sometimes dictating who sang here and who sang there, and even controlling who promoted in certain areas, the television monster began to demand more than the team could deliver. Other groups went on television, most of them locally, but syndication gave some the massive outlet they had been searching for. The LeFevres syndicated a show and hit the big markets. Others did the same.

The Florida Boys finally scored the biggest strike with the *Gospel Singing Jubilee.*

The years of 1956, 1957, 1958 were down years for most quartets, other than the team, and one of the reasons for that was the dominance of the Blackwoods and Statesmen.

The Florida Boys' first television hit was a syndicated program called *The Gospel Songshop*, which went on the air in 1959. They did the Gospel Songshop from Pensacola, Florida, for a year, using the Greenville, South Carolina, area, which included Anderson, Greenwood, Spartanburg, and Asheville in its viewing area, for a test market. Then they moved the show's base to Nashville for its final two years because facilities were much better in Nashville, and the expertise was there to make the show a hit.

Out of the Songshop grew the Jubilee. The Songshop never was an across-the-board national production, but the Jubilee was—and it scored big numbers from the first. The Florida Boys secured the right to buy time on any station in any market area, and at one time the Jubilee was shown in every major market in the United States. That coverage at least matched that of the Statesmen's NABISCO show, and far outstripped everything else gospel groups were doing in television.

The Jubilee was a lucrative promotion, not only for the Florida Boys but also for those other groups that anchored it, like the Happy Goodman Family and the Inspirations.

It began in 1964 and grew quickly to national attention, and when it had run its course, eleven years had passed.

The Jubilee's format was simple—colorful backdrops, a minimum of talking, as much good singing as could be crowded into an hour—and it hit with a smash.

It was not the elaborate production that the NABISCO show was. The Statesmen often sang with Wade Crager's Orchestra, which played the Biltmore Hotel in Atlanta. Crager's orchestra was a good dance band whose members knew and loved gospel music, and they backed the Statesmen with a relish. NABISCO had the show on about 150 television stations, and perhaps 50 more sold the show to local sponsors and aired it that way.

The Jubilee did not diminish the prowess of the Statesmen and Blackwood Brothers. It simply helped other groups catch up.

The Cathedral Quartet gained national attention singing on the widely-syndicated telecasts of Rex Humbard's Cathedral of Tomorrow in Akron, Ohio.

Local groups began to grow more powerful by singing on local television channels. A good example of this was the Kingsmen Quartet, which sang variously on Asheville's WLOS-TV and Greenville's WFBC-TV. Television helped Eldridge Fox make up his mind to turn the Kingsmen into a fulltime group which was soon voted the Number One quartet in America by the fans.

At the same time that these good professional groups were narrowing the distance between themselves and the Statesmen and Blackwood Brothers, television also helped to drop gospel singing from whatever national recognition it was beginning to enjoy. It became too easy for local quartets to get on local television, and soon there were groups on the air that had little business being there. Some were whoopers and hollerers and others chose to preach rather than sing, railing and ranting over the airwaves, forcing thousands of viewers to change channels quickly.

Before too many years passed, gospel singing wore itself out on television, and with the discontinuance of this revenue many groups sought refuge in the church again. The All-Night Singings disappeared as many inner cities became unsafe for nocturnal dalliance, and too many people who attended the singings previously, would rather not take the chance of venturing downtown, risking their parked automobiles to various stages of destruction, and sometimes even taking their lives in their hands while walking from the singing back to their cars.

There were other reasons, too, for gospel singing's passing from television. One was the advent of the Christian station, which programmed vast quantities of gospel music. The stations that programmed the big syndicated shows began to say that smaller Christian stations were fulfilling the people's needs for gospel music, and gradually eliminated quartets from their programming. Unfortunately, most of the Christian stations, some fed by those big "eyes in the sky"—satellites—could not reach wide enough markets to make the programming pay.

Some gospel groups, particularly those of old-time vintage, will say that preaching was the undoing of gospel music on television—and, indeed, the undoing of massive public concerts in many towns and cities. Too many groups took stage time to shout and preach rather that sing, and countless thousands of fans began to disappear.

"One thing we've never tried to do," said Les Beasley, "is get past the basic plan of salvation in our song presentation, because when you do that you're getting past our basic reason for existence. Our singing is for Christian entertainment and spiritual uplifting. Christian people need a form of wholesome entertainment, which will help them forget their problems for a while, but when you start trying to sell them a particular religion, or your set of do's and don'ts, then I think we are stretching what we are trying to do." The Florida Boys have never tried to preach from stage.

Les made this statement at a *Singing in the Smokies,* which the Inspirations promote every summer in Inspirations Park on a mountain outside of their home base of Bryson City, North Carolina.

"We used to work just cities," Les said, "and we all liked to work the big cities—Nashville, Atlanta, Birmingham, Chattanooga, Memphis, Houston, Fort Worth, Indianapolis, Detroit. And the smaller cities like Greenville and Asheville and Pensacola. But look at us tonight. Here we sit on a mountainside, seventy miles from Asheville, in a cow pasture, and there are thousands of people here. It used to be that the people in Bryson City had to go to Asheville or Knoxville or Atlanta to hear gospel music. Now people in those towns have to come to Bryson City to hear us.

"So times change," Les concluded. "But the music should not. Nor the presentation. Not that much, anyway. Our approach has to be different, but I don't think we have to change the music."

J. D. Sumner's thoughts on this subject are even more succinct. "People can get up Sunday morning and go to church and hear the best preachers in the world for free," he said, echoing Riley Smith's words. "Why should they come to a singing on Saturday night and have to pay ten dollars to have somebody who doesn't know anything about preaching preach to them? They pay to hear us sing. Our ministry is in song. We should sing to the people and hope they get a blessing from it."

Dad Carter of the Chuck Wagon Gang used to say, "This is the way I make my living. I am an entertainer."

There are two distinct schools of thought on that subject, and those who adhere to evangelizing on stage point to the fact that more and more quartets are singing in churches now in an effort to make ends meet.

So the industry has almost run full cycle. It started out in churches and schoolhouses, then Wally Fowler brought the singing into huge auditoriums with his All-Night Singings, and then the better quartets made their way onto national television, and now they are returning to singing in churches to pay their bills.

Les is right. Times have changed. The business has gone full cycle.

CHAPTER THIRTY-ONE

End of an Era

The end of the era of gospel music as pure Christian entertainment came with the breakup of the Statesmen-Blackwood team. It did not come overnight, but as a gradual loss of dominance by the team. Perhaps it was a different kind of gospel music—or a different feeling among the singers—that forced one era out and another in. The new era bore much more spirituality than the old one, and considerably less entertainment. More groups began to look upon their work as a ministry rather than as a Christian entertainment medium.

Hovie Lister actually began this era in such a subtle way that possibly even he did not sense the coming change. He began it with his great stagemanship, with his ability to wind up every Statesman performance with the crowd solidly in the palm of his hand.

He did this in a most simple way. The Statesmen came on stage like Halley's Comet, singing the latest songs in their great and tuneful way. If by chance their singing failed to move the crowd, Hovie cracked a few jokes, and if his humor, too, fell a little short, then he preached a while. Between the three he never failed to captivate the audience.

Being an astute observer of the passing scene, and always a man who knew what was going on around him, Hovie recognized the swing toward spirituality—and certainly his peers saw what was going on—and they all bent with the wind.

Too, as Buck Rambo once said, when he and Dottie came on the scene in the middle 1960s, gospel singing up to that point had been largely four men standing at a piano singing.

Some groups dared to make it different, and those groups who were different actually brought about the changes.

Television was responsible for the change, but before change can be made, there must be something to change to.

So. . . .

When the Rangers Quartet broke up, who can ever forget the Rangers Trio that followed—David Reece, Roy McNeil, and Clarke Thompson? Singing without a bass voice, they made the great crowds tap their toes as often as did the finest quartets. Reece wrote a lot of the trio's material, keeping the repertoire fresh, and the crowds loved the three. They were as different from the Rangers Quartet as night was different from day.

Then there were the Sons of Song—Bob Robinson, Calvin Newton, and Don Butler—who also made it to the top without a bass singer. Their sound was different, a clipped, sometimes almost brooding rhythm. They were masters of inflection and dynamics. How harmonious they were!

And after these two moved off the center stage, along came the Rambos, Buck, Dottie, and Reba, and completed the change from the Golden Era of Gospel Quartets to the modern era of mostly mixed groups who sing more salvation songs than the old quartets did.

And all the time, there were Wendy Bagwell and the Sunliters singing and laughing their way around America.

The Sons of Song came together rather by accident one evening in 1957. The Revelaires had just disbanded and Don Butler was loose, not singing with anyone. Bob Robinson had been with the LeFevres in 1954 and 1955 and had played piano for the Deep South Quartet for six months in 1956.

Robinson and Butler bumped into each other on Peachtree in Atlanta one night and as they stood on a street corner talking, Calvin Newton came tooling along in a snappy little convertible. Butler and Robinson waved, and Newton executed a neat U-turn and pulled over to the curb to talk. He was playing and singing in a club on Memorial Drive and had just gotten off work.

The three decided to get together and see what they sounded like singing. Calvin was a tenor, Robinson a good lead and pianist, and Butler a deep baritone.

When they ran through a few songs, they liked the sound they achieved, and decided to drive to Birmingham that weekend and crash Wally Fowler's All-Night Singing.

They worked up eight songs, rented matching tuxedos, and drove to Birmingham, but they ran into what almost amounted to a stone wall: Wally discouraged them.

"Fellows," Wally said, "we've got a full program. I honestly don't have a spot for you."

But their adrenalin was flowing so thickly they couldn't take no for an answer. They insisted that Wally give them a chance, and finally Wally laughed and said, "All right, I'll tell you the only thing I can do: I can put you on at intermission."

"We'll take it," said the three. All they wanted to do was get on stage.

Calvin found the light man and asked him to douse the house lights as soon as Wally introduced them.

When intermission came, people got up to leave, and Wally introduced the Sons of Song. The house lights went down, and people stopped in the aisles. A pin-point spot hit the Sons of Song, and they began to sing "Sometimes I Cry." A hush settled over the house, and many people made their way back to their seats. The Sons of Song sang their eight songs and several more. They sang with a magic they hadn't known they had, a magic that held the crowd at rapt attention—and they sang for forty-five minutes.

The crowd burst into tremendous applause, shouting for more, and when the Sons of Song left Birmingham that night they had enough dates booked to fill their weekends for almost the rest of the year.

They were different, and the crowds loved them. They sang across the country, adding something different to the quartet lineup at the All-Night Singings. They heralded the coming change.

Tragedy struck the Sons of Song late in 1958. En route to Miami to sing at a disk jockey convention, they ran up under a tractor-trailer loaded with watermelons.

Bob Robinson woke up in the hospital nine days later, severely injured. Don Butler never fully recovered from back injuries, and finally gave way to Les Roberson and then Lee Kitchens. Calvin was banged up too, but he slipped out of the hospital and went on to Miami. He was the one who most savored the roar of the crowd.

The Sons of Song sang on until 1964 when they teamed up with Jake Hess's new quartet, the Imperials, but broke off after a while and disbanded.

The Sons of Song were great stylists. A learned man once said that most of the great singers in Nashville starved while the stylists made money.

That's the way it was with the Sons of Song. They took some of the attention away from the quartets of the day, including the two team quartets, the Statesmen and the Blackwood Brothers.

Just as the Sons of Song got their start by singing that intermission gig in Birmingham, the Rambos got their big boost at the National Quartet Convention.

Buck Rambo was converted in a service in Western Kentucky in which Dottie sang. They were married in 1950 and Buck intended to support his family as manager of a supermarket. He had never sung. But he found that he could sing with Dottie.

Reba came along in 1952, and the three sang a lot together, but didn't really launch out until Reba was thirteen years old in 1965.

"Gospel music was still four men and a piano," Buck said. "We came along with an accordion and a guitar, and we didn't know you couldn't do that. Many of the quartets were the same, but we were different. I think we got booked a lot because we were different, and promoters liked that."

The Rambos, singing as the Gospel Echoes, went to the National Quartet Convention in 1967, but J. D. Sumner, who ran the convention, told them they couldn't sing because they were a trio and this was a *quartet* convention.

Someone—probably James Blackwood—interceded with J. D., and Buck and Dottie and Reba went on. Before that, J. D. had turned down Bill Gaither and his trio and several other groups that were not quartets.

The Gospel Echoes sang Dottie's new song, "He Looked Beyond My Faults And Saw My Needs," and the crowd went wild. They sang more of Dottie's songs and the cheering continued.

"I thought we weren't gonna get 'em off stage," J. D. said.

When the Gospel Echoes left the convention they had all the bookings they could handle.

For ten years or a little more the Rambos, who soon dropped the name of Gospel Echoes and used their family name, were one of the dominant groups on the gospel scene.

And during that time they were influential in ending that old era and ushering in the new one.

"Ours became what we felt to be a ministry," Buck said, "and that's why we left the circuit and went out on our own to sing in churches. When we went to a concert, J. G. Whitfield, who promoted most of the singings in which we appeared, would have six or seven other groups on the program; and we didn't have the time to do what we felt the Lord wanted us to do. We weren't having a good time; so we quit."

When they left the circuit, they did not have a date booked. There were thirteen people on the Rambo payroll, and during that first year, Buck said he lost $200,000. But the Rambos persisted, overcame the obstacles, and prevailed in doing what they felt they were really called to do.

"We didn't want to cause any trouble," Buck said, "and we weren't mad at anybody, but we felt we couldn't do what we wanted to do."

Mostly the Rambos sang Dottie's songs, and her music seemed to have a little more reverence than most.

Other groups followed the Rambos' style, and before the Rambos made their exit from the circuit, the dominance of the Statesmen and Blackwood Brothers was broken and gospel music changed eras.

Hundreds of family groups came upon the scene. The number of male quartets diminished, and gospel singing was never to be the same again.

We applied the word "different" to the Sons of Song and the Rambos. Perhaps we should have saved it for Wendy Bagwell.

How could one begin to describe Wendy Bagwell?

Wendy is an entertainer, a troubadour, a minstrel. With a full appreciation of life gained on the perilous sands of Iwo Jima and Saipan, he injected into many of the songs he wrote and sang the fullness of life, the humor of it all; and he, more than any other, became the epitome of folk gospel, because of the way he sang of the things around him.

He was different, to be sure. He knew what life and death were about. On Saipan he had been forced to dispatch thirty-six enemy Japanese who threatened the existence of both himself and his friends; and on Iwo Jima he and another Marine slipped through the Japanese lines to come up behind the enemy, and there, like Samson wielding the jawbone of an ass, he slew eight more Japanese who had his company pinned down.

Wendy came home from the war a blessed man, figuring himself extremely fortunate to be still alive.

"A lot of my friends were killed in the war," he said, "and I found out then how to really get close to the Lord. My daddy used to say, 'In good times a Christian is one thing; but in bad times a Christian may be another.' He told me, 'During the depression you could not believe how close I stayed to the Lord. I was actually afraid we were going to starve to death; so I was convinced the Lord sends depressions to get us close to Him.' After the depression was over, my daddy felt he wasn't as close, his prayers weren't as fervent, his meaning wasn't as great. It's the same in war. Brother, if you are one point of a second from death every second, you can flat do some tall, gettin'-down-to-it praying."

Wendy did not begin singing to repay the Lord for his life. He began singing because it was fun. He liked the way Geraldine Terry and Georgia Jones sang in church, and he began to sing with them. One day, he thought they were singing so well that he exclaimed, "We ought to get on the radio!" So they did—and they've been singing since. Dot Pressley replaced Georgia Jones, and Virginia Williams replaced Dot, and then Little Jan came along, and the real Sunliters were born.

In 1961, Wendy and the Sunliters played Carnegie Hall in New York. Wendy jokes that "everything was downhill from there."

He began to sing and recite novelty tunes, and they became in great demand. He could extract laughter from any audience.

Sometimes the big push for an entertainer comes by accident. That was the way it was with Wendy when he and the girls went into that Kentucky snake-handling church unaware of what they were getting into. What happened that night in a snake-handling service gave Wendy the tune he wrote about "Here Come The Rattlesnakes," and he had a million-seller on his hands, one of the few that gospel music can claim.

He followed it with several other hilarious ditties, and his niche was carved in gospel music.

If gospel music has a poet laureate, Wendy Bagwell is it.

He is different even from those who are different from the rest. Know what I mean?

But it's like the old man said, "It takes all kinds."

Not any of these groups fit the *status quo*. They took attention away from the quartets because they were new and refreshing and different.

Difference often leads to change.

It did this time.

CHAPTER THIRTY-TWO

'How Could We Complain . . . ?'

One of gospel music's best partnerships has been between George Younce and Glen Payne, a pair who seemed to be cut out to perform together.

They sang for years with different groups until Glen and Bobby Clark and Danny Coker formed a trio in 1963 to sing for Televangelist Rex Humbard in his Cathedral of Tomorrow in Akron, Ohio. Eighteen months later, in November of 1964, George Younce left the Blue Ridge Quartet—Elmo Fagg, Kenny Gates, Bill Crowe, and Ed Sprouse—and joined the trio, making it the Cathedral Quartet.

He and Glen have been together since, through a lot of thin and some thick.

George Younce and his older brother, Brudge, were named for presidents of the United States. Born in 1926, Brudge was named Eugene McKinley for President William McKinley. George came along on February 22, 1930, George Washington's birthday, and his pappy just couldn't resist naming him George. He added a middle name of Wilson—not for Woodrow, but for the doctor who delivered the baby—and thus we have George Wilson Younce.

Brudge's first recollection of his little brother George was at the age of five when, in Patterson, a cotton mill village where they were born near Lenoir, North Carolina, George would sing and dance on the storehouse porch, "just astompin' away," Brudge said. When George finished, he'd pick up the pennies tossed on the porch by onlookers and quickly turn them into candy in the mill store.

On Sunday, the Younces went to church and afterward George would mimic the preacher, preaching from a chair or on top of the table.

Just after World War II, when George was in his teens and working in a furniture factory in Lenoir, he got off from work at 4:30 in the afternoon and broke his neck racing the two hundred yards home to lie on the floor and listen to the Blue Ridge Quartet singing over a Burlington radio station, little dreaming that in a few years he would sing bass for that same quartet.

At age fifteen, George sang with a local quartet called the Spiritualaires. He sang lead until he got up one morning and started to sing, and, as he put it so succinctly, "I thought somebody had cut my throat." His voice change dropped him immediately into the bass range—and before long he was singing in that low bass register.

After turning himself into a full-time singing professional, George did duty with the Blue Ridge, the Weatherfords, the Florida Boys, and the Homeland Harmony quartets.

Just before that, he sang with the Watchmen in Beckley, West Virginia, where he met his wife, Clara; and prior to that, he was in the army. In 1953 he went to Camp Desert Rock, Nevada, and witnessed the awesome explosion of an atomic bomb.

Meanwhile, Glen Payne was already singing professionally, and had been for some time.

Glen was a Texan who got his early training and his start in quartet singing in the Stamps School of Music in Dallas. He sang a year with Frank Stamps and the Stamps Quartet in 1943, and then, like millions of other Americans, he went to war. When he returned to civilian life in 1946 he went back to singing with the Stamps Quartet in Dallas—with Haskell Mitchell, Clyde Garner, and Roger Clark, with Jack Taylor playing piano—and in 1951 he switched over to the Stamps-Ozark Quartet and moved to Wichita Falls, Texas, to sing with bass Fred Bennett, baritone Charles Bartlett, first tenor Pat Garner, and pianist Henry Slaughter.

That group disbanded in 1956 in the midst of the quartet-singing depression, and the following year Glen moved to Akron and joined the Weatherford Quartet, singing lead with Earl and Lily Fern Weatherford, the baritone and soprano, bass Armond Morales, and Henry Slaughter at the piano.

"As far as I'm concerned," Glen said, "that was one of the finest quartets that ever walked on stage. We didn't have a romp-'em, stomp-

'em, hand-clapping style quartet, but if you came to hear real smooth harmony, which I still like, then you enjoyed the Weatherfords."

In Akron, Glen met Van Lua Harris, with whom he fell head over heels in love, and they were married by Rex Humbard on his national telecast, at Humbard's request.

"We had more than three thousand people at our wedding," Glen beams.

Both Glen Payne and George Younce are considered by their peers to be two of the best singers in the business today. Both know how to sing because both took the time to learn the rudiments of their trade correctly.

"I don't believe I'd be singing today," George said, "had it not been for Lee Roy Abernathy. Years ago he had nothing and I had nothing. I'd spend a week at a time with him and Louise, bless her heart, and she would do for me. She would even wash my clothes.

"About two or three in the morning, me and Lee Roy would start to work. He'd say, 'George, you look sleepy enough to work on those low ones,' and we'd work the rest of the night. He trained me. He showed me how to use my voice; he actually taught me how to sing."

George said his greatest encouragement came from Elmo Fagg, who ran the Blue Ridge Quartet the five years George sang with it from 1959 to 1964.

"I joined the Blue Ridge when I was green as grass," George said, "and never once did Elmo say angrily, 'Younce, you're not doing this right.' He'd say, 'Younce, I believe I can help you.'

"I was indeed fortunate to meet some of the people I met while learning to sing."

Glen's musical education was a bit different—it was forced. "In my earliest deal with V. O. Stamps," he said, "I had to take a voice lesson whether I wanted to or not. I studied under some of the great teachers. I think that was probably the greatest thing that ever happened to me vocationally, but I didn't believe so at the time.

"I believe kids nowadays don't know the importance of studying and learning how to sing correctly. I would recommend it highly. If somebody's gonna have a singing career, he has to have a good voice first, and then voice instructors can teach him how to breathe and keep the words out front.

"Too, I've never had a sore throat from singing. I have never had laryngitis. I attribute that to proper training."

Thankfulness and friendships often enter the conversations of George and Glen. Both have been around a long time, and as the years add up, both feel a sort of indebtedness to their peers in the business and to those who pay to hear them sing.

George said, "There is no way in the world we can sit here and be thankful enough for what we have been able to do—to put clothes on our kids, raise our families, send 'em to school, live in a comfortable home, drive a nice car, eat good food. How in the world could we complain about anything? All we can do is praise God. We can say, 'I'm so thankful that God has blessed me like He has,' but that's not enough."

"We're indebted to a lot of folks, that's for sure," Glen said. "We have to be very careful, too, in our relations with others. If we meet someone in a hallway and, for whatever reason, we appear to snub him, it hurts him. It hurts if we're not friendly to our fans. I don't know of anybody who'd snub anyone on purpose, but we do it sometimes without thinking, because we're in a hurry to get somewhere or we've got something pressing on our minds. They don't realize we might be saddled with problems. All they want to do is show how much they love us."

Some of the closeness has gone out of gospel music because today's groups do not work as much with each other as groups did in bygone days.

"We used to go into towns together," George said, "stay together, play golf together, clean up and dress for the program together. We were close."

"We don't work with each other a lot now," Glen added. "We don't see Les Beasley, for example, as much as we'd like to. We work with the Kingsmen a little more than the Florida Boys, but not too often even with them. I don't think we show enough love among ourselves—not like we used to. I want to know their problems. It really hurts me when I hear of their problems. I care for them."

"Maybe it's the age factor, too," George said. "I tell Eldridge Fox that I love him, and I tell Les Beasley I love him. It's not just something to say, not just words, because I do love those guys—but we don't see a lot of that in the young guys in our field. When I get to thinking why they don't show the kind of love that we old-timers show, I realize they haven't been here as long, and they haven't been through what we all went through together. They don't appreciate the importance of it as much as we do."

That closeness is part of the appeal of gospel music. Closeness between the singers, closeness with the fans.

Often some of these old-timers go head to head on stage during a concert. Like George Younce and J. D. Sumner, trying to outsing each other on a program. They love to do that. They used to do it constantly—and the fans were rewarded with the greatest singing on earth.

There was a competitiveness that projected itself to the audiences. And while competition was present on stage, there was great love between these men off stage. They had worked together, lived together, hurt together, shared each other's joys and heartbreak, and had been like brothers—some even closer than that—over the years. Those things cannot be dented by competition on stage. Fans draw lines and claim superlatives for favorite individual singers, and possibly begin to snub their competitors, but you won't find a smidgen of ill feeling toward each other among a majority of these old-timers.

They've been through the mill. They've conquered adversity. And they've become the stronger for it.

There is a camaraderie among these gospel old-timers that isn't found in any other part of the music world—at least not to the extent that it's found here.

CHAPTER THIRTY-THREE

Views from the Top

We could hear the water lapping gently outside the cabin window. A sailor would have called the window a porthole, for we were on a ship, the *Emerald Seas*, bound for Nassau out of Miami. The occasion was the "Singing At Sea," that annual excursion in which a thousand people spend four days sailing, visiting exotic tropical islands and listening to several quartets and mixed groups sing gospel songs.

Eldridge Fox, owner and ofttimes baritone singer of the Kingsmen Quartet, stretched in one bunk, and Rex Nelon, major-domo of the Nelons, sat in a comfortable chair. A tape recorder sat on a table halfway between them. They talked for hours. Both Foxy and Rex go back to the 1950s in gospel music. Both manage their own groups, and both are wise in the ways and in the later history of gospel singing.

"I went with the Homeland Harmony Quartet in 1955," Rex said. "The Statesmen and Blackwood Brothers were riding high, and the Homeland Harmony and the Harmoneers were nearing the tailend of their careers. Some of the more popular groups were the Speers, the Oak Ridge Boys, the Rebels Quartet. The Oaks were ten years old but hadn't reached the popularity peak yet; but they were up-and-coming. Little Johnny New sang with Wally Fowler in the Oak Ridge, and Wally had Curley Blalock and Glen Allred. Then along came Carlos Cook—that was before Smitty Gatlin—and Bob Weber. Herman Harper took Weber's place. This was after Calvin Newton was gone.

"In the Homeland Harmony," Rex said, "we ranged as far as Texas and Oklahoma, riding in a Roadmaster Buick. We didn't have a stretch limousine like the Statesmen and Blackwoods had. We would ride three or four days in that Buick and we looked a mess. That was before wrinkle-free clothing.

"I thought the Statesmen were the best quartet in those days. No doubt in my mind—in the fifties era. They were the most professional group I had ever seen: They looked it, and they acted it. When you saw one of the Statesmen in a town somewhere, you always found him in a suit and tie. I mean, talk about playing the role, they did! From the very first to the end, they played the part. Plus, they worked and practiced. Every day they weren't on the road, they rehearsed. They had everything; they had new songs, they had great voices, and to my way of thinking they just had it all—everything it took: showmanship, professionalism. And when Denver Crumpler came along, he gave them a dignity they'd never had. But they maintained it after Denver died; they kept it to the end."

"Things were different then," Eldridge said. "Things began to change from the fifties on. There are many, many more groups today. Up to and including the fifties, all groups got their material from songbooks. Mosie Lister wrote a lot of songs, and Vep Ellis, and Albert E. Brumley, and, of course, Lee Roy Abernathy. They turned out some great songs. And J. D. Sumner and the Big Chief came along, and they were terrific songwriters, too.

"Back then, there were a lot of good songs like 'You Sho' Do Need Him Now' that must have come from black gospel. Those were show songs, and it's hard for us to do anything today that reminds people of blackness. That's taboo.

"A lot of things were different then, in that respect. The Sunshine Boys, when J. D. was with them, would do 'Steal Away and Pray' and J. D. would do black preacher recitations on it. Then they did a song called 'Read That Book' that had a recitation. Some of those songs were just comedy routines, but they entertained the crowds during their day and time.

"Back then, we didn't have the amount of material we've got now. There are all kinds of groups recording now, probably a hundred times as many groups doing full albums, and we have to have more material today. Since we have more to choose from, there is more room for error. We miss a lot of good songs today. Actually, we missed a lot back then, too. When I worked with the Statesmen and one of my jobs was to scout for material, I turned down Marshall Pack's 'One By One,' which became a tremendous hit. I turned down 'Scars In the Hands of Jesus.'

"We've got some songwriters today who can really write," Eldridge said. "'Midnight Cry' is one of the best songs ever."

"But a lot of today's writers," Rex joined in, "are one-time writers. They write one big song and that's it."

"Yes," Eldridge said, "but Squire Parsons, Joel Hemphill, Ron Hinson are really prolific—like J. D. used to be. Yet even with a wealth of material today, we have trouble finding good songs because there are so many groups looking."

"We cared about material then," Rex said. "I wasn't into gathering material when I was with the Homeland Harmony in 1955 and 1956, but Connor Hall would say 'We're gonna do this song,' and I just automatically thought that was what we were supposed to do. A bit later on I began listening to songs for material, and I brought a song to Connor I thought was an awful good song. Connor didn't like it, and I gave it to Big Chief. It was a song called 'I Wanna Know,' and the Statesmen recorded it on a forty-five. On the other side they did 'My Heavenly Father Watches Over Me,' and they just killed the world with both songs."

The subject switched to voices.

"Back then," Rex said, "if a quartet lost its bass singer, it got Aycel Soward or Pappy Waits, or someone like that, and the quartet knew it had probably bettered itself. It's as hard to find good voices today as it was back then.

"In the 1950s and 1960s," Rex continued, "we had more trained voices, more people who had gone to school and learned to sing right. A lot of people really wanted to be good singers then, and they worked hard at it. Like Jake Hess, who studied voice as long as he was with the Statesmen in Atlanta—fifteen years—and you could call his style corny or whatever, but technically Jake was one of the finest singers I ever heard in my life.

"Singers came out of those Stamps' Ten-Night Singing Schools. That's where Glen Payne came from. He learned to sing correctly from some of the great voice teachers, and that's the reason he will tell you today that he has never even had a sore throat from singing."

"As a whole," Eldridge said, "singers today are not prepared like singers used to be. When singers went on the road then, they were prepared. They knew how to sing."

"There are some awfully good voices today," Rex said, "but we did have more good trained singers then per capita. Today, they're mostly self-taught, but a lot of them can sing.

"It was hard to sing with somebody like Connor Hall because you had to practice the song, had to practice the timing, when to clip the words and when not to, when to hold them, how to say the words, and he'd catch somebody breathing when everybody else was singing, we'd start all over again and he'd say, 'We don't breathe there, we breathe here.'

"Today, they just get together and sing and when you run out of breath you catch one, and let the other person catch a breath when he can. They don't work on that as much as we used to. Not many know to do that. If you don't practice something like that, then you forget about it—you forget what you're supposed to do."

"Singing schools were important to people then," Eldridge said, "in many ways. That was before television and superhighways, before cars attained the popularity they have today. You'd have two hundred people in church, all of them singing shaped notes, and the teacher could point to anyone of them and he'd sing the verse. That was a lot of our recreation."

Rex said, "That's all I thought about. On weekends I knew where all the singing schools were and the singings. We could go to a singing on Sunday afternoon and another on Sunday night."

"Rex is different from most bass singers," Eldridge said, making a point. "Rex is an octave-low lead singer. He has a fantastic bass voice, but he uses it like a lead singer. George Younce is a great bass singer. But the big, robust basses like Arnold Hyles and Aycel Soward are not there anymore. Bob Thacker could never sing right on pitch but he had a great voice. During that era there were a lot of those big, big voices. I guess that came from training."

"Pappy Waits," said Rex, "sang with just about everybody in the business. He was a salesman. He's the one who started this trombone-blowing through his fist. He was the first real communicator in our business.

"But Pappy had his idiosyncrasies, too. Connor and Urias LeFevre used to talk about Pappy in the old days when some quartets were singing with Stamps-Baxter and some with Vaughan, and there were big, big rivalries. They said if a quartet got out there and really tore the place up before Jim Waits could get on, Jim would get sick. But if he ever got on first, it was Katie bar the door. He was about six feet and kinda slim—and he could sing bass!

"In most of Pappy's early singing, he didn't want to sing anything lower than an E flat (two octaves below middle C), and if you could get a song up in his range he could really sell it. When he was still around in the sixties, he was hitting even lower, some big, big B flats and A flats.

"I don't know that my own voice has deepened very much," Rex said. "I'm a pretty solid C most of the time, but some of the time B flat, and I can hit an occasional A. But we have girls singing so high in our group there's nowhere for me to go, so my voice has always been strange. It has never seemed to settle down and stay one way all the time. Tonight, I might be able to do a low C and tomorrow I might have trouble with an E flat. I never have understood that. It's something I've got to live with, I guess. And I can tell the minute I get out there what I can do and what I can't.

"Wide ranges have always amazed me," Rex said. "One of the widest ranges in our business was Shorty Bradford. He could sing either a high C or a low C."

It was past midnight and the ship glided through the Caribbean. Most aboard were asleep, but Rex and Eldridge were just getting wound up.

"Aycel Soward was out of the business when I came in," Rex said, "but I had heard him enough from the beginning to know that there was something there that I have never heard anywhere else to this day. He could do things that were so different. He was an awesome bass singer to me. Back then, what he was doing was low, but today it wouldn't have sounded that low. He had a fullness in his voice from the bottom to the top.

"When London Parris first left Lee Roy, he was hitting some of the biggest notes I have ever heard in my life. The A, I believe, was his most solid note. He could fill up a building with his A's, and they would ring in your ears for days.

"J. D. has never had the fullness some other bass singers had, but nobody's ever come close to him being low. Most of the bass singers who tried to sing as low as he does had pitch problems, but J. D. never suffered from that. He has a good ear, and his lows are unheard of. I've hit my lowest note a lot of times and J. D. would drop it an octave on me. I don't know what makes a voice do that. It has some gear I've never been able to find."

"It's a God-given talent," Eldridge said. "You can't develop it. If you can sing it or growl or holler it, you can develop it, but you can't push it to the extreme when it's not there to begin with."

Rex said, "I've got some old, old records made by the Sunshine Boys when J. D. was with them, and he was about a C or maybe a B flat, but he just kept working his voice deeper someway."

"Rex is a stylist," Eldridge said. "There has never been a bass singer like Arnold or London or J. D. who could take a song like a spiritual and sing it like Rex. He's got a low bass lead voice. He sings a lot of country. He's the only one I ever heard. And he can lay a good foundation."

"I've got three high voices I sing with," Rex said, "so I have to be careful. But when I was with the Homeland Harmony, I had to sing a different way. They were all big voices, and I had to learn to be heavy with them. When I came with the LeFevres, they wanted a thin voice; so I had to thin out. They had to have a thin voice to match theirs; they were all thin. Urias would keep pushing me back from the mike, and I'd back up and sing a little harder, and he'd back me up again. I sang with him twenty years. Turned down a lot of jobs. Turned down the Oak Ridge job three times. I guess I just hated change.

"Speaking of different," Rex said, "Buford Abner and his brother, Merle, made the Swanee River Boys different. They wrote their arrangements that way, too. Buford tried to style his group like an old-time black group, singing softer and with a certain beat, and he could do it as well as anybody I've ever heard. Most of their stuff was just old-time black spirituals with a beautiful soft harmony. The Jordanaires were like that, too, but not that far. They were just very precise singers."

Eldridge said, "Cat Freeman was a great singer."

"I liked the sound of Cat's voice," Rex said.

Eldridge added, "I thought Denver Crumpler was the greatest tenor who ever lived. He gave an addition to the Statesmen that they never had before. In harmony, I thought Cat was better than Denver at blending. Denver was really at his best with the Rangers; he was beginning to tail off just a bit when he came with the Statesmen—but he was still great."

"While we're speaking of being different," Rex said, "we ought to mention Dwight Brock. He revolutionrized piano-playing for quartets. He showed all the other pianists how to pick it up on the fly. Back then, the piano player stopped after the introduction and picked it up only when the quartet began to sing the verse. But Brock didn't stop. He'd just roll right into the verse and the singers had to pick it up on the fly. Man, that really changed quartet singing!"

"It did," Eldridge agreed, "but the one who changed quartet music the most was Jackie Marshall. He took it from choir music and made it something else. I guess it was the song 'Hide Me, Rock of Ages' when we started switching parts, and Jackie developed that. The lead singer always sang the lead line and the tenor sang the alto line, and on 'Hide

Me, Rock of Ages' Jackie made the tenor take the lead an octave high and inverted the harmonies. That's technical, I realize, but until Jackie came along, the piano-player had just played what the group sang."

They spoke of the uniqueness of gospel music.

"It's the most unique business in the world," Rex said. "We have our own tour. The contemporary people don't have it like we do.

"And when J. D. engineered the first custom-built bus, he revolutionized the entire entertainment industry. Buses have done two things for certain: They've made it easier to travel, and they've put a lot of groups out of business."

"That's true," Eldridge said. "If you're not real careful, you'll be singing to pay for your bus."

"Kids come into the business today," Eldridge said, "and don't believe what we went through to get where we are—wherever that is! They have no conception of what it was, and they don't want to hear it. Now you get on a nice bus and go somewhere and sing and get paid a certain amount of dollars. They ride in air-conditioned buses and fuss if the air-conditioned buildings in which they sing aren't cool enough.

"There isn't a thing in my quartet that I haven't done," Eldridge said. "Set up records, set up sound, drive the bus, get the bus fixed, and it gets kinda funny sometimes when youngsters come and say they can't do this and that. I've never asked one to do anything I haven't done a hundred times.

"It never entered my mind to quit or that I would fail. It was just what I had to do."

"Most singers are on salary now," Rex said, "and they know they're going to get paid enough to live on. When I was with the Homeland Harmony there were times we didn't have anything. I could go down to this restaurant called the Pickwick that Lester Maddox owned, and he'd let me eat and I paid him when I worked. I hadn't been in Atlanta too long and I learned to stretch a big, economy-sized jar of peanut butter and a loaf of bread a long way.

"We usually found time to make extra money," Rex added. "I set up a sideline business doing carpenter work. My specialty was back porches and steps. There weren't many houses that didn't have back porches and steps, and they'd rot away. I did that and painted and caulked windows, things like that.

"We were based in Atlanta, and we envied the Statesmen. They were riding high while we starved to death."

"That was when the Statesmen and the Blackwood Brothers had

their team," Eldridge said. "That team tried to put everybody else out of business and darned near did. If you didn't have their blessing, you didn't hardly work."

"You didn't work out West," Rex said. "Not in California, anyway. You didn't work the North, either. Anywhere they worked regularly, you didn't work unless they said so. We didn't. The LeFevres didn't. They froze us out.

"But when the Caravan and the Jubilee hit television," Rex said, "that changed things. We went into all those places on TV, and no longer could they keep us out of an area. Television broke up that team's dominance and brought a parity to the business again."

Rex told how he got his job singing bass with the Homeland Harmony in 1955.

"I had bought all the records I could find," he said, "and I knew everybody's songs. I memorized them while playing those records. Riley Smith, the promoter in Asheville where I lived, told me that Lee Roy Abernathy had split away from the Homeland Harmony and was forming his own group. Riley thought I should call Lee Roy and see about singing bass with his new group.

"I called Lee Roy, but he said he already had London Parris. He thought I should call Connor, so I did, but Connor said, 'Well, I've got somebody right now. I've got Aycel Soward.' But Aycel didn't stay long, and Connor got George Younce. George didn't stay long, either, and Connor called me. I didn't know it at the time, but the reason George left was that he was starving to death. That didn't make any difference to me. I wasn't trying to get the job to make money. I just wanted to sing. I would have paid Connor to let me have the job.

"Anyway, I went down for a tryout before George left the quartet. Remember that I had memorized every song the Homeland Harmony sang. Connor called off several songs and asked if I knew them. I said, 'Well, sir, I've never sung them, but I think I can get through them.' Two of the songs were tough ones, 'There's A Little Ringing,' and 'Sing Your Blues Away.' They were Homeland Harmony specials.

"Connor gave me the music for the two, but, of course, I just looked at the music and made out that I was singing by sight when I was really singing from memory. I didn't miss a note, and I got the job. Old George Younce left there shaking his head. He went back to West Virginia and told some folks, 'I don't know who that old boy is that Connor got. He's not too low, but he's the best music-reader I've ever seen.'

"Connor hired Jim Cole out of West Virginia to sing the lead, and Jim and I took a room upstairs over an apartment Jack Clark had. Jack was our piano-player, and he'd just got married. Jim and I would go down and eat one meal every day with Jack and we paid him so much a week for it. Sometimes that one meal would be all Jim and I had to eat all day, and Jack and his wife wouldn't have had enough money for groceries if Jim and I hadn't paid them for that one meal. So it was a matter of all of us sharing what we had to keep from starving to death.

"But we kept on singing."

"Yes, sir," Eldridge said. "Right to this day."

Both Eldridge and Rex were yawning frequently. Rex made his way to the door, mumbling that he'd see Eldridge tomorrow, and before he was out the door, Eldridge had the light out and was beginning to snore softly. . . .

Before he went to sleep, he looked at his watch. It was three in the morning.

CHAPTER THIRTY-FOUR

Elvis Missed His Chance

There is something about the Kingsmen Quartet that brings on unusual things. They are rather like a full moon—wherever they are, things happen. Personnel has nothing to do with it; being a Kingsman does. In the years since that escapade at the Shellanes Motel in Sheffield, Alabama, the Kingsmen changed all personnel, with the exception of Eldridge Fox, who owns the quartet, but found it could not change its ways.

The new guys are just as nutty as the old ones.

The Kingsmen were singing in Waynesboro, Virginia, and Garry Sheppard and Arthur Rice were talking backstage before they went on.

They happened to be standing near the backstage fire alarm.

On stage the program had just begun, and the first group was singing.

There was nothing complicated about the fire alarm. It was a simple gadget on which a person only had to pull a release valve at the bottom and get out of the way. The alarm would do the rest.

Standing deep in thought and conversation, Arthur began unconsciously fumbling with the fire alarm, and in a moment he pulled the release valve all the way down. The alarm, however, didn't go off; so Arthur pushed the valve back up.

"Boy, you're lucky," Sheppard said to Arthur. "What would you have done if that alarm had gone off?"

AND THEN IT WENT OFF!!! IT ALMOST DEAFENED SHEPPARD AND RICE, AND EVERYBODY IN TOWN HEARD IT.

The master of ceremonies, who also happened to be the town's police chief, rushed on stage, took the mike from the singing group, and yelled, *"FIRE!!! FIRE!!! EVACUATE THE BUILDING IMMEDIATELY!!!"*

Before he could ask that the building be evacuated in an orderly manner, everybody leaped up and made a concerted rush for the exists.

It looked like the Oklahoma Land Rush!

Arthur ran on stage, shouting, "False Alarm! False Alarm!" His words were no more than a puff in a hurricane. "False Alarm! There's no fire. It's a false alarm!"

He must have realized that he sounded like Gomer Pyle shouting, "Citizens arre-ust! Citizen's arre-ust!" for he suddenly shut up and watched the exodus with astonishment.

People plunged through the windows and out the doors in droves.

"That's amazing!" Arthur said to himself. "I've never seen anything like that."

He was appalled, however, to see senior citizens, white heads bobbing, running at full tilt, and people pushing other people in wheelchairs, the riders gripping both handles, chins jutting forward, holding on for dear life as they rushed pell-mell for safety.

When the fire department arrived with all of its available equipment, the crowd was standing outside looking for a fire.

But there wasn't even any smoke!

No one knew where Garry Sheppard and Arthur Rice were; they were conspicuous by their absence.

When order was restored, the crowd rushed back inside to reclaim seats, and several fist fights almost broke out for front-row seats.

And it was with much trepidation later in the afternoon that Sheppard and Rice ventured on stage to sing with the Kingsmen.

In all of gospel music there has been nothing funnier than some of the incidents that have occurred to men who wear hairpieces.

The reason that a lot of guys wear hairpieces is not altogether because they are sensitive about their bald pates, but because the heavy stage lights reflect off bald domes and create problems for people in the audience who are trying to see.

At least, that's what some of the guys say who wear artificial hair.

If baldness was ever an embarrassment on stage, it no longer has to be. Some of the guys in gospel music wear toupees that cannot be detected, and others wear another brand.

Anyway, wearing artificial hair solves some problems but it isn't all glamor. Ask Derrell Stewart of the Florida Boys. He sported a fine head of someone else's hair for many years.

Once when a tornado hit Pensacola, where the Stewarts live, it damaged the walls of his house and he had to have the house repainted.

At that time, Derrell owned two hairpieces. One was at the barber's being restyled, and the other lay hair down on the kitchen table.

One of the painters went inside to drink a cup of coffee. He also lit a cigarette, and after a few puffs cast about for an ashtray. Spotting the upturned hair on the table, he flicked the ashes of his cigarette in it. The plastic on the inside of the hair formed a cup. Then, when he finished the cigarette, he crushed it out in the hairpiece, burning a hole through the plastic.

Derrell walked in about that time and yelled at the painter, "What are you doing? That's my hairpiece!"

"Hairpiece?" said the painter. "I thought it was an ashtray."

The Florida Boys made the most of Derrell's wig. Once at a singing in Texas, Derrel's head began to itch and, while playing a song, he reached up under his hair and scratched his head. Until that moment, the audience had not realized that he wore a hairpiece, but they caught on quickly, and gave Derrell such a going over that the Florida Boys made a routine of it. One night, when Les Beasley was talking on stage, Derrell lifted his hair and scratched under it and Les kept on talking. Derrell took the wig off and laid it on the piano and Les pretended to see it for the first time and did a double take. The crowd loved it.

Eldridge Fox, Jake Hess, Shaun Nielson, Wally Fowler, Tim Riley, and others, all wear other people's hair.

And they have fun with it—most of them.

The writer Joseph T. Catring telephoned Eldridge one day, and Eldridge's daughter, Terri Lynn, answered the phone. "Daddy's not here right now," she said.

"When will he be there?" Catring asked.

"Oh, he'll be right back," Terri snickered. "He and Mother had to go back to the bus. He forgot his hair."

Eldridge keeps his hair on the nightstand beside the bed when he sleeps. He was awakened one morning by his little feist dog, growling like crazy. Coming out of the fog of sleep, Eldridge got out of bed to quiet the dog and discovered that the sounds were coming from under the bed.

When he looked, he saw his dog tearing his hair apart. The hairpiece apparently had fallen off and frightened the dog, which attacked it with such ferocity that he certainly defeated it.

Eldridge has always taken a lot of kidding about his hair and has joked about it himself. He wore hair from the time good hairpieces were perfected. He once went to a barber in Atlanta who apparently knew little about artificial hair. Climbing into the chair, Eldridge winked at others waiting and said to the barber, "Gimme a flat-top," whereupon the barber took him at his word, ran his electric clippers up the back of Eldridge's head, and ruined his hairpiece.

Not much has happened to Eldridge's hair on stage. Once, when the Kingsmen took a bow in Tampa, Florida, Frank Cutshall, standing beside Eldridge, flipped the back of Foxy's hair as they bowed, and the hair came unglued and fell in Eldridge's face.

Others have had more trouble on stage. The Statesmen were singing in Osage Beach, Missouri, and Hovie Lister told Sherrill Nielson to open the second half of the program by playing and singing a solo. Sherrill bounded on stage, tripped over the top step, and his hair flew off and landed across the stage.

Offstage, Hovie covered his eyes and groaned, but calmly Sherrill retrieved his hair, put it back on, sat on the piano bench, and said to the audience, "I'll bet you didn't even know it was portable."

The second week Jake Hess wore a toupee, he was on stage with the Statesmen in Macon, Georgia, trying to hide behind Doy Ott and trying to look as inconspicuous as possible. He was terribly self-conscious about the hair. A fan in the balcony dearly loved to hear him sing, and after Hovie failed to feature Jake on one of the first half-dozen songs, the fan yelled down and said, "Hey, Hobie, let that kid with the wig sing one."

There is a bit of discrepancy between J. D. Sumner and Jake Hess over how Jake came to wear artificial hair. J. D. said he and Jake were sitting in the dressing room about 1955 and he told Jake, "Your hair's getting thin. You ought to get a toupee."

"Aw, George," said Jake, who has always called J. D. George, "I ain't gonna wear one of those stupid things. I like the way I look."

J. D. took out his upper teeth and said, "I like the way I look, too, but what if I didn't wear any teeth? You gonna be as stupid-looking as I am without teeth?"

J. D. said Jake went to a wiggery that afternoon.

Jake recalls going with the Statesmen to record a television show in New York, and the producer, a man named Harrison, began stuttering and stammering. "Jake," he said, "I need to talk to you about something."

"What is it?" Jake asked.

"You see those other guys," Harrison said. "They have full heads of black hair—and, well, we're going to have to put dulling compound on your head before we can roll the cameras."

"Do you want me to wear a toupee?" Jake asked.

"Yeah," Harrison said. "That's it."

"Tell you what," Jake said. "You buy it; I'll wear it."

For the next three days, while the Statesmen filmed for NABISCO, Jake said a man worked with him, making a hairpiece. NABISCO paid for it.

Jake said he had never been troubled by his hair coming loose. "The kind I wear," he said, "I don't worry about it coming loose; it sticks so good I have to worry about getting it off."

"That's the truth," J. D. said. "I walked out of a hotel with him in Detroit one night and the wind was blowing so hard it blew my overcoat off and didn't even muss Jake's hair."

Derrell Stewart wasn't that lucky. He came out of a hotel in Birmingham into a crowd of people and a hard wind blew his hair off and sent it rolling down the sidewalk. "I just ran it down and stomped it," he said, "and took it back to the hotel."

Les Beasley said Wally Fowler was in a wreck once and was thrown out of his car. "He went bouncing down the street on his butt," Les said, "trying to steady himself with one hand, and holding his hair on with the other."

Someone suggested that J. D. Sumner wore a hairpiece. "Nobody could have a head of hair like that at his age," the fellow said.

"It's really my own hair," J. D. said.

"I'll vouch for that," said Hovie Lister. "God ain't that punishing. He wouldn't have made J. D. that ugly and taken away his hair, too."

"I dunno," J. D. said. "Look what He did to poor old George Younce."

Fun? Yes, they'll make you laugh. Some of their jokes are kid's stuff. Like when Jim Hamill was young and singing with the Weatherfords. He slipped a big, black, rubber spider into a songbook in church and handed the book to Lily Fern Weatherford. When she opened the book, she screamed and alarmed the whole church.

Then there was the time the Weatherfords were going down the highway at a rapid clip and Hamill, sitting up front in the limousine, lit a two-inch red firecracker, from which he had extracted the powder, and threw it in the back seat. Those back there tried to bail out of the car at seventy miles an hour.

Hamill outgrew most of that stuff, though he still loves a good story or a good joke on someone. He realizes the camaraderie that binds people in this business is more than superficial. They may get on stage and sing their hearts out, trying to outdo each other—but they'd fight for each other if the chips were down. They are, indeed, special friends.

"Young guys coming into the business," Hamill said, "have no idea what we all went through in the early days. Like the first professional quartet I was in, I made fifty dollars a week. That was in 1953 and we were the Melodymen. We did two live radio programs a day, one at 7:30 a.m. and the other at 10 a.m. on KMA Radio in Shenandoah, Iowa, the same station the Blackwood Brothers were on a few years earlier. In the month of May that year we worked twenty-eight out of thirty-one days in concert, traveling in a car, five of us, working every night. That'll either make friends or enemies out of you."

In most cases, it makes friends. Even refusals for singing jobs didn't dent friendship among these people.

The most famous refusal came in the early 1950s and involved Jim Hamill and Cecil Blackwood who sang in their own quartet in Memphis, Tennessee. They called themselves the Songfellows.

This shy kid from Tupelo, Mississippi, whose family had moved to Memphis, kept hanging around. His name was Elvis Presley, and he had a job driving a truck. But he wanted to sing.

He hounded the professional quartets that came to Memphis. J. D. Sumner always let him come in the stage door to the monthly Memphis sings because Elvis usually didn't have the money to buy a ticket.

Elvis braced Hamill and Cecil Blackwood for a tryout with their quartet, and they tried him out. Then, the story goes, Hamill put a fatherly arm around Elvis's shoulders, led him away, and as gently as he could, broke the news to Elvis:

"Son, you better stick to driving that truck. You can't sing a lick!"

Hamill says it didn't happen exactly that way. He admits that he and Cecil turned Elvis down, but only because he couldn't sing harmony.

"When he learned to sing harmony," Hamill said, "he had already signed that contract with Sun Records. Me and Cecil went to him and tried to get him to break his contract and sing in the quartet with us—

but he wouldn't. Or couldn't. That was the contract that RCA Victor bought—and Elvis rose to international stardom."

But just think! Elvis missed his chance! He could have sung with the Songfellows. And then, one day he might have been good enough to sing with the Stamps Quartet, or the Cathedrals, or the Kingsmen.

And do you know what?

He would have been happy.

And maybe still alive!

CHAPTER THIRTY-FIVE

Going Home

One of the principal themes of gospel music, and the subject of thousands of songs, has been "going home." Almost all of those men and women who pioneered gospel singing in the 1920s have now followed the lead of what they sang about for so many years: They have gone home.

Otis McCoy is still around at this writing. He is in his nineties, still singing, and he still loves to bowl. Undoubtedly there are a few more around. But most are dead.

What a choir could be formed among those who have gone on! What singing they did here! How well they paved the way for those who sing the gospel now.

What a magnificent bass section, for example, lies in the grave— Big Chief Jim Wetherington, Big Jim Waits, Aycel Soward, Frank and V. O. Stamps, Adger M. Pace, Bill Lyles, Johnny Atkinson, Burl Strevel.

Most of the Statesmen Quartet have been reunited in death: Big Chief, Denver Crumpler, Cat Freeman, Doy Ott, Bobby Strickland. Only Hovie Lister and Jake Hess of the Statesmen most folks remember are still with us.

The men who became the movers and shakers of gospel music, James D. Vaughan and the Stamps brothers, are gone.

But the heritage they bequeathed us remains.

And so does their music. Much of it was preserved on recordings, some of which still exist, and if one knows where to look he can find recordings of those quartets that sang in the twenties and thirties, and certainly can find plenty of recordings of those great post-war quartets of the 1940s and 1950s.

The voices, then, of Dad Carter and Kieffer Vaughan and Frank Stamps and Dad Speer live on. Even the voice of Homer Rodeheaver, who recorded gospel songs before World War I, is still around on record.

Gospel music has tried to honor its forebears by establishing a hall of fame, but like so many other such halls it has only scratched the surface of the number of those who deserve to be enshrined. The Gospel Music Hall of Fame, coordinated by the Gospel Music Association in Nashville, has become mired in internal politics, particularly in the split between what is now known as Southern Gospel and Contemporary Gospel.

The hall has no home, no place to house the mementoes of the great singers of gospel music, things that the public would like to see.

For the record, here are the names of those enshrined in the Gospel Music Hall of Fame at the time of this writing:

Those voted in while living: Big Jim Waits, Albert E. Brumley, Lee Roy Abernathy, James Blackwood, Brock Speer, Mosie Lister, Eva Mae LeFevre, George Beverly Shea, Connor B. Hall, John T. Benson Jr., Ira Stanphill, Thomas A. Dorsey, William (Bill) Gaither, Hovie Lister, Ralph Carmichael, John W. Peterson, Rev. James Cleveland, Wally Fowler, W. B. Nowlin, J. D. Sumner, P. J. Zondervan, Jake Hess, Cliff Barrows, Les Beasley.

And those voted in posthumously: G. T. (Dad) Speer, Lena Brock Speer, James D. Vaughan, Denver Crumpler, J. R. Baxter Jr., E. M. Bartlett, John Daniel, Adger M. Pace, Homer Rodeheaver, A. J. Showalter, V. O. Stamps, Frank Stamps, W. B. Walbert, R. E. Winsett, G. Kieffer Vaughan, Fanny Crosby, George Bennard, Big Chief Wetherington, Mahalia Jackson, Ira Sankey, Clarice Baxter, John T. Benson Sr., Marvin Norcross, Cleavant Derricks, Charles Gabriel, Haldor Lillenas, B. B. McKinney, Lowell Mason, John Newton, Tim Spencer, Urais LeFevre, D. P. (Dad) Carter, Paul Heinecke, Lloyd Orrell, Clara Ward, Ethel Waters.

The list is small for twenty years of voting, and the names of dozens of giants are conspicuously absent. It is possible that a hall of fame could not be built large enough to house those who truly deserve to be enshrined, for every man and woman who sang the gospel professionally did his part to bring the business out of its infancy. Some were better than others, better singers, better musicians, and that is the criterion for the hall of fame, of course; but they all contributed tremendously to the growth of a new folk form of sacred music.

They all deserve recognition.

Take a moment and think back to other days.

Think of the Statesmen walking on stage, Hovie Lister waving a big red bandana at the crowd and five hundred people in the audience waving red bandanas back.

Think of the Rangers Quartet, laughing like maniacs, pulling Arnold Hyles out of a ditch in the middle of the night.

Think of the thousands who swarmed to the Vaughan and Stamps-Baxter schools of music to learn a special kind of singing.

Think of twenty great professional quartets singing on the same program.

Think of how your seat shook and the rafters rattled when J. D. or Big Chief went down to the bottom to get the note.

Think of the Blackwood Brothers, naked and all soaped up, standing beside their bus praying for the rain to start again, so they could finish their shower.

Think of Frank Stamps kicking the plug out of the wall to kill the mike and silence the Melody Masters, a rival Vaughan quartet.

Think of. . . .

The Statesmen and Blackwood Brothers rolled along a paved country road in South Georgia at a fair rate of speed. This was in the early 1950s before J. D. invented the customized bus. Big Chief Jim Wetherington drove the Statesman limousine, and Wally Varner was at the wheel of the Blackwood Brothers' car, trailing Big Chief.

"Big Chief was a fast driver," Wally said. "He always rolled along about seventy-five miles an hour. He believed in getting there without wasting any time."

On this day, the speeding limousines came suddenly upon a fork in the road, and Chief didn't know which way to go. The road markers were rather confusing, and before he could get it figured out, he got into the loose gravel between the forks of the road, and then crammed on the brakes. The limousine spun about four times, round and round, and came to a stop over against the pumps at a gasoline station. A startled attendant, paralyzed with fear, stood frozen about four feet from where the limousine stopped.

Big Chief quickly rolled down his window and calmly said, "Fill 'er up!"

No one ever said gospel music would be boring.

Index